The Times We Had

The Times We Had

LIFE WITH WILLIAM RANDOLPH HEARST

by

Marion Davies

Edited by

Pamela Pfau & Kenneth S. Marx

with a Foreword by
Orson Welles

The Bobbs-Merrill Company, Inc.
Indianapolis/New York

Designed by Jacques Chazaud
Manufactured in the United States of America

First printing

Library of Congress Cataloging in Publication Data

Davies, Marion, 1897-1961.
   The times we had.

    1.   Davies, Marion, 1897-1961.   2.   Hearst, William
Randolph, 1863-1951.   I.   Title.
PN2287.D315.A35   1975   791.43'028 0924   [B]   75-7015
ISBN 0-672-52112-1

Introduction

Marion Davies recorded the notes for this book on magnetic tapes in her Beverly Hills home. With the assistance of Stanley Flink, a Time-Life correspondent, she began work in the summer of 1951. On August 14 of that year, William Randolph Hearst died, ending their thirty-two-year affair.

For ten years and thirty-nine days after he passed away, Marion lived with her memories. But this work was withheld from publication while she lived, because she felt she may have revealed too much.

After W.R.'s death, W. A. Swanberg compiled and wrote Citizen Hearst, published by Charles Scribner's Sons in September 1961. And Fred Lawrence Guiles researched and wrote Marion Davies, published by the McGraw-Hill Book Company in 1972. Those two books are certainly the standard reference works on their subjects.

This book is a personal memory. It is possibly an autobiography, but probably not. Marion said what she had to say, then put it aside and never went back to it.

She was born Marion Cecilia, the youngest child of Bernard and Rose Reilly Douras, and she would become a major American film star of the 1920s and 1930s, helped by her friend, publishing and real estate tycoon, art collector and film producer William Randolph Hearst. He would supervise most of the forty-five films she made as she became the richest actress of her time.

Against the background of the great worldwide depression of the thirties, Marion and W.R. lived in a style that rivaled the grandeur of European royalty, and indeed they traveled in those circles.

When Marion tired of working in films, prior to World War II, she gave herself over to W.R. as a constant companion, carrying out his wishes both in business and in pleasure. After his death in 1951, although she was only fifty-four, it seems her life lost its momentum. She dabbled in real estate and built her fortune to an estimated value of twenty million dollars, then wavered between constructive charities and destructive drinking.

Her films were forgotten as time passed, and her fans found new idols. The Hearst newspapers faded, too, in the glare of electronic journalism and labor problems.

But the properties remain. San Simeon, the most famous, was given to the State of California. Not the several hundred thousand acres of land around the castle—which still are operated as a cattle ranch—but the buildings at the top of La Cuesta Encantada, the enchanted hill. And now it is a true California spectacle. Opened to the public, cautiously at first, it soon gained an overwhelming response. The landmark generates a profit for the State's general fund. Tickets for the tours are sold out weeks *in advance as tourists from all over the world jam the facilities of the few towns along that part of the coast.*

We have heard that San Simeon was W.R.'s favorite home, built in honor and memory of his mother, but it was only when Marion reigned as hostess that it dazzled the world. There were sixty guest bedrooms and a constant flow of people arriving and departing. While they visited they had such diversions as pools, tennis courts, the beach, a zoo and a cocktail hour with Marion—which W.R. ignored.

Everyone took meals in the Refectory at a monastery table three hundred years old. Marion and W.R. sat opposite each other at the middle of the long, laden board. The guests would find their place cards moved farther and farther from the center of the table as their stay at San Simeon lengthened. It was a gentle reminder that time was passing, and they could go home.

For the guests, there were also newspapers to read and movies to watch. Mostly W.R.'s publications and mostly Marion's pictures.

For those who were never guests, there were many books and articles and movies that built upon the legends and accounts and realities of life at San Simeon.

Orson Welles wrote, directed, produced and acted in a film which the world believed was based on the lives of Marion and W.R. It seemed fitting, then, that he should write the Foreword to this book. Nonetheless, his only meeting with Marion and W.R., as we understand it, was an occasion after the film was released, when they shared an elevator in a San Francisco hotel, going up in silence. Today Citizen Kane is shown in theatres and at film festivals, and continues to attract and polarize comments on its subject.

We think that film influenced W. A. Swanberg and his publishers in their choice of a title for their book.

Marion has taken some liberties in this book. For instance, the older Marion got to be, the later the date she was born. Beginning at that point, the editors have taken some liberties, too, but only to make sense where there seemed to be confusion or to supply the details lost in the lapse of time.

Readers of this collaboration are reminded of Aaron Burr's statement:

> *I would not wish to possess that*
> *kind of memory which retains with*
> *accuracy and certainty all names*
> *and places. I never knew it to*
> *accompany much invention of fancy.*
> *It is almost exclusively the blessing*
> *of dullness.*

Indeed, we wish we had had the great privilege of knowing Marion. Working with her, but without her, we have come to respect her view that there is only one true four-letter word in the English language: dull. And she is never that.

—PP & KSM, New York City
July 1975

Foreword

Comparisons are not invariably odious, but they are often misleading. In their enthusiasm for this truly fascinating book, early readers called Marion Davies and William Randolph Hearst "the Jackie and Ari of their day." And why? Because they had "more glamour, power and money than anyone else." The truth is that Hearst was never rich in the way that Onassis was rich, and the power of Onassis resided solely in his money. He could buy himself an airline, an island or a Greek colonel, but his place in history is recorded largely in the gossip columns. Hearst *published* the gossip columns; he practically invented them. The difference is immense.

If Hearst was not a great man, he was certainly a towering figure in the first half of this century. If he had been ten times richer than he was, he would not now be primarily remembered for his millions. Onassis was neither a great man nor a great force in the world; he was—quite simply and purely—a celebrity. "You make the money," Hearst might well have said to him, "I'll make the celebrities."

This, of course, is a paraphrase. When Frederick Remington was dispatched to the Cuban front to provide the Hearst newspapers with sketches of our first small step into American imperialism, the noted artist complained by telegram that there wasn't really enough shooting to keep him busy. "You make the pictures," Hearst wired back, "I'll make the war." This can be recognized not only as the true voice of power but also as a line of dialogue from a movie. In fact, it is the only purely Hearstian element in *Citizen Kane.*

There are parallels, but these can be just as misleading as comparisons. If San Simeon hadn't existed, it would have been necessary for the authors of the movie to invent it. Except for the telegram already noted and the crazy art collection (much too good to resist), in *Kane* everything *was* invented.

Let the incredulous take note of the facts.

William Randolph Hearst was born rich. He was the pampered son of an adoring mother. That is the decisive fact about him. Charles Foster Kane was born poor and was raised by a bank. There is no room here for details, but the differences between the real man and the character in the film are far greater than those between the shipowner and the newspaper tycoon.

And what of Susan Alexander? What indeed.

It was a real man who built an opera house for the soprano of his choice, and much in the movie was borrowed from that story, but the man was not Hearst. Susan, Kane's second wife, is not even based on the real-life soprano. Like most fictional characters, Susan's resemblance to other fictional characters is quite startling. To Marion Davies she bears no resemblance at all.

Kane picked up Susan on a street corner—from nowhere—where the poor girl herself thought she belonged. Marion Davies was no dim shop-girl; she was a famous beauty who had her choice of rich, powerful and attractive beaux before Hearst sent his first bouquet to her stage door. That Susan was Kane's wife and Marion was Hearst's mistress is a difference more important than might be guessed in today's changed climate of opinion. The wife was a puppet and a prisoner; the mistress was never less than a princess. Hearst built more than one castle, and Marion was the hostess in all of them: they were pleasure domes indeed, and the Beautiful People of the day fought for invitations. Xanadu was a lonely fortress, and Susan was quite right to escape from it. The mistress was never one of Hearst's possessions: he was always her suitor, and she was the precious treasure of his heart for more than thirty years, until his last breath of life. Theirs is truly a love story. Love is not the subject of *Citizen Kane*.

Susan was forced into a singing career because Kane had been forced out of politics. She was pushed from one public disaster to another by the bitter frustration of the man who believed that because he had married her and raised her up out of obscurity she was his to use as he might will. There is hatred in that.

Hearst put up the money for many of the movies in which Marion Davies was starred and, more importantly, backed her with publicity. But this was less of a favor than might appear. That vast publicity machine was all too visible; and finally, instead of helping, it cast a shadow—a shadow of doubt. Could the star have existed without the machine? The question darkened an otherwise brilliant career.

As one who shares much of the blame for casting another shadow—the shadow of Susan Alexander Kane—I rejoice in this opportunity to record something which today is all but forgotten except for those lucky enough to have seen a few of her pictures: Marion Davies was one of the most delightfully accomplished comediennes in the whole history of the screen. She would have been a star if Hearst had never happened. She was also a delightful and very considerable person. The proof is in this book, and I commend it to you.

Orson Welles
Los Angeles, California
May 28, 1975

The Times We Had

Marion and her sister Rose.

1

A fire in Brooklyn. Early days. The man who owned Campbell's Studio. A bicycle ride in Palm Beach. Carl Fisher calls from Miami. The Ziegfeld girl. Mr. Hearst signs a contract. A stop at Cartier's.

I was born in 1905.*
I was born in Brooklyn, at home. My mother had a great enormous house at Prospect Park.

One night when she and my father came back from the theatre, the house had burned to the ground. I had just been born. My mother wondered where Rose and I were, and she fainted dead away when she saw the ashes. My brother Charlie had set the house on fire with a box of matches.

After that, my father decided that if he didn't get us out of Brooklyn, Brooklyn would go to pieces. So I never lived in Brooklyn. As I say, I was born in Brooklyn, but I woke up in New York, at Gramercy Place.

I saw my brother Charles only once—in his coffin. I was very young when he died. It was after his holy communion. He had taken a rowboat with another little boy when he was told not to. The rowboat overturned. It took four weeks of poling the lake to find him.

When I got a bit older, my mother decided that I was kind of a problem. Because I stuttered, no school wanted me. When I'd get up to recite, all the kids would laugh at me. So my mother decided to put me in a convent—Sacred Heart, on the Hudson River.

But that didn't work out, so then my mother took me to France and put me into a convent there. It was near Tours, in the Chateaux district. When my mother came there to see me, all the nuns and the

_____
* Marion was born at six in the morning, Sunday, January 3, 1897.

1

My father was then a city magistrate.

Marion, age thirteen. *I wanted to go on the stage. School was dull.*

mother superior would spy on us. They wouldn't like me to say this, but there were peek holes.

My mother would say, "How are you?"

I said, "Fine."

She asked, "Like it here?"

I said, "Love it."

But when I squeezed her hand, she said, "I want to talk to the mother superior."

So the mother superior came down. She said, "What's wrong, Mrs. Douras?"

"I don't think my child is a very good influence in this convent, because she doesn't like it."

My mother was instinctively a very fine woman. She took me back to New York, and I was the happiest person in the world.

Then it was the Riverside Drive houses at 103rd Street, and then Chicago, and back and forth.

My father was then a city magistrate and my grandfather a district attorney. My grandfather owned two blocks from 12th to 14th Streets. He also had an enormous place at Saratoga, where he had race horses, and my grandmother owned an enormous estate in Upper Montclair.

I was living in Gramercy Park in 1907. My parents went to Chicago to see my sister Reine, and I was left in the care of a janitress, Mrs. Mower, who lived in the basement. I used to call her the cockeyed janitress. She didn't like that.

Over the basement was a living room and a dining room, and then over that was my mother and father's room, and over that was my room.

The house, sort of a gray stone, was right on the park and quite near Stanford White's house. My parents knew Mr. White, and they both had a great deal of respect for him. They thought he was a very nice man, that the stories told later on were absolutely untrue—about the cake and the naked girl dancing out of it, who was supposed to be Evelyn Nesbit.

Stanford White, the architect who designed the original Madison Square Garden and many other noted New York City structures, was shot and killed in 1906 in a dispute over actress Evelyn Nesbit. Her irate husband, the young Pittsburgh millionaire Harry K. Thaw, shot him three times during a performance of the comedy show MAMSELLE CHAMPAGNE at the Roof of the Garden. Evelyn Nesbit did not appear in the show, and it would only be much later, at a party given by Earl Carroll, that she would rise nude from great quantities of cake and prohibition champagne.

Well, Mrs. Mower had quite a job cleaning the whole house, so she'd say, "Here's the key. Go over in the park and play, then come right back." This was after school.

I was not supposed to be left on my own at that age. I think they suspected me already. But she'd say, "Here's ten cents for you: five cents for a can of sardines and five cents for a bottle of sarsaparilla." She thought that was enough for my luncheon at school. Of course I was little, so I didn't require much, but the combination of sardines and sarsaparilla—I think she believed in the two S's instead of the three R's.

At school I had a great precedent over the other children. I was the only one who was in the dunce seat all the time. I always had to sit in the corner with that thing on my head.

When I got home from school I'd look for Mrs. Mower. She'd be busy, so she'd give me the key and say, "Go into the park."

Outside the park, there'd be rag-gedy-looking little boys and girls. They were all screaming and throwing stones at the kids and nurses inside, and it seemed to me they were having more fun than we were—than I was, anyway, because I was always locked in. So I decided to join up with the outside forces, and since I had the key, I just went out and joined them. Nobody pays attention to youngsters who don't belong to them.

It happened to be Hallowe'en, and the kids had stockings filled with flour. Some of them had bricks in them, too. Well, they said, "You won't do what we do."

"I bet I will."

"We're going to Lexington Avenue, and on the way up we're going to steal some vegetables."

I was all in favor of that. I thought, Why shouldn't I? They were having fun, and I wanted to be in their set, which I thought was very, very elegant. My set was dull—the social set. So I went with them all the way to 26th Street. Imagine how far that was from the park at 19th Street.

We went to this big brownstone house and they said, "One of us will run up and ring the bell, then run down. Whoever answers the door, we throw at him." Well, a big fat butler opened the door. We gave it to him, all the vegetables, and then we started running. But the butler had a police whistle in his hand, and he blew it.

I thought I could run fast, but a policeman grabbed me by the pants. As he hung me up in the air he said, "Who are you? Where do you live? Where's your mother? What are you doing out at this time of night?"

I said, "It's Hallowe'en—just fun."

"Fun? All right, that's fine." He had a big Irish accent. "I'll tell you what we're going to do with you. We're going to put you in jail with all the other criminals."

"I didn't do anything."

"We caught you with the others." So he took me into the jailhouse. I was so frightened I wouldn't say a word.

It was the first time I'd ever been arrested.

They let me loose, but they wanted to see where I lived. I had the key, and when I went into the house they said, "Where's your keeper?"

"She's asleep downstairs."

Well, the door shut, and I went into the dining room and put the key on the table. I looked over in the corner, and there was a big rat. Because I was so little, he seemed really big, sitting up, looking at me with big black eyes.

I ran outside, slammed the door—and locked myself out of the house. I slept underneath the staircase all night long. Nobody found me.

Then my mother sent for me to come to Chicago. I guess the police had called them and said, "Your daughter's molesting an important citizen's house." That's how I found out that it was Mr. Hearst's house at 123 Lexington, at 26th Street.

It was just a coincidence that the kids picked his house that night.

Ten years later I ran into Mr. Hearst's car on my bicycle. I never believed in fate, but I think that was it.

Marion was envious of the exciting and glamorous life of a New York showgirl. Her elder sisters were then on stage—as was her friend Marie Glendinning. And Marion was able to talk her mother into sending her to Theodore Kosloff's ballet school.

Dancing is a rather different thing from school.

There's a huge mirror and there's music and you feel that you're doing something. You have on your toe slippers and you go up and down and you can see yourself with a hundred other kids. To me, that was life. But school wasn't. School was dull.

But my mother insisted that I go to school. Well, it didn't work out. She finally decided she had had enough. She asked me what I wanted to do. I said, "I want to go on the stage."

Then I went to Kosloff's school.

My father didn't like it, and my mother liked it even less. She stayed with me every second, but she was really heartbroken. She just didn't like the idea of anybody going on the stage so young.

I thought it was very good training for me. I believe people should get out and really start working when they are young. If you don't get started young, you get into a sort of lazy mental condition.

My mother still regarded Rose and me as kids. She couldn't figure out why we wanted to go on the stage. The reason was that our sisters Reine and Ethel were on the stage. We just wanted to ape our elder sisters. Rosie and I even wore their clothes when they weren't looking.

My sister Reine wanted to have a stage name. One day, while driving from her place on Long Island, she saw a real estate sign: DAVIES REAL ESTATE. She thought, "That's me."

We all took on the name automatically.*

My first job on the stage was the one that Marie Glendinning got for us. I was not quite fourteen when we went to Lee Herrick's Agency, and we got the job and the contract. My mother

---

* Real estate agent J. Clarence Davies had emigrated from the Netherlands, changing his name from Davries. His business is still evidenced by nameplates seen on buildings in Manhattan and by a collection of historical prints and photographs displayed at the Museum of the City of New York.

His son, Valentine Davies, went to California, wrote many motion picture scripts, became president of the Screen Writers Guild, and won an Academy Award for *Miracle on 34th Street*.

said, "I'm going to frame this contract, because every time I look at it, it's going to break my heart." I was in the pony ballet and Rose was a showgirl.

The showgirls were tops. The pony ballet not only had to shine the chorus girls' shoes, but they had to wait on the showgirls too.

They would just run around and say, "Hey, come here, kid. Come here, now. How would you like to lace my shoes? How would you like to help me on with my costume?"

No matter what work we were doing, we had to stop to help them. I mean, behind the scenes. That was the routine that always went on in the pony ballet. But we didn't mind. Youngsters always have adoration for elders, even when they are only older girls. We used to think, "Oh, how glamorous they are." If the chorus girls were glamorous, the showgirls were super glamorous. "Can we do anything for you?"

They'd say, "Yes. How would you like to go and get me a glass of water?" Something like that. So we were constantly waiting on them.

I never got tired, because I loved it. I loved the theatre, the smells, the greasepaint. When they'd say, "Half an hour! Fifteen minutes! Overture!" then you'd run like mad down the stairs to get on the stage.

My first show was Maeterlinck's *The Bluebird*. It opened in Washington.* My family was there in the audience.

On opening night, mothers are not allowed backstage at all; they make the kids nervous. So Reine and my mother and Ethel and my father were in a box watching my maneuvers. They had to have a spyglass to see me, because I was way in the back.

When you were in the pony ballet,

---

* In 1910, when Marion was only thirteen.

My sister Reine wanted to have a stage name. . . . She saw a real estate sign—DAVIES REAL ESTATE—and she thought, "That's me." We all took on the name. (Photo courtesy Mrs. Valentine Davies.)

I was not quite fourteen and I was in the pony ballet.

When I got out of the pony ballet I became a Ziegfeld girl.

The girls in the show told me who he was. They said W.R. was a wolf in sheep's clothing.

you were not mentioned at all; the programs just said *Ballet*. But I got this big batch of telegrams from Calvin Coolidge, Senator Knox, Woodrow Wilson, Andrew Mellon and others.

It was very exciting. Thinking I'd make myself a big shot with the big showgirls, I said, "I have a lot of telegrams."

When they looked at them they said, "Hmmmm—get a load of her." And then they started laughing. I didn't know what they were laughing about.

I thought, "There's something rotten in Denmark here."

They said, "Isn't it funny that they all came from the same place?" From Claridge's Hotel, New York.

My sister Reine had sent all the telegrams.

My first real admirer while I was on the stage was called the "Boston Millionaire." That's how it is when you're on the stage; you get admirers and proposals of marriage or something. It doesn't matter what your face looks like; it's all how you look from across the footlights. And every girl in a show looks glamorous to the audience. Now this one was a bachelor. He sat in the first row and was very elegant. But he had to have an introduction, through my mother.

Ziegfeld would always insist that the stage-door-Johnnies had to be introduced properly. And there were so many, and all with proposals. It was preposterous, in a way, because they were looking over the footlights. When we looked the other way, into the audience, no matter how well dressed a man was, it wasn't as exciting as the stage. The glamour was all on the stage. And I hated to leave the stage after a performance.

What restaurant, even the Ritz-Carlton, could give the glamour that the stage did? I wanted to just go home at night, because everything else looked dark. Nothing was interesting.

When I got out of the pony ballet, I became a Ziegfeld Girl. Some were dancers and some were showgirls. I was one of the dancers, but they picked out little special things for me to do. I failed in every one of them.

I had long curls, practically to my waist, and Ziegfeld thought I looked like the *Spirit of Spring*.* I was supposed to walk down a staircase in a gorgeous costume of blue tulle with sparkles on it and a maribou hat and say, "I am the spirit of spring."

I said to my mother, "I don't think I can say that line. Because I st-st-stutter."

"You stammer."

"What difference does it make? Stutter, stammer, it's the same th-th-thing."

But she said, "I think you can make it."

On opening night she gave me a glass of champagne. It tasted kind of bitter. Mother said, "I know you don't like it, but it'll help you. You can do it."

The big music started, and I was supposed to come down in that gorgeous costume that Ziegfeld had spent a thousand dollars on.

But they had picked the wrong girl.

When I got down the stairs—this was the curtain, the finale—I looked around and I started, "I-I-I-I-I-I . . ." So they pulled the curtain.

The next day at rehearsal they chose somebody else. My heart was broken, not because of that line, but because they had taken the costume away from me. I was back in the back line again. Opening night, I was in front; second night, I'm in the back row.

There are lots of tragedies in the theatre, but I really did love it.

I never liked young men, which was the funny part of it. The stage-door-Johnnies I didn't like. Especially those

_____

* The final production number of a Ziegfeld show.

8

who came from Yale. Princeton wasn't too bad; Harvard was a little bit on the boring side.

Once, a show I was in was playing New Haven, and the Yale boys took a dislike to the play, and especially to the leading lady, Gaby Deslys.

We were there for two weeks. On the last night the Yale boys brought all the vegetables they could think of— rotten tomatoes, eggs and everything— and started throwing. Gaby Deslys got a tomato in her face, and all the ponies were spottsy. We were lucky to be in the back row that night.

Then they started dragging up the seats, and they had to get the fire hose on them to get them out of the theatre.

I didn't know Mr. Hearst then, but he always sat in the front row at the *Follies*.* The girls in the show told me who he was. They said, "Look out for him—he's looking at you. He's a wolf in sheep's clothing."

That was so ridiculous, because he wouldn't have hurt a fly, but I didn't know him then. He sent me flowers and little gifts, like silver boxes or gloves or candy. I wasn't the only one he sent gifts to, but all the girls thought he was particularly looking at me, and the older ones would say, "Look out . . ."

The next thing that happened—I was asked to have some special photographs made at Campbell's Studio.** I was elated by the idea, but my first thought was, "What am I going to wear?" My mother said, "You've got to ask the dresser if you can borrow some clothes from the show."

I got the clothes, and we went to

---

* At the New Amsterdam Theatre in New York.
** At 530 Fifth Avenue, New York City.

I had some pictures taken at Campbell's Studio, but I had to borrow some clothes from the show.

At Campbell's Studio, Marion held up the backdrop. She had been in a piece called *Little Butterfly from Japan*.

Campbell's Studio. My mother fixed my hair, and the photographer knocked on the door and asked, "Are you ready?" So I went out and he told me where to stand.

I had two or three pictures taken before I saw Mr. Hearst. It was hard to see past the bright lights, and he was sitting right under the camera. He was dressed very conservatively, in a dark blue suit. If his suit had been in any other kind of color, I might have seen him sooner.

I ran into the dressing room because this was the man I had been warned not to talk to. I said to my mother, "Lock the door—the wolf is here!"

"What wolf?" she said. Then Mr. Campbell knocked on the door and said, "Aren't you ready?"

"She's a little nervous," said my mother.

When we got out in the studio, Mr. Hearst had left. He hadn't meant any harm, and he owned Campbell's Studio. But he had the most penetrating eyes—honest, but penetrating eyes. He didn't have a harmful bone in his body. He just liked to be by himself and just look at the girls on the stage while they were dancing..

I think he was a very lonesome man. But that was not my first meeting with him, because I didn't actually meet him.

The next time I saw Mr. Hearst was down in Florida at Jim Deering's house, after the show had closed.

His place was called Vizcaya Villa. It was in Miami, on the bay—Biscayne Bay, I think.

An interesting coincidence of names was that W.R. had played a strong, if unsupportable, role in demanding war when the American ship Maine *was sunk in Havana harbor. At the time of the sinking, a Spanish warship, paying a courtesy call on New York, was an-chored off the Battery. In the wake of public indignation, courtesies were scuttled, and the ship, the* Vizcaya, *sailed for the open seas.*

Vizcaya was an enormous white marble house that looked like a Venetian palace. Outside, there was a sort of canal with Venetian poles and a big marble ship. There was a huge garden on one side, and the swimming pool was half indoors and half outside. On the other side was a sand beach—just an imitation beach, not a real one.

The floors inside were all black marble. There was an enormous dining room and a big patio where we used to look at movies. It was very formal. Inside was Empire, outside was Venetian. It was a beautiful place.

We often went there in the winter—Ethel and Rose and I. Never Reine, because Reine was always busy doing something else. I had a strange room, but very nice. It was all black marble, pink satin, and ostrich feathers. Can you imagine anything like that! It was called the *Little Princess* room. Jim Deering used to reserve it for the younger degeneration.*

Everything had to be ver-ry, very dignified with Jim. He was absolutely proper; nothing out of order. Nobody would ever say anything that was wrong—not the slightest bit off-key.

Jim was very austere; much, much too formal. After dinner we'd see a picture on the patio; after that we'd go swimming; after that, breakfast in the morning. And everybody should be on time.

The routine was really annoying. It made me want to break jail. That sort of behavior ruins your indigestion.

I said to my mother, "I'm terribly

---

* In 1975 a communication from Vizcaya, now the Dade County Art Museum in Miami, noted, "There has never been such a room as the *Little Princess* room at Vizcaya."

I was down in Florida at Jim Deering's house, Vizcaya Villa. (Photo courtesy Miami-Metro Department of Publicity and Tourism.)

It looked like a Venetian palace. Outside there was a sort of canal with Venetian poles and a big marble ship. (Photo courtesy Miami-Metro Department of Publicity and Tourism.)

bored here. What a lot of grumpy people." Well, I won't mention any names, but this was no place for anybody who wanted to have fun. Jim Deering's ruling was that anybody who was his house guest had to be his house guest. And if they didn't like it, they could . . . you know. So I jumped over the wall one night.

Marion was presumably bound for the amusements of Palm Beach, probably to meet her friend from Philadelphia, socialite Ella Widener, who would take her to Bradley's Beach Club and Casino.

Colonel Edward Riley Bradley ran the club from 1898 to 1946. The location, by the Flagler Bridge, is now called Bradley Park, in his memory.

The small house of games is gone, the fixtures drowned in the Atlantic Ocean by the terms of the will of Bradley, who was also an artist, civic leader and philanthropist. Later, Joseph P. Kennedy would eulogize, "When Bradley's went, this place lost its zipperoo."

Well, of course I had to go back. My mother said, "Jim is furious. There's a car down there for you. You had better get back here." So I went back to the same dull people.

Bertie McCormick* was there. He was married, but I can't think of how many times he had been married. At that time I think he was in the procedure of divorce. I'm not positive.

He was a rather husky man, rather on the heavy side, with a white mustache. He was very nice: jovial and amusing. I didn't appreciate his humor at that time because I was a brat. But

he had everybody at the table laughing all the time.

He must have been a middle-aged man, because at that time he looked older than W.R.

Ruth Bryan Owen, who was the Ambassador to Sweden or Norway or something, and Mr. and Mrs. Harry Winston were there, too.* Jim was very fond of Mrs. Winston. As for the rest of the people, although it was a very small group, I didn't even know their names. I wasn't interested in them one bit. But I knew that they were supposed to be the social elite of Miami.

Whenever I'd make a wrong move, W.R.'d always come to the rescue. But I'd never see him. I mean you don't speak to someone unless you're properly introduced. He was always a shadow. But it didn't do any harm. He helped me many times when I unsus-

---

* Ms. Owen would become a United States Congresswoman from Florida in 1928. The Winstons were jewelers.

---

* Colonel Robert McCormick was the publisher of the *Chicago Tribune* and a partner in Deering Harvester, the farm equipment manufacturing company later to be split into the John Deere Company and the International Harvester Company.

The women of the Douras family in 1918. From the left: Marion, Irene (Reine), Mama Rose, Ethel and Rose Marie.

Sister Reine owned the Rolls-Royce. Marion, in a promotion for the Ziegfeld *Follies*, drove an Overland Cloverleaf in Central Park.

pectingly got myself into some kind of a jam.

Like the time I went to Bradley's. I was there with Mrs. Widener. She always used to gamble a lot—ten thousand on the black, twenty thousand on the red.

Suddenly I got a note—kind of a thick note. I opened the envelope. There was fifteen hundred dollars in it. That was a fortune to me. The place was all very alive, everybody gambling, and Mrs. Widener said, "What have you got there?"

I looked around, and behind one of the red curtains was W.R. I thought, Oh, I can't accept it. But Mrs. Widener said, "Give it to me. I'll put it on— Where did you get that?"

I said, "My mother gave it to me." Well, she put it all on zero and lost.

I still didn't know W.R. It was still to be a long, long time—too long. I wish I had that time to live over—it might have been sooner. I saw him many times, but there was no conversation. It was like Svengali, or Pygmalion and Galatea.

The first time I really officially met W.R. was in Palm Beach. I had gone bicycling at the country club one day. Gene Buck was with me.*

It was very hilly there. We started going downhill, and I lost control of the brake. Lickety-split I went up in the air—my panties showing—and then I was lying flat. I still have the wound from that morning. I just missed a car by inches. The car stopped, and W.R. got out. He said, "May I help you?"

"Noooo . . . I can make it."

In the meantime Gene Buck had gone in the other direction and fallen on his can, too.

W.R. said, "Your bicycle's broken." It was practically split in half. He picked up the bicycle and tied it on the back of his car. Then he told the driver to take me to the Royal Poinciana.*

Now he recognized me. He'd seen me at Campbell's Studio in New York. But all he did was stick his head in the car and say, "Mrs. Hearst, will you kindly get out and walk?" And they just walked off, after he'd fastened the bicycle on.

And that was really our first meeting.

I tried to talk to the chauffeur. I said, "Nice day, isn't it?"

He said, "The usual procedure."

"What do you mean by that?"

"Everybody says it's a nice day. But it isn't, really." And he took me back to the hotel.

Another time I was supposed to be selling something at a bazaar. And Mr. Hearst was sitting there with his family.

He came up to me and said, "I'll pay five thousand dollars for your watch." It wasn't worth it—it was just a black band—but W.R. bought it.

At times W.R. would telephone Jim Deering's house. Or his valet would call to ask if Miss Douras was there.

Then Jim Deering's valet would say that a man had called and asked for me. At dinner one evening Jim said, "Someone has called and asked for a character at the table here whom I don't wish to mention."

Everybody looked at each other, because Jim was very austere. He said, "Marion, do you know a Mr. Carl Fisher?" I said no.

And Jim said to the others, "Well, somebody here does, because he keeps calling all the time."

---

* Gene Buck wrote the music for the 1915 *Ziegfeld Follies,* which Marion played in.

* Said to be the largest resort hotel in the world in the 1920s. It had a Cocoanut Grove Restaurant and a Palm Beach railroad stop. It was also the largest wooden building in the world.

The next day Jim pulled the same routine on the patio. He said, "Mr. Carl Fisher called up again."

I said, "Who did he ask for?"

"He asked for you."

"But James, I don't know any Carl Fisher. Where did he call from?"

"He said Palm Beach."

"I know someone in Miami."

"Well, it could have been that he was at Palm Beach at the time."

"I don't know," I said.

Then Jim said to my mother, "Why don't you tell her to keep quiet? She talks too much." He wouldn't let anyone talk on the phone.

Carl Fisher was a Miami real estate tycoon. People used to call him Mr. Miami. Hearst would often use his name as a joke.

When we went back to New York, I saw W.R. at a party given at the Beaux Arts Building on 42nd Street, where the artists lived and had their offices. There was an enormous restaurant down below which was supposed to be very exclusive.

That was where the party was held. I was with Angie Duke, Doris's cousin,* and quite a number of people were there. W.R. was in white tie and evening dress. It was a society-charity party—I forget which charity.

I couldn't stay very late because I had to work the following morning. When it was time to go, Angie asked for my wrap. While we were waiting, a voice behind me said, "May I say good night?" I turned around and it was W.R. He said, "May I shake your hand?"

"Certainly," I said.

We shook hands and he said, "Good night, Miss Douras." I felt something in my hand. I thought, What the heck

is this? Then he left, and Angie took me home.

I didn't open my palm until I got home.

It was a diamond wristwatch.

The next night I had to go to Boston for the rehearsals of a new show, which turned out to be a flop. But after rehearsal at the theatre that night it was snowing like mad, and we went screaming down the street, all of us laughing, and I lost the wristwatch.

I was staying in Boston with a friend, Pickles St. Clair,* and another girl, and they said, "We'll look for it." And starting from the theatre we looked all over, picking up all the snow, trying to find the wristwatch.

Well, I was crying because I'd lost my wristwatch. I shouldn't ever have accepted it—I knew that; I was in the wrong. But when I lost it, I was digging up the snow, retracing my steps back from the Copley Plaza to the theatre. Finally, Pickles said, "You'd better call up Mr. Hearst."

"I wouldn't dare do that. It doesn't sound right to me. I can't possibly do it."

Pickles said, "Then I'll call him."

"Don't you dare!"

But she did, and—I think it was the next day—I got another one. Not a note, not a word, just another diamond wristwatch.

But this one wasn't as pretty.

I said, "Look, Pickles, you keep it. I don't want it. But when I told you not to call him, why did you? It looks like I'm cheating—and I'm not a cheater."

After the *Follies,* I was in a show playing in Wilmington, Delaware. The manager of the show was Charles Dil-

* Angier Biddle Duke, a society figure and one of Marion's beaux, had just returned, wounded, from World War I.

* Pickles St. Clair was a showgirl with Marion in the revue, *STOP! LOOK! LISTEN!*

lingham, and the show was called, I think, *Misinformation*. I had a very big part in that show. I held up the back-drop.

Well, on the train coming back from Wilmington, Dillingham walked out and said to us, "What punks know how to play cards here?" That time we weren't called ponies. And none of us knew how to play cards. But he picked me out, and another girl. We went into the drawing room, and there was old Colonel Dupont—or maybe he was a general. He was very tall, with a mustache. We said we didn't know how to play poker, but he said, "I'll take you on for just one game."

I said, "All right, but what are the stakes?"

He said that, just to be kind, we'd make it a dollar. When we got through, he said, "You lost."

"How much?" I asked.

He said, "Twenty-five dollars." Now that was a fortune to me. I was making eighteen dollars a week, and I had with me about thirty dollars. Part was my salary from the last week, which I was going to take home.

Well, I gave it to him. And that was that.

But the story he told to various friends was that he felt so sorry for me and was so ashamed that, as he was getting off the train at Grand Central, he was looking for me. He said, "That poor little girl, who doesn't have any money . . . and I had to take twenty-five dollars from her." As he was walking to his Ford car, which was waiting for him, he saw me, the poor little pony, getting into a Rolls-Royce. "Then I didn't feel sorry," he told them.

Well, it so happened that my sister Reine owned that Rolls-Royce. She had come to the station to meet me.

I never saw Dillingham again, but I heard the story from various people. Even Mr. Hearst heard the story, and he told it as a funny story. But I didn't think it was.

Florenz Ziegfeld was always looking for the most beautiful and the most

Marion with Matt Moore in her first film, *Runaway Romany*. It was released in December 1917.

fascinating, to be in his FOLLIES. These productions became more and more elaborate with the addition of special effects.

Ziegfeld had discovered something red and green and new and tried it out just before intermission at the *Follies.* But we first saw it at dress rehearsal.

It was an experiment—a motion picture shown on a big screen after the first act of the show. Everyone wore glasses with one red and one green lens.

The film showed animals having a big fight, and a gorilla looked right into the camera, bared his fangs and went "GGGRRRRrrrr . . ." right up to your face. Every night the audience would scream.

When we saw it, we nearly killed each other trying to get backstage. I don't know who screamed the loudest —I think I did. We all ran like mad. I know I was the first back in the dressing room.

Now they call them three-dimensional films, but no one can say they are new. Ziegfeld had them then. But W.R. never got into that setup. He did become interested in making motion pictures a short time before I came on the scene. He got more into it afterwards.

Marion already had spent several years on the stage—first as a FOLLIES girl and later as a showgirl in road-shows. Contrary to her modest remarks, Marion was a very successful showgirl, not always the star, but a featured performer and a singer and dancer.

She worked in several films before she signed the first contract with W.R. And she even wrote the story for the first film in which she starred, RUN-AWAY ROMANY, produced in 1917 by *her brother-in-law's Ardsley Art Film Company.*

I had my first actual conversation with W.R. when I was called to the International Studios at 127th Street, in New York, where they were making motion pictures.

I still didn't know him at all except to say, "How do you do"—that was all.

At the studio I had to wait in the office, as everybody else did, until finally I got in to see Carl Zittel, the studio manager. He said, "I've seen your picture. It rather stinks."

"Yes, it does . . . I guess."

"But I want to make a test of you and see if you're worthy," he said. "I know you can't act, but I'm going to give you a chance."

"What sort of test?" I asked.

"What did you get for *Runaway Romany?*"

"I got fifty dollars."

He said, "I might give you a contract for about, say, five hundred dollars a week."

"Well—I don't think I'm worth that."

"Think it over," he said. "Now go— I'm busy."

Later, I went back to look at the tests I had made. I was sitting in the darkened projection room, waiting for the projectionist, when a little man came in with a briefcase and sat down next to me. My tests were flashed on the screen, and I was awful. I said, "I'm ashamed of it; let's shut it off."

He said, "Oh, it's all right."

When it was over he said, "I've come here with a wonderful contract for you. Also, Mr. Hearst has rented the Harlem Park Casino. He rented it from a widow for five hundred dollars a week for ninety years."

I said, "It looks like he's going into production." Then the man was called in to see Mr. Zittel, and I sat there while they ran my tests over again. I didn't like seeing them, and I thought, I'd better get out of here.

When I got to the elevator, W.R. was there. He said, "How do you do?"

And I said, "How do you do?"

Then he said, "I'm buying a new studio—or renting it for a thousand dollars a week—to make pictures. We'd be very happy to have you among the stars."

"A thousand dollars a week?"

"Yes. I'm going in now to sign the contract."

"Look," I said, "I don't know you very well, Mr. Hearst, but it isn't a thousand—it's five hundred. I talked to the lawyer in there, and he said five hundred, for ninety years."

"Did he say that?"

"Pardon me if I'm out of turn, but he told me he was very happy about the widow getting five hundred a week for ninety years. She can't live that long."

"Would you mind waiting here for a minute?" he said.

"No, I'm sorry, I can't. I've got to go."

"Have you got a car?"

"Certainly I have a car. I don't walk all the time."

We went down in the elevator, and he saw me to my car. Then he called Zittel.

Well, Zittel got fired. I didn't mean to do anything, but it happened accidentally, and I thought, How can people be so crooked? Five hundred dollars a week for ninety years! He couldn't live that long either. But he had two contracts. Five hundred dollars a week for the widow and five hundred for himself.

Mr. Hearst always placed his faith in people who had no faith.

I waited, and finally W.R. rang up my father and said, "I would like to start some productions with your daughter at any amount of money."

And my father said, "Well, I don't know. Did you see her first picture? She really was no good on the screen."

That was my dad. And I agreed with him, but apparently the answer was yes. W.R. sent a contract to the house for me to sign for five hundred dollars a week for one year with an option. I signed it, because on the stage I was only getting forty-five or fifty dollars a week.

We went into production immediately.

I did I don't know how many pictures. In those days they made them in a hurry. Eleven days was about it. And Mr. Hearst always used to look at the rushes, and then he would express an opinion, or send a note. Occasionally he did come on the set.

He used to call up my mother and ask if he could come for dinner. And we'd sit around afterwards and listen to the radio or play cards or something silly like that. It got to be a very friendly affiliation.

He told my father that he was in love with me, and my father said, "It's up to her. She went on the stage of her own volition, and her life is in her own hands. Her career, whatever she wants to do, whatever my daughter decides —it's all right with me."

And my mother felt the same way.

W.R. said he would try to get a divorce, and he did try. He spent hundreds and thousands of dollars trying. But there was the Catholic religion, and I think his wife felt that it said, "I will not accept a divorce." But instead it says, "If you are divorced, you cannot get married again in the Catholic Church."

In New York there were no grounds for divorce except adultery, and since

MARION DAVIES'S JEWELRY COLLECTION
AT THE TIME OF HER DEATH

	VALUATION
RINGS	
Platinum marquise solitaire ring, approx. 21 ct.	$50,000
Cabochon emerald ring with 10 diamonds	700
Emerald solitaire ring, approx. 17 ct.	21,000
2 genuine pearl rings	1,600
3 genuine sapphire rings	1,500
NECKLACES	
Genuine pearl necklace (46 baroque pearls) with 18-diamond clasp	3,000
Platinum diamond and emerald choker, emeralds approx. 70 ct., with 281 diamonds	6,500
Ruby and diamond necklace	7,500
Carved emerald necklace	4,000
Diamond choker, 15 marquise diamonds and 2 pear-shaped diamonds	22,500
Sapphire necklace	12,500
1 three-strand semi-baroque cultured pearl necklace	40
BRACELETS	
Emerald and diamond bracelet, beads and diamonds	2,000
Platinum ruby and diamond bracelet with 3 rubies	7,000
Platinum diamond bracelet (4 large diamonds with numerous small diamonds)	6,500
Marquise diamond bracelet with 2 square diamonds	15,000
Emerald and diamond bracelet with 22 cabochon emeralds	4,500
Platinum diamond bracelet	2,500
Emerald bracelet containing 19 emeralds	12,500
Sapphire diamond snake bracelet	4,000
Cabochon emerald diamond bracelet	1,110
Cabochon ruby and diamond bracelet	5,000*
Ceylon sapphire and diamond bracelet	10,000*
BANGLES, CLIPS AND BROOCHES	
Trabert & Hoeffer cabochon emerald bangle with 38 diamonds	1,100
Emerald diamond clip with 10 emeralds and 46 diamonds	350
Platinum diamond clips	1,800
Diamond buckle brooch	3,000
Platinum sapphire brooch	6,500
Ruby and diamond clips	5,000
Emerald and diamond brooch	5,000
1 pin—American flag	750
1 pin—ballerina shape (gold, platinum and pearls)	200
1 brooch pin—horseshoe design	300
1 magistrate's badge—City of New York	10
PENDANTS	
Cabochon emerald pendant with 50 round diamonds, approx. 3 ct.	2,000
Pear-shaped diamond pendant, approx. 29 ct.	90,000
MISCELLANEOUS	
Platinum diamond watch	1,200
1 gold finger ring	50
1 gold chain with gold charm ballerina	25
Gold toothpick	10

All of the above items with two exceptions (*) were sold in open court in 1963 to E. B. Kislinger for $407,500, which was the top bid for the entire lot.

her cousin was the chief of police, he would let her know if she was being watched. Naturally, she was very cautious.

They were estranged before I met him—W.R. was fifty-eight when we met—and he was lonely. That was why he'd go to the shows, and the girls would think he was a wolf. But he was not.

Of all the innocent people, he was the kindest, most innocent, naive person you'd ever want to meet. He wouldn't have harmed anybody, ever.

I remember that once W.R.'s valet, talking to one of the maids, said, "Mr. Hearst is the cleanest man I've ever seen. Or smelt. He doesn't have to take a shower; he's just—clean." And he was clean mentally as well as physically.

W.R. would say, "I'm in love with you. What am I going to do about it?"

I'd say, "Well, let it ride. It's all right with me."

You can tell by a person's look whether he's in love with you or not. Definitely, he was. And he said, "I don't like it this way." But he was always hoping.

And he never, never once said anything wrong, and he never made any passes—but I could tell by his eyes that he loved me.

My father liked W.R. He said he was an honest man. My parents thought he was honest because ours was purely a friendship. It was just a friendship for quite a long time. And it was a very nice sort of friendship to have.

He would come maybe once a week for dinner. Maybe a month would go by. But always he'd bring Guy Barham or Frank Barham or Orrin Peck.* He was never alone. Maybe he was just

------

* They were close friends of W.R., and the Barhams would soon work for him as publishers of the *Los Angeles Herald*. Orrin Peck was a celebrated portrait painter.

protecting himself; I don't know. He was fifty-eight when I was sixteen.

And so their love affair began. Times were different then. It was not acceptable to be seen in public with another woman's husband . . .

We'd go to a restaurant, and as long as another man was along, no one could accuse Mr. Hearst of being indiscreet. But we could always sit in a corner and talk. I was in love, and I know he was, too.

I think W.R. was a little jealous of my leading men. But I told him, "That's silly. Everyone has to do a little embrace in pictures, just for the audience's sake."

But he used to cut out all those scenes, and the pictures would end up with no embrace. No kissing at all, even though it was supposed to be a happy ending. He said, "Mary Pickford's always made very fine, clean pictures. And I want you to do the same."

It was the same way when I was on the stage.

Once Henry Bull called up my mother and said, "The Prince of Wales is in New York, and we're giving a party tomorrow night for him." And at that time everybody was excited about the Prince, and I wanted to go to the party after I left the theatre.

When I came out of the matinee, W.R. was waiting, and he said, "May I drive you home?" It was snowing, and my mother wasn't there, so I went with him. We drove up Fifth Avenue, and he stopped at Cartier's.

He went in, and in no time he came out with two things in his pocket. Of course I didn't know what they were at the time. Then he asked me, "Are you going to that party tonight that General Vanderbilt's giving?"

I said I was.

"Would you rather have some jewelry than go to the party?"

"What?"

He showed me a diamond and pearl bracelet and a pearl and diamond ring. He said, "If you don't go to the party, these are yours."

Now what was I supposed to do? Bird in the hand, you know.

He was afraid I might fall in love with the Prince of Wales. I had to make a quick decision. I said, "I won't go." In other words, "Gimme, gimmee, gimmeee."

He let me out at the house, and I decided I'd really pull a double-double. I'd keep the jewelry and still go to the party. But he had detectives outside of the house, watching, and I couldn't get out. I called Henry Bull and said, "I'm awfully sorry—I have a headache and I can't go." So I missed the Prince of Wales's party.

W.R. admitted he was jealous, and then I was trapped. I thought, No, I don't want to meet him, but I really did. Everybody in New York wanted to meet him.

Later I met the Prince when we were down at Sunnydale at his house outside London. He was then going around with Lady Dudley Ward. It was just before he met Wally Simpson.*

I was hoping that someday W.R. and I would marry, but, as I said to him, "Love is not always created at the altar. Love doesn't need a wedding ring."

For years he tried to get a divorce,

* Henry Bull was a partner of General Vanderbilt. The Prince of Wales did have a romance, not with Lady Dudley Ward, so far as is known, but with Gloria Vanderbilt's aunt, Lady Thelma Furness.

and because he couldn't, he was miserable. I knew what he was trying to do, but he wasn't getting anywhere.

Not only did he have the detectives working, but he tried to put a law through that any married couple who had not lived together for the past ten years was automatically divorced. In his case, he could have made it twenty years, but the Catholic Church barged in and killed that.

But I was very happy the way we were. I had great respect for him and he had respect for me. We were together, and that was all that mattered.

There was his work and there was my work. He was interested in my work; he was on the sets, he went over the dialogue, and he even used to direct some of the scenes.

I was interested in his work, but there was a little difference. He had more intelligence about my work than I had about his, and that was really true.

We were going along just the way I wanted it to be. I wanted to be Marion Davies, having the great privilege of knowing Mr. William Randolph Hearst. That was all I wanted.

I might have accepted marriage, had it been possible; I might not have. I had seen enough of marriage, and to me it didn't mean anything at all. It was just based on a ring, and suppose the ring breaks? You don't base everything from God on a wedding ring.

W.R. didn't think so. He wanted to make me an honest woman, which was rather ridiculous. But he felt very deeply on the subject. I didn't. I would dodge it all the time, as a matter of fact. When people get married, they get into a lapse of indifference. The husband thinks he can go out and do what he wants, and so does the wife. I used to see that all the time. Why should I run after a streetcar when I was already aboard?

Marion in *Young Diana*, in 1922.

2

Silent pictures. The Great Marion Davies Murder. An opening at the Cosmopolitan Theatre. Marion moves to California. Terrified by a lion. A party for the King of Siam. Mr. Hearst puts all his eggs in one basket.

I couldn't act, but the idea of silent pictures appealed to me, because I couldn't talk either. Silent pictures were right up my alley, and that's how I got all the bad notices, except for the one that Louella Parsons wrote.

She was working on the *Morning Telegraph,* and W.R. apparently read her review. Everybody else said, "Stinking." But Louella said, "Give the girl a chance." W.R. immediately hired her for the New York *American,* because of that one review.

W.R. always said to me, "Never read any bad reviews about yourself. Read only the good ones." Of course I thought, What if there are no good ones? Then I'm really in the dumps. I'd rather read the bad ones than the good ones anyway, because at least there are more of them.

And you might find out what's wrong. If they say this scene or that scene is not good enough, or if the comedy is lacking, maybe you can perk it up.

If they only say, "You're shining, blooming, blah, blah, blah . . ." you have nothing to go on, except conceit and ego, which doesn't help work at all. I liked criticism, but W.R. said, "I never read any of it."

I thought it was an incentive to prove the critics wrong, and you need that needling in the theatrical business. Nobody's perfect, and if they said, "She was wonderful in her performance; nothing could have been better," then I may as well have packed up and gone to bed.

23

After I'd made about six or eight pictures, W.R. started the Cosmopolitan Pictures Company, and then he signed a contract with MGM. But that was after about two years.

The first Cosmopolitan production, made for an MGM release in 1924, was YOLANDA. By then Marion had made seventeen feature films, released by Select Pictures, Graphic Films, Pathé or Paramount.

Little Old New York and *When Knighthood Was in Flower* were very successful. They made money. The other pictures we made did not.

When *Knighthood* opened at the Criterion Theatre and we were all there in a box, I had a speech prepared. But after the picture ended, the lights went up and everybody left the theatre, so I didn't have a chance to speak. I was so glad, but all through my dinner I had been trying to memorize the speech and I couldn't eat.

I had to learn fencing for that picture. Every day for four hours, for four months. I had a mask for the first month and buttons on the ends of the swords. Then they took the mask away and then they took the buttons off. I was frightened stiff. And my legs were stiff, too, from lunging.

It was awfully hard on the back and the legs.

But I was supposed to be disguised as a boy, and I'm in an inn in England in *Knighthood,* and they think I'm not quite a boy.

I had escaped from my brother, who was Henry the Eighth.

So I had a drink and ate the meat, with my hands, and then somebody said, "How about a duel?" So then I had a duel—with five or six men. You could have five eyes knocked out. You have to be *en garde* all the time. Well,

it took four months to rehearse that scene, and I thought it was kind of fun, in a way. I didn't mind the work, but my legs and my back did. The preparation was harder work than the actual production.

I was so stiff I couldn't walk, but the director thought I walked just like a princess. That was Bob Vignola and he was a very good director, and I did about six pictures with him. I was like a racehorse. Once I got started I wanted to run, and once I stopped I just wanted to lie down and read a book, with my hooves on.

But I did a lot of pictures. I worked harder than I thought I did, but it was a very happy existence. The parties, the dinners, not much rest. But sleep wasn't important. It was one big merry-go-round.

I really wanted to give up when the talkies came in. I was all right in silent movies when I just had to make faces at the camera. But I wasn't interested in silent films. It wasn't really work. When the talkies began, I realized I had to work; I couldn't stall around anymore. But even when I worked hard, I still wound up at zero. I had tried, anyway.

It's a pretty rugged life for a person. You have to admire actors. It's a wonder they have any hearts left, the way they work. They get so excited when they go through emotional scenes.

I didn't have it. When we would see a play, W.R.'d say, "I think you could have done that better." But I knew perfectly well I couldn't have done it even half as well. But he was prejudiced, which was understandable. And I rather liked him for that. He made me feel comfortable when I was uneasy.

Now the critics didn't quite agree with his theory, so he didn't read any of the criticisms. I thought I had to read the critics just to know how I

Marion in *When Knighthood Was in Flower,* 1922. She played the role of Mary Tudor. Lyn Harding portrayed the elder brother, King Henry VIII.

The fencing scene from *When Knighthood Was in Flower*.

In New York City, the Prince of Wales said *Knighthood* was wonderful. In London, *it was a terrific failure. . . . The English paid a lot of attention to their critics.*

was. W.R. would say, "I know you're all right." But he was just one critic.

Some of my pictures did get some critical approval. *Operator 13* did, *Little Old New York* did, *Peg o' My Heart* did and *Knighthood* did, except in London, where they said, "Why should an American girl play Mary Tudor?" They thought it was horrible for the sister of Henry the Eighth to talk like me— and they tore me apart in London. But the English are the ones who should watch their diction. I can hardly understand them or their films, and I'm very proud of my American accent.

Well, the English paid a lot of attention to their critics, and *Knighthood* was a terrific failure in England.

We could have made *Little Old New York* in less time, but the whole studio

had burned down, with my costumes and everything. We had to move over to Fort Lee in New Jersey and I had to get new costumes.

And another thing happened when I was doing *Little Old New York*. There was the Freeport murder. And that happened the same day that the studio burned.

I was sleeping at my mother's house. I had to get up early in the mornings to go to work, and the newspapers had EXTRAs on the street. The boys were outside yelling, "Read all about the Marion Davies murder!"

So we sent for a newspaper. There was a story: "Woman shoots husband because of jealousy of Marion Davies, who was at her sister's home at a birthday party for her father."

I was nowhere near Freeport. I was at Riverside Drive. I said to my mother, "This isn't true. I can't understand it."

Then my mother rang up Reine, who said, "What happened was, my neighbors, a mile away, decided to have a fight. And she chased him around the lawn and she shot him. But all she did was knock his false teeth out." Papa Ben rushed out immediately and called the police.

I threatened to sue the papers. Every one of them headlined me. They called it the Marion Davies murder. And I had two witnesses to the fact that I was not there: my mother and the butler. None of my family even knew the people. I think their name was Hirsch.

All I wanted from the newspapers was a retraction. I rang up every newspaper myself. They all said, "No retraction."

Then I wrote the papers a letter, and still I got no retraction. It may have been a slap at Mr. Hearst, but I don't really think it was. I didn't want the publicity, but I got it. Bad publicity.

So my father said, "You've got to sue. You have to go into court and fight for your rights." Well, I'd never been in court in my life, and I was afraid I'd stutter. He said I'd better get ready. So I sued the newspapers. Each for a million dollars, just to scare them. I wanted any kind of a retraction.

And I went to court as the main witness. The whole place was jammed, outside and in.

Reine was on the witness stand, and my mother was with me, but I was afraid. If you stutter, the implication is that you're guilty—immediately.

I got up and ran for the car and went home. When my father got home, he was furious. He said, "Judge Simpson can't understand your actions. You were called and called... Don't you know that that is a breach of court? You might be thrown into jail for not appearing on the witness stand."

I said I couldn't help it. I couldn't do it.

He said, "You've certainly spilled the apple cart. Haven't you got courage enough to get up on the stand and tell the truth? What are you afraid of?"

"Nothing," I said.

He said, "Well, you lost your case."

I didn't want any money. I just wanted to be cleared. My father said he'd see to that. And they did print the retraction, but you had to get a spyglass to read it, and it was way back, practically with the classified ads.

W.R. said I should have gone ahead with the lawsuit and made them retract the story on the front page, just the way they had printed it. But I couldn't.

His papers didn't print the story at all. Never said a word. But W.R. thought I might have been there that night. He was a little bit dubious about it. But I was looking at the rushes with my mother, nowhere near Freeport. I had to work until nine, look at the rushes until midnight or maybe one o'clock, and then be back at the studio in the morning. I had to be up at seven.

So they called it the Marion Davies murder, but all his wife did was shoot his false teeth out.

Then there was almost a tragedy at the opening of *Little Old New York* at the Cosmopolitan Theatre, which Mr. Hearst had bought just especially for the opening. We were having a banquet with the Mayor,* and I think Will Hays was there, and Joseph Urban, who did the decorating. Urban was saying, "Don't go in—until the theatre's finished." I was supposed to sit with the Mayor in one of the loges that had been fixed up in the theatre. It looked like a little jewel. At the last

_____
* John Hylan.

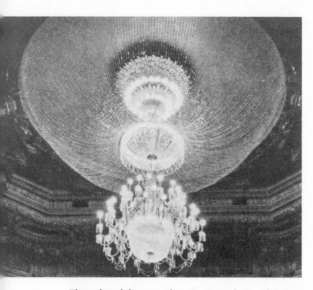

The chandelier at the Cosmopolitan Theatre, when *Little Old New York* opened in the summer of 1923. *I didn't look at the picture because I was looking at that chandelier all the time.* (Photo courtesy of Bob Board.)

minute there was a chandelier they couldn't get up. And it cost about sixty thousand dollars. It was already 8:15, and we were being stalled off while they were trying to finish the job with big ladders.

There were people outside waiting, and cars all around, and W.R. said, "It has to be now or never. We can't keep the people waiting. Let's take a chance." So we went in.

I didn't look at the picture, because I was looking at that chandelier all the time. It was an enormous thing, and all the audience down below would've been killed if it had fallen.

The Mayor said it was a very good picture, and he was very conservative. But I bet they were glad to get rid of us. After the premiere we went to California.

When I first arrived in Hollywood I didn't like it. I decided to live in Santa Barbara and make pictures up there. I didn't know anybody, and I couldn't understand the big wide spaces. I was a city girl, and I was afraid of everything.

After a while I learned to like California, so that when I went back east, I didn't like New York anymore. I think you like either one or the other, but not both. In New York I got to feeling crowded in, crushed; there was no fresh air, just gas fumes and coal dust. So I switched my affections. It did take a while, but when I got broken in I stayed broken in.

All the family had come along, and we rented Mrs. Somebody's lemon ranch—only she wouldn't let us pick a lemon off a tree. That was in Montecito.

A studio which had been empty for years was being fixed up. I was there a year without ever shooting a scene. We just sat around and talked about the story, which didn't mean much—it was about a love piker, sort of a sucker. I didn't care for it, but we were supposed to do it. Poor Frances Marion would work on it and get headaches, and then we never made it. Of course I knew nothing about pictures, so I couldn't put my two cents in. Whenever I said anything, it was so dumb they would look at me in amazement.

THE LOVE PIKER was made in 1923 as a Goldwyn-Cosmopolitan Production, but Marion Davies was not in it.

Writer Frances Marion, in her autobiography OFF WITH THEIR HEADS! (Macmillan, 1972), noted that after W.R. had hired her, her father sent her a note: "So you've gone from bad to Hearst." But in a career that would include 137 film credits and many other published works, Frances Marion went ahead and worked on the screenplays of seven of Marion Davies's films: THE CINEMA MURDER (1920), THE REST-

Reviewers dismissed *Young Diana* as little more than a fashion show. It was one of six feature films Marion made in 1922.

LESS SEX (1920), ZANDER THE GREAT (1925), THE RED MILL (1927), BLONDIE OF THE FOLLIES (1932), PEG O' MY HEART (1933) and GOING HOLLYWOOD (1933).

They couldn't figure out what to do with me, so they dumped me on Louis B. Mayer. The next thing I knew I was at MGM, working on *Zander the Great*. Frances Marion wrote that play and she did a wonderful job.* Hedda Hopper played my mother in that picture.** I was supposed to be an orphan kid, and I had to fight a lion in a lion's cage.

The big job was to get me into the cage. With the lion there. Frances Marion's husband, George Hill, was the director. He said to me, "Now look, we've got a big sheet of glass here, between you and the lion. All you do is get into the cage, and get near enough so that the audience thinks you're kissing the lion. Then he'll roar and you'll climb up the side of the cage."

Like a monkey, I guess.

Somebody said they'd taken all the teeth out of the lion. But they hadn't. That lion had teeth, and he was mad because they had brought him over from the zoo. And he was kicking up a bit.

They wanted a rehearsal. I was courageous and went into the cage, and the lion went "RRRRoooooaaaarrrrrr!" I started climbing, and when I got to the top of the cage I was yelling, "Help!! Murder!!"

It was just one of those stunts for a laugh. That was the big idea, but I think a lion can go right through glass, which I had forgotten was there.

Whoever whipped that one up

---

* The screenplay by Frances Marion and Lillie Hayward was based on the play by Salisbury Field.
** Hedda Hopper played Mrs. Caldwell, Marion's foster mother and Zander's real mother.

didn't like me. But Charlie Chaplin came over and did the scene for me, in my clothes. And that was the first time I ever met him. He did the whole scene in two shots and then he left. Then I did my close-ups alone, in the cage, without that lion.

But they thought up more stunts for me. They wanted me to ride backwards on a bicycle, when I couldn't even ride forwards. It was a story that was mixed up with the West and the circus. They said it was funny, but George Hill committed suicide a little while after. I hope it was not because of the picture.

When Marion began working at MGM, W.R. assigned a young reporter to cover her, releasing him from his regular duties at the Los Angeles Examiner. *And he would stay with Marion, handling her publicity material, throughout her working days at that studio.*

When I first started to work at MGM, I used to see a man on my set, all the time. I didn't know the setup, and I wouldn't ask anybody. So finally I asked him, "Who are you, please?"

He said, "I'm from the publicity department."

"Yeah?"

"Now don't get me wrong. I don't want to be here any more than you want me here. But I'm stuck with you. If you can take it, I'll try to."

"Is it going to be as hard as that?"

"Pretty tough, I think."

"What makes you think so?" I asked.

"Well, I've been here for about a month, and you've just looked at me and said mentally, 'Throw that punk off my set.' "

I said, "No, I didn't do that . . . What did you say your name was?"

"Wheelwright. You know, wheels, like on cars. Of course, if you don't

He wanted me to ride backwards on a bicycle when I couldn't even ride forwards.
Marion was making Zander the Great in 1925.

like that joke, I'll walk out and come back again the other way. But I've really been sold down the line. I'm in Siberia as far as you're concerned. There are other stars I'd rather be on the set with than you. It seems I'm nailed to the cross."

"Well," I said, "it looks that way to me, too. I'm nailed up, too, but I don't mind the nails."

"Well, it all depends. If you'll treat me like a human being and won't look at me like I'm poison . . ."

I said, "Now look, let's not be facetious about this."

"Oh, you know that word, too. Well, I'm stuck with you, so let's try to make the best of it."

"Okay," I said.

When I saw him the next day I said, "Hello. What's your name?"

"Hello, Miss Nobody."

"What is your name, really?"

"Call me Ralph."

I said, "Are you sure?"

He stayed with me for every picture I made. His boss was Howard Strickling. Howard and I had one thing in common: we both stuttered. When Ralph introduced me to his boss, I was saying, "How-how-how-how-how are you?" And Howard was saying, "How-how-how-how are you?" So he also said, "I've met my enemy."

When I was in the *Follies* back in New York, I had a faculty for looking out from the wings, which I was not supposed to do. Joe Frisco, who was in the show, had a cigar, and he was lighting it before he went onstage. I watched him like a punk, two nights in a row. Then I walked over and asked him, "Why-why-why-why do you light this cigar?"

He said, "Jeez, get away from me. I won't be able to speak a word." When he went onstage, he couldn't talk. Stuttering is contagious, from one stutterer to another stutterer.

So I became known as public nuisance number one-one-one.

Vincent X. Flaherty and I had a good time together, because he stuttered very badly. He'd say, "P-p-p-p-p-put me away from her." And George Hearst was the same way.

And Somerset Maugham was the same way. Frances Marion reports that he once thought Miss Davies was mimicking him. Outraged, he stormed away from her, saying, "Fre-fre-fresh b-b-b-bitch!"

Life in California got to be very gay. There was work and some sort of a party every night. And I got to love MGM, I really did; but I didn't realize it until I left. I was ten years at the studio and I knew everyone. There was always something to do.

Frances and Sam Goldwyn would have dinner parties, and he was always very nice and amusing, without meaning to be. W.R. also liked Sam and Frances. She was wonderful, and very intelligent.

Mary Pickford was the great hostess. At least she had that honor. She did give good parties—a little bit on the dignified side, but otherwise all right. You couldn't take off your shoes and dance, like you could at Lord Beaverbrook's house in London.

I don't think anybody actually gave wild parties. But you always had at least one or two drunks at a party.

I'd have dinners at the beach house, and we'd go to the pier at Venice, or the Cocoanut Grove, or to the Biltmore Hotel after a football game. That would be a madhouse. You could hardly get in the lobby, what with the carrying-on by those lovely little football characters. Then there was also the Montmartre Restaurant, but only for lunchtime. And there was the Roosevelt Hotel in Hollywood.

There was a country club where the

Life in California got to be very gay. There was work and some sort of party every night.

younger degeneration used to go, and we would go there every once in a while, for a dance. There was also the Embassy Club, and one time we went to Palm Springs, when the Ambassador to Spain* was there.

One night Mary Pickford called me up and said, "I'm having a party for the King of Siam." I said I'd be there.

I was a little late, so I went running up the steps. She was standing with a chap I thought was the butler. I had an ermine coat. So I threw my coat to him and said, "I'm sorry I'm late."

Well, he was the King of Siam. He was all dressed up with a white jacket.

She was very disturbed; she thought I had done it on purpose, but I hadn't. I was upset at being late.

She put me at an odd table, but then the King asked Doug [Fairbanks] if I could sit next to him. I didn't move. I put on a pout until Doug asked me to sit next to the King.

Then I went over. But it was just like talking to a wall. He understood English as much as I understood Chinese. He wanted to explain that he wasn't angry, but it was a horrible thing for me to do.

That was just before Doug and Mary got their divorce.

When I first got to Los Angeles, I stayed at the Ambassador Hotel. Then I rented a house in Beverly Hills that belonged to Norman Kerry, the actor, and his wife, Rosine.

Then we moved into the house at 1700 Lexington Road.

My mother bought it, and that's where we lived. That's where we had the most fun.

* Alexander P. Moore had been the United States Ambassador to Spain in 1923.

My mother was very quiet and reticent. She didn't seem to fit in with the motion picture people. She was very nice and polite, but she couldn't understand their sense of humor and would take things seriously. We'd drive her crazy with the victrola or the radio and our friends coming over at night and playing cards. She couldn't sleep, and one night she lost her temper. She leaned over the balcony and said, "Everyone go home, please."

But we were all there, and it was like the Sanger Circus, with Ethel, Rose and her daughter Pat, and Reine and her daughter Peppy and her son Charlie, who had just graduated from the University of California at Berkeley at the age of sixteen.*

We all lived at 1700 Lexington, and Mr. Hearst stayed there too. I had been working for him in New York, and he had turned over the Cosmopolitan Film Company to me. Then he made a contract for me at MGM, and my salary

* He hadn't graduated; he'd just dropped out.

Irving Thalberg was the boy genius in charge of MGM. Marion signed a contract paying her $500,000 a year and said, "Who wouldn't?"

was very good. It amounted to about half a million a year. Who would turn that down? But it was too much money, because my ability was not equal to it at all.

He had said, "I guess I'm putting all my eggs in one basket." And I was the basket.

At MGM they thought maybe they had something in me. To their sorrow, they found they didn't. And it was a ten-year contract, and there were supposed to be four pictures a year.

As it happened, it was set down to two pictures a year because I didn't want to make any more. But I worked at MGM for almost ten years.

W.R. made me the president of Cosmopolitan Films, and I was supposed to get half of the profits. And they went for that.

I had lots of fun at MGM, and no problems, because they had figured out that either I was sort of an idiot or I had a protector.

They never argued with me.

La Casa Grande at San Simeon. (Photo courtesy State of California.)

3

The MGM studio. A fight with Lillian Gish. Terrified by a cow. Harry the perfect gentleman. Eddie the carpenter. Gandhi discovered in Bad Nauheim. Mr. Hearst builds San Simeon.

At San Simeon, W.R. built a castle. It soon became known throughout the world for its extravagance and splendor, and for enhancing a barren part of California's coast that up until that time had disdained civilization's progress. W.R. would insist that it was a ranch, not a castle.

As work on the hill at San Simeon progressed, so construction burgeoned around Los Angeles. The movie industry had moved from New York to California to take advantage of the free sunlight and the open spaces. There were many new film companies in action, and though most relied on a single charismatic figure for their success and vitality, some companies were beginning to stabilize and to organize continuing schedules of work.

At MGM, Louis B. Mayer and Irving Thalberg planned one new picture a week to keep theatres supplied and audiences habituated to regular attendance.

We all had our dressing rooms in a wooden building at MGM. The women were on the top floor: Norma Shearer, Greta Garbo, Joan Crawford, Sally O'Neill and me. The men were underneath, and there was a sign: NO MEN ALLOWED TO GO UPSTAIRS. Why it was that way, I can't understand. They had that sign, but my God Almighty, we were not pushovers. I took my father upstairs one night, but that was all right. He was my father.

It was the craziest idea, that the male stars would come up and

Overleaf: San Simeon as it appears today. *W.R. didn't like anyone calling it a castle. It was always the ranch.* (Photo courtesy State of California.)

attack the female stars. Most of the male stars didn't even care for the female stars. It was like professional jealousy. They'd just say, "How do you do," or "Good morning," and that was the way it was.

I think it really meant that they didn't trust the girls, so they locked us up in the cloister. Even the assistant directors used to yell, "Hey, you're wanted on the set!" They wouldn't dare come upstairs.

The arrangement didn't give Lillian Gish much protection, because Jack Gilbert would stay downstairs with a bunch of violets in his hand. He might as well have waited for the sun to come out at night, because she was dodging him. They were making *La Boheme* and he was madly in love with her.

Jack Gilbert was the sort of person who took the movies seriously. When he played in a love scene with somebody, he fell in love with her. So he'd be down there, standing with a bunch of violets, waiting for Lillian. But she was only there for the one picture.

The story about the fight with Lillian Gish was just a story. It went on, like a mothball, then a snowball. It got bigger and bigger.

The problem was that there was only one room up there with a toilet. That was supposed to be mine, because I needed one. And the others didn't have any toilet. But Lillian Gish had gotten that room. Apparently she had been promised it. So I said to Louis B. Mayer, "I've got to have that room." I took her things and moved them out, and I stayed there. I wouldn't leave, not even to go on the set. Well, Lillian got furious, and she wouldn't leave my room. She said to me, "Yughh." Now for a nice, sweet little girl she was very nasty. But finally she thumped out and I locked the door. Lillian went to the front office.

We all had one dressing maid, Lulu, and she said, "This is going to be a big fight."

But I had the key, and I was going to stay. When they wanted me on the set, I said, "I don't care. I'm going to stay and claim my room."

Then the phone rang and some woman asked, "What room are you in?"

I said, "I'm in the room I was assigned, and I'm going to stay here."

This woman says, "Oh, what's happened?"

"Lillian Gish was in the room I was supposed to have."

"Well, I told her which room she was supposed to go to. But she took your room?"

"Yes. Now tell her to stay out of here. I'm not complaining; I just don't want to be annoyed. I'm not going to share my toilet. There's one down at the end of the hall." I'd been inspecting the joint, so I knew.

I don't know whether Lillian created a fuss or not, but I don't imagine she liked it very much. I heard she was biting her nails about it, but I don't believe she did.

I never did see her again. She only did that one picture, and she paid no attention to Jack Gilbert with his violets —none whatsoever.

Well, I got tired of running up those steps, so I built the bungalow. I had a great big lawn all to myself, and I could roll on the grass and kick and groan and scream and roar and holler.

I was doing two pictures at the same time, *The Red Mill* and *Tillie the Toiler*. That meant I could work from nine to five on one and from six to four in the morning on the other. That was for six weeks. I had to sleep at the bungalow, on a couch. There wasn't a bed there.

One morning they wanted me to go out on the lawn and milk a cow, with

The view from Marion's bungalow. *I had a huge lawn and I liked to play somersaults. It peps you up. So I'd do a few somersaults before I'd go on the set.* The stages had glass walls then, to provide light for the cameras. When talkies began, the walls were covered with insulation, and interior scenes were electrically lit.

I was doing two pictures at one time: THE RED MILL and TILLIE THE TOILER. I would work from nine to five on one and from six to four in the morning on the other.

my back to the camera. I thought, Well, I've done worse things in my life. I'd almost killed myself in other pictures, so I might as well go for the cow's left leg. They said, "Just put your head around and look at the camera and start doing this . . ." They showed me, and I said okay.

Well, the cow went "MOOOOOO" and kicked over a pail. I ran. I jumped over the fence and hid behind a bush, and they couldn't find me. The property men were looking all over the place. But I had taken off with my pigtails in the air. I had to go on the other set—so I got my stand-in to do it.

I was shaking all day long, I was so frightened. I thought, Fear creates fear. Roosevelt didn't originate that statement.

I would usually take a chance on doing anything. In *The Red Mill* I was supposed to grab the windmill and go around on it, once, twice, and then faster. I had to hang on, and it was all wet and slippery, and I thought if I fell I would get cut into two pieces. But I wasn't afraid. I was silly. They should have gotten a double to do that thing.

The director was just thinking about the scene, not about anybody getting hurt. They would think it was simple, but I should have been thinking about my life. The two things didn't jibe. I guess I was a daredevil. I'd do anything they asked me to.

I was at MGM for ten years and I was never late. After luncheon I'd walk to the set, which was better for the digestion than riding over. Sometimes I wouldn't eat and I'd get to the set earlier.

I met Harry Crocker, an actor in *The Big Parade*, one day when I was sup-

Louella Parsons, Harry Crocker and Marion. *Louella never complained about him because Harry was a perfect gentleman.*

posed to be working on the back lot. I'd just taken a driving lesson. It had been raining, and I got my car stuck in the mud and didn't know how to get it out. Harry walked up and said, "May I help you?" I said yes. And he got the car out, which was very nice.

Two nights later at a party at the Ambassador Hotel, Elinor Glyn* introduced me to him. I said, "We've already met," but at first I couldn't figure out where; he looked so different in a white tie. We've been friends ever since.

Harry went to work on the papers with Louella Parsons. He'd get a scoop, and he'd ring up Louella and say, "Here—it's yours." Louella never complained about him, because Harry was a perfect gentleman.

---

* A noted English novelist and film writer whose screen adaptation of her novel *It* starred Clara Bow—who thus became the original "It" girl.

I started working at MGM about 1924, and that was the first time I ever went to San Simeon. I think Bebe Daniels and Ben Lyon were along, and Connie Talmadge.*

The reason I didn't go earlier was that W.R. said, "It isn't finished yet." Of course it's not finished even now; the back of it will never be finished. But when I was young, the place didn't interest me at all. I'm glad I got old so I could appreciate the beauty of things. It's a gorgeous place.

When I used to go to Europe, I'd look at the Doge's Palace and I'd just think, Oh, it's sinking on one side. I was bored stiff. All I wanted was an ice-cream soda or a Coke. And you couldn't get those things in Europe. Even now they still don't know how to make ice-cream sodas. They look at you and think you're crazy.

---

*Bebe Daniels and Ben Lyon were husband and wife. They both started working in films in 1919, and by the mid-1930s, when they retired, they had appeared in more than a hundred pictures—though seldom together. Connie Talmadge was the sister of Norma Talmadge. Both were major film stars, and Norma was married to Joseph M. Schenck, a top executive at MGM.

I was constantly thinking of myself, nothing else. Young people never appreciate the beauty of things. Maybe I was the one and only, but I'd look at things in a gallery or a museum and I wouldn't see them. It was a long time afterwards that I realized they were marvelous.

When we went to San Simeon we'd take the train and then a car from San Luis Obispo. Sometimes we went by plane. W.R. had three planes, and if I was working late on a Saturday, I would fly up. When I wasn't working I'd stay at San Simeon, and then I'd wish I were working because there were so many people there and the routine got tiresome—laying the place cards and meeting the visiting characters.

George Hearst and Blanche, his first wife, were the first of W.R.'s family to come up to the ranch. I had a profound affection for both of them. They asked W.R. if they could meet me, and I was tremendously flattered. We got to be friends from then on in. I liked them both, but I always especially liked

George, Bill, W.R., John, David and Randolph Hearst at the circus party in 1937.

George. Most of the family thought he was null and void, but he was not. He always was very kind, and I always regarded him as my best friend among all of W.R.'s boys.*

I guess Mr. Hearst didn't want them there, but I felt it was their due, that they should see their father. And I felt that I was in the way of that. But W.R. didn't feel that way at all. If they wanted to see him, they had to come to San Simeon and, inevitably, bump into me. It was too bad it had to happen that way, but he wouldn't meet them anywhere else.

George was the oldest son and the smartest. He was the first one to be nice to me—and so he was in. Well, George and Blanche were in the dining room when W.R. walked in with me, and George tried to smile. W.R. said, "What are you doing here? When you come, you should notify me beforehand. And get up and say 'How do you do?' " That was the way it went. It was a delightful life. I was embarrassed all the time.

Then Bill came. Afterwards, everything was all right. I suppose they didn't do it for any other reason except they knew who held the money-bags. They realized that their mother wouldn't give them a cent, so they had to rely on their father. But they used a little diplomacy.

Visitors to San Simeon were usually fascinated by the hospitality of W.R. and Marion. Employees of his newspapers were often invited to join the other celebrities who came up to the ranch.

Winifred Sweet Black Bonfils had pioneered in the technique of the sob story, writing for Hearst publications under the pseudonym of Annie Laurie. At the ranch, in this construction period, she introduced Marion to a mythical carpenter.

Winifred Bonfils was a charming woman, a nice little old lady. She had diabetes, and she wasn't supposed to eat anything with sugar in it. After dinner she would beg me, "Could I have some ice cream?" Outside in the pantry, she meant.

She lived in San Francisco and she'd come to visit occasionally. One time she said, "Marion, I had the funniest experience. I was lying in bed. I had been ill, and suddenly I was awakened by some little fellow who came right through the door. I asked him, 'What are you doing in my room?' He didn't answer. So I watched him. He came over to the bed. He was very short, but he had a long tape measure, and he measured me for width and height. I said, 'Now, what are you doing?' But he didn't answer. He just disappeared.

"Next night, same thing. Same routine. I was getting mad. Finally he said, 'I'm Eddie, the carpenter.' I said, 'Now look, I don't know any Eddie the carpenter, and how dare you come into my room?' He said, 'I'm measuring you for a coffin.' So I got rid of him real fast and haven't seen him since."

Well, it had been a dream, of course.

About two weeks or maybe a month later she came back to the ranch. She had written an article entitled, "Is It Fair To Steal from the Blind?" It was a beautiful piece about a close friend you place all your trust in.

Mrs. Bonfils had had a secretary, but on this visit she came alone and had to

---

* There were five boys. George was born in 1904. William Randolph, Jr., in 1908, and John Randolph in 1909. Randolph Apperson and his twin, Elbert Wilson (who would change his name to David Whitmire), were born in 1915. In the mid-1970s, Patricia, one of the five daughters of Randolph Apperson, would gain celebrity after she was kidnapped from her Berkeley apartment by the Symbionese Liberation Army, used for a ransom paid in food, and then converted to the cause of her abductors—winding up on the FBI's wanted list for her alleged part in a California bank robbery.

be helped all the way. She had gone totally blind.

I asked, "What happened to your secretary?"

"How did you know?" she asked.

"What do you mean? I thought she was so devoted to you."

"I didn't mention any names in my story."

"You said somebody you thought was honest had turned out otherwise."

"I'll tell you, but nobody else," she said.

It seems the secretary would say to her, "Here's a check for the household. Will you sign it?" And she had trustingly signed the checks, and now she didn't have any money left, not a cent. She started to cry.

"That's horrible," I said.

"That's life," she said. She was heartbroken. Two months later she was dead.

That was how I met Eddie the Carpenter. Every time I didn't feel well, I'd say, "Send for Eddie."

When W.R. decided to build San Simeon, he said he wanted to pick out a spot with a good view. His father had left him the property. His mother had a house there in which a cousin, Randolph Apperson, lived. Apperson was the overseer.

While the house was being built, W.R. would go up to the site and stay in a tent. The work proceeded so slowly that Constance Talmadge said, "A brick a day keeps the bricklayer in pay." And yet it was awfully hard for them to get the material up that hill.

When I first saw San Simeon, those back wings were finished and the hall part was completed. It was an awesome thing. I'd seen Versailles and palaces in Europe, but nothing could compare. San Simeon is so beautiful, with the view of the mountains and the ocean.

I'd go up on weekends, and there'd be twenty or thirty guests, possibly forty or fifty. The train would leave Los Angeles at eight-fifteen and arrive at San Luis about three in the morning, and we'd motor on up. We'd come back on Sunday to be at work Monday.

Pete was the man who owned the limousines in San Luis. Several cars were needed, and it was about an hour and a half's drive. W.R. would pay for the train and for the cars.

When we arrived we'd have breakfast and a rest. Luncheon was about two-thirty and dinner about half past eight at night. Saturday night we'd watch a movie.

Before breakfast on Sunday we'd play tennis or go horseback riding—the usual things, the sporting life routine. Or we'd swim. There were two pools, one indoors and one outside, all mosaics. And there was an old Grecian temple on one side.

W.R. had his office in a separate building, House A. There was a House B and a C, but why they didn't have a D and an E I'll never know. He was too busy, I guess.

W.R. would come out and join the guests and go swimming. And he played tennis and went horseback riding. He was excellent at riding.

Nobody was allowed to ride in the area where the wild animals roamed. There were lions and tigers; leopards and bears of all kinds; honey bears and spider monkeys; camels, deer, water buffalo, zebras and elk; emus and ostriches. W.R. thought it was picturesque. There was an elephant named after me. I was insulted.

They had named the elephant Marion, but in order not to hurt my feelings they called her Marianne. That was still the name of a movie I

The Refectory. The guests dined under banners from Siena and a French tapestry, but there was no tablecloth, and W.R. thought paper napkins were more sanitary. *And it saved the laundry.* (Photo courtesy State of California.)

Above right: San Simeon. The Roman pool was indoors and was decorated with 18-carat gold-filled tiles made in Venice. (Photo courtesy State of California.)

Right: San Simeon. A bedroom in the north wing. The Doge's Suite at San Simeon contained a seventeenth-century Italian bed, a Sarouk carpet, and pieces of art created during the European Renaissance. (Photo courtesy State of California.)

San Simeon. The Neptune pool holds 345,000 gallons of mountain spring water, warmed to 70°. (Photo courtesy State of California.)

Old oak number 7. The state has them inventoried and maintains them with cement and wires.

Carrara marble copies of classic Roman and Greek sculpture, in the gardens of San Simeon.

had made, my first sound movie. (My middle name was Cecilia, and I'd made a movie in which I was Cecilia of the Pink Roses. I didn't like my middle name, so I'd changed it to Violet.)*

There were signs, too; DO NOT TEASE THE ANIMALS. Of course that was just the very thing we'd do. Especially the apes. One was called Jerry and one Mary, and they were married and had a little papoose, the first one born in captivity. But it only lived six months.

Jerry was enormous and quite a character. We used to throw stones at him, or we'd get a rope and give him one end and we'd all be at the other end. One jerk and we'd all go right down. Then he'd get mad and shake the bars, and we'd all run. All this was under the sign, DON'T TEASE.

But Jerry did some naughty tricks. He did something to Marie Dressler. He did something in his hand, and when she wasn't looking, he threw it at her, and it went all over her.

He hated everybody, but he had his reasons. We wouldn't hurt him, just make faces, but he'd get mad. It's a good thing Jerry never got loose.

W.R. never allowed hunting. He'd inspect the animals regularly, and he had fifty or sixty cowboys looking after them, and the cattle.

At the house there were three butlers and God knows how many maids. You had to have help with a place like that.

There were probably a hundred workmen, but I didn't see a brick a day being put in. W.R. did things on a big scale, and he didn't care about money at all. There were sculptors and artists to paint the ceilings and to do the rooms over, and over again.

He took great pride in San Simeon,

watching over it and inspecting it. He wanted it to be a museum. He didn't like anyone calling it a castle; it was always the ranch. No tablecloths; always paper napkins. On that one, he thought it was more sanitary, and with so many guests he was probably right. It saves the laundry, too. And I got the habit. And I've always used paper napkins. They don't look so good—but what's the difference?

I think W.R. liked House A better than any of the other houses. And he liked the Gothic Suite, way upstairs in the main house, underneath the Celestial Suite, right over the library.

Picnic luncheon at San Simeon. W.R., in riding boots, may indeed have ridden a horse while his guests rode in cars.

* Violet was a character Marion played in the film *The Belle of New York* in 1919.

There was an enormous oak tree near House A. One day as W.R. came out of the house the tree knocked his hat off. So he called the caretaker and said he wanted the tree moved about ten feet over. He was told it would cost a thousand dollars a foot to move it. He wouldn't let them destroy that tree, although it took months to move it. It was fascinating just to watch it being moved.

The meals were really wonderful. There were three chefs, and at least one of them was bound not to miss. We'd have picnics down at the beach, about five miles up the coast toward San Francisco, or we'd go on camping trips over at Mel Peters's ranch. We'd go on horses for about eight hours. If you didn't want to ride horseback, there were about twelve cars and drivers.

Anyone who had the courage to swim in the ocean was crazy. It was too ice-cold, all the year round. I'd just sit around awhile and then go back up the hill.

W.R. owned a little over three hundred thousand acres, but the government owns it now. They took a hundred thousand acres.*

We were always having parties—costume parties, birthday parties, even weddings. We had at least four weddings there. Mary and Bill Curley, who was from the *New York Evening Journal*—he wasn't the Mayor of Boston. And Maitland Rice and Noreen Phillips. George Hearst married Lorna, his second wife, at San Simeon, and Patricia and Arthur Lake got married there.

The ceremonies were held in the living room. We'd have flowers and decorations, and bridesmaids. But nobody

ever spent their honeymoon there. I had to order the dresses for Mary and Bill Curley's wedding. Doris Duke, Mary Sanford and I were the three bridesmaids, and Mrs. Hal Roach was the matron of honor. I rang up Orry Kelly and said I needed the gown in just two days, and he produced the stuff. Everything arrived all right, even the wedding ring.

Among the guests, somebody was always having a birthday, and I'd whip up a party. We'd send for the musicians and even the presents. I'd get gifts for the other guests to give, because they wouldn't know we were having a party.

Clark Gable was another guest. Women were always running after him, but he'd just give them a look as if to say, "How crazy these people are." And he stayed pretty much to himself.

The society people always wanted to meet the movie stars, so I mixed them together. When they say that society people are higher than the stars, that isn't so. Society always wants some celebrity at their parties, and they are lucky if they can get one, because theatrical people are very particular who they go with.

I think the covered-wagon costume party* was the biggest party we ever had at San Simeon. We had over a hundred people there for the weekend. A big tent was set up outside near the back entrance, close to the breakfast room. Not as far away as the tennis courts.

We had to get extra beds and fix up things in practically no time. With well over a hundred people coming, it was most everybody in the motion picture industry: the Gary Coopers and the Thalbergs and the Warners and Gable and Bill Powell, and a lot of the newspapermen, publishers and editors.

---

* The United States government purchased 153,-840.45 acres from the Hearst Corporation for two million dollars on December 12, 1940. This land became the U.S. Army's Hunter Liggett Military Reservation.

* April 29, 1933. The party celebrated W.R.'s seventieth birthday.

Clark Gable posed with Ziegfeld *Follies* dancer Mary Libby, who married MGM story editor Samuel Marx and became the mother of one of this book's editors.

At the ranch for W.R.'s birthday party in 1933, cowgirls Dorothy Mackaill, Constance Talmadge and Eileen Percy.

Adela Rogers St. John. She would later write *The Honeycomb* and many other works.

Gary and Rocky Cooper posed with film director Richard Boleslavski, who would not dress for the covered wagon party, and his wife Norma.

But not Chaplin. He wouldn't go to any party. You'd call him, and he wouldn't talk on the telephone at all. His secretary would say he'd come, but he'd never turn up. He'd occasionally come to the beach house, and we'd play charades and have a lot of fun. He said he'd rather walk the streets of Los Angeles alone at night than go to anybody's party.

That was the stand he took, and since that included everybody, people got tired of asking him. He was temperamental, I suppose, but I don't think there's anything wrong with him, except that he's a little cracked.

Chaplin was very arbitrary. When someone said yes, he'd say no; if you said no, he'd say yes. He always wanted to take the opposite side of an argument.

Every once in a while we'd get a comedian in the group. The real practical joker of San Simeon was Eddie Kane. Not the actor, but a playboy from New York society, a clown. He was really fun, and he'd keep everybody in stitches of laughter. He's dead now, poor Eddie.

And Bob Hope was up there a long time ago. So we had a lot of laughs.

There were some men who were a bit strenuous in their pursuit of me. That happened occasionally, but the moment W.R. would arrive, they'd all run for shelter.

Nobody ever dared to stand up to him, and I didn't ever give anybody any encouragement. I was a jolly, happy, free catch with everybody. I'd say hello, and that was as far as it ever went.

It was quite romantic at San Simeon, and over a jigsaw puzzle there'd be five or six people and you'd look up and you'd see an eye looking at you. It was cute. Somebody might say something like, "You're divine and such and such." But the moment W.R. would appear, *whoosh,* they'd disappear.

I was supposed to be the matchmaker of Hollywood. I took great delight in promoting romances. I was always a bridesmaid but never a bride. I would say, "You know, he's crazy about you. But the trouble with you is that you're a little indifferent. Just go up to him and sort of look at him and say, 'Hello . . .'"

They'd say, "Do you think so? Why, he hasn't even looked at me at all."

So I'd go to the man in question and I'd say, "Why, she's crazy about you. She thinks you're gorgeous."

"Really?" he'd say. "How do you know?"

"She told me." Then I'd be careful. "Do you like her?" So it would work into a romance, and then there'd be a wedding, and I was a bridesmaid again.

I just did it to get a new dress. I liked a change of clothes occasionally.

Jean Harlow came up to San Simeon quite frequently. She was very nice and I liked her. She didn't have an awful lot to say.

She was crazy about Bill Powell; she waited on him hand and foot. I thought they were going to get married. It looked that way. He had just been divorced from Carole Lombard. But then Harlow died. What she died of, I don't think anybody knew. Somebody said sunburn; somebody else said makeup poisoning. Nobody but the doctors actually knew.

Needless to say, all the men used to flock around her. She was very attractive in an evening dress, because she never wore anything under it. One time, up at Wyntoon,* when some

---

* Wyntoon, a medieval manor house on the Mc-Cloud River in northern California, was built by W.R.'s mother, Phoebe Apperson Hearst, in 1903. Over the years, W.R. added to the manor until it became a village with a total area of 67,000 acres.

When Louis B. Mayer's daughter Edith married William Goetz, Marion was a bridesmaid, second from the left.

When John Considine, Jr., married Carmen Pantages, Marion was a bridesmaid, third from the left.

When Constance Bennett married the Marquis de la Falaise de la Coudray, Marion was a bridesmaid, sitting second from the left.

Jean Harlow with William Powell. *I thought they were going to get married. But then Harlow died.*

staid people from Washington were visiting, Jean had on a white chiffon gown that was a little bit too open. W.R. said, "Will you please tell Miss Harlow to go back to her room and get dressed?"

"But," I said, "she has an evening gown on."

He said, "To me it looks like a nightgown."

So I said to her, "Do you realize your dress is a little . . ."

"So what?"

"Well, Mr. Hearst doesn't like it. Couldn't you change and put on something else?"

"All right," she said. She went back up, then came down in a coat, which she wore all during dinner. She wouldn't change her dress.

In the main living room at San Simeon, two big iron flower pots stood alongside the big fireplace, which had come from Stanford White's estate. One day Helena* started barking and tried to get into one of the pots.

W.R. investigated and found a little mouse in the pot. He grabbed Helena and said, "Take her out of here!" I held onto Helena while W.R. caught the mouse, then went through the dining room and into the pantry. He came back holding a big spoon and went outside. It was threatening to storm.

He was gone for about half an hour. When he came back I asked him what he had done.

He said, "I dug a little hole for the mouse and put leaves over it so the mouse will be warm.

"The mouse is frightened. I don't want it to be around where Helena is, because Helena's a mouse-killer. Now nobody will find it."

---

* W.R.'s dachshund.

After dinner W.R. asked for some cheese and went outside to feed the mouse. That night it really stormed and was very windy, and W.R. was worried about the mouse.

He went out to check and came back and said, "The mouse is fine. Nice and warm." That mouse was warm because W.R. had taken a scissors and cut off part of the little blanket I had on my chaise lounge. He had ruined my lovely blanket just to keep that mouse warm. And the next day at luncheon he was very happy. The mouse was fine.

This went on for two days. The third day W.R. wouldn't come to luncheon, and nobody knew where he was. I asked his valet to find him. Well, W.R. finally walked in, and you never saw such a gloomy face. He said, "The mouse is gone."

I said, "Well, with all the food you've been feeding him, you kept him so full, he probably thought he'd like to go get a little fresh air and run around and see life."

W.R. said, "I hope—I really and truly hope that's it."

He really loved animals. I think it all started with the little white mouse that he had had as a pet when he was a child. He'd carry it around in his pocket.

I felt the same way about animals. Children, too. There happened to be quite a controversy one time.

Some doctors apparently didn't like Irene Castle* and the vivisection thing and they brought my name into it. They said that people who were against the vivisection thing were not humanitarians. They didn't care about human lives, only about dogs.

Well, that was no argument. That was too ridiculous.

I said that the way I felt about dogs

---

* Irene and Vernon Castle were a famous dance team.

The Assembly Hall at San Simeon. The ceiling came from the Palazzo Martinengo in Brescia, Italy. The fireplace at the end of the room was sixteenth-century French. On the right, two mantels were stacked to form another fireplace. The tapestries were Flemish, lending a casually sumptuous elegance to the cement-block walls. (Photo courtesy State of California.)

also went for rats and mice and even as far as cockroaches. At least people get a chance to have a drink or something to put them out of their agony. At least they don't know what's happening.

They were taking poor little animals and cutting them apart when they didn't even get a chance to get a drink of vodka. And they agreed with me at the hospital. W.R. felt the same way. Everything has nerves in its body, even the fish that you catch. So I should have been a vegetarian.

I had an agreement with the hospital to cut vivisection out. Dean Warren said, "Nothing. Not even a mouse or a rat. We won't do it."

Marion's humanitarian instincts were to find many forms of expression. She had established a children's clinic for medical research and treatment. In 1960, Dean Stafford L. Warren of the UCLA Medical School said, "We are extremely grateful to Miss Davies. Her warm, cooperative spirit and dedication to improving the conditions for the treatment of ill children made it possible for us to launch a training and research program. . . . Her generosity has now made possible the expansion of the Marion Davies Children's Clinic program in a splendid new facility as part of the University."

The $2,656,556 building is at the Westwood campus. It replaced the original Marion Davies Clinic, established in 1932 at 11672 Louisiana Avenue, West Los Angeles. Marion had donated $2,100,000 to the project. Additional funds came from the U.S. Public Health Service.

The original clinic. Having no children of her own, Marion played godmother to tens of thousands. When this clinic was demolished to provide space for a highway, she wrote a check for a new clinic, now part of the UCLA Medical Center in Westwood. (Photo courtesy UCLA Medical Center.)

The entrance to the original children's clinic on Louisiana Avenue on the west side of Los Angeles. (Photo courtesy UCLA Medical Center.)

W.R. always maintained that if you have a dog, for instance, and you leave the room and shut the door and say, "I'll be back," the dog doesn't understand that. The dog thinks you're never coming back.

Now a child can understand, maybe. But the dog can't and keeps worrying, "Will he come back?" That's why I took my dog Gandhi everyplace I went. I got to be a menace to everybody.

I got Gandhi when I was at Deske's Grand Hotel in Bad Nauheim [in Germany]. Mr. Hearst was taking the cure there. We were all supposedly taking the cure, a whole bunch of us. George Hearst and Lorna, Peggy and Charlie Lederer, Bill Hearst and Harry Crocker, and I think Mary Carlisle was there. Buster Collier was along, and John Hearst and Gretchen.

The routine was that at eleven o'clock you had a massage for half an hour. Then you took a carriage over to the bathhouse. They were called badhouses, but they were only for baths.

You go in and there is a clock and you have just eight minutes. You go into a wooden tub; it was all bubbly—like soda. After eight minutes you rang the bell, and a woman rushed in and got you out and wiped you down. You then went back to your hotel to sleep for one hour. No coffee or no tea was permitted. A little Rhine wine was okay, but just a little.

It was one day with the bath and two days without. That was the treatment. So for the extra two days, we would go down the Rhine River and stop at the wineries.

There was one in Mainz where there were round tables. A little taste was twenty-two dollars. You were supposed to just taste it and spit it out. Well, we didn't taste it; we drank it all.

Tables and tables of wine, all kinds of wine. We were well filled up, and a wine merchant had given us a wonderful luncheon, with cocktails, which they don't usually have.

So afterward, we were testing the wine, drinking it, and there were these big hollow empty vats. Bill said, "I can get through the little slat." But it was a pretty big slat, and he got through and inside the vat and out again. I said I'd go next.

When I got inside that vat, I was gassed by the smell of the dead wine, and I came out groggy. I was singing on the way home. "Why was I born? Why am I living? . . ."*

"Are you tight?" W.R. asked me.

I said, "Not any tighter than you are."

"I didn't drink a bit of wine."

"I did."

Well, that night Dr. Greudel arrived, and I was supposed to be the nurse. I was the one who had to take the specimens. The doctor walks in and we're all laughing and he looks at all the wine bottles we'd bought. Well, he asked me to get the specimens, and he gave me the bottles labeled for everybody. I'd go knock on the doors and say, "Would you mind . . . ?" I was most embarrassed with the men.

One day at the bathhouse they asked me if I wanted to try the Emperor's bath. And I did. It was all tile, a big sunken bathtub. It cost a little bit extra, but that was all right; it was gorgeous, and I felt very rich and elegant. I was lying in it and looking at the clock, but the clock wasn't working. The bath hadn't been used since the Kaiser's time, and I was the first one to try it, and I didn't know what time it was. I rang the buzzer, but there was no answer.

I thought they had forgotten me. Finally some old woman, about three

---

* And the next lines of the Jerome Kern/Oscar Hammerstein II song were, "What do I get? What am I giving?"

W.R. helped navigate along the Rhine.

ble, because they shrink the heart down, and a large heart is not very good. The hot bath pulls it down, and then it can start all over again. Mine was the size of a dime. I was lucky I was still alive. But it's a wonderful cure.

Then Dr. Greudel wanted to see me about the specimens. He said, "I have some very bad news to tell you."

"What is that?"

"Mr. Hearst is very sick. He has the worst case of kidney trouble I have ever seen. But it's most peculiar. I have examined him. His heart is okay—he is a little overactive. But this kidney trouble I can't understand. It's very bad, very bad."

I said that I didn't even know about it.

The doctor said, "Don't tell Mr. Hearst; it will frighten him. I want another specimen. Do you mind?"

I said, "Couldn't you get somebody else?" It was rather embarrassing for me to say, "Here's a bottle. Do it."

He said, "No. No. You have to do it."

"All right," I said. I went back to the hotel and said to W.R., "Give me another specimen."

"What? I'm tired of this."

"The doctor wants it. So go on and just push it outside the door." Which he did, and I took it back.

The doctor said, "This doesn't match. This is blond and that was brown."

My nephew was the culprit. He had taken his label and put it on W.R.'s bottle. And Charlie had kidney trouble, so it was just a joke. Very funny, driving Dr. Greudel crazy, because he didn't know what the hell was going on.

It was in Bad Nauheim that Charlie decided that he would go and have all his hair shaved off. He wanted to look like Mahatma Gandhi. Well, that was where I got Gandhi.

Harry Crocker found him. He said to me one day, "There's a poor little dog here, a nice little dog that was left be-

hundred pounds, comes in. I'm screaming my head off. And she drags me out. I'm droopy, but I didn't feel any different. The doctor examined me and said, "You have no heart."

I said, "What's the matter?"

Well, he couldn't find my heartbeat.

Of course, that's the idea of the baths. They're marvelous for heart trou-

cause his owner owed five hundred marks to the hotel. The manager will sell him." I said I'd like to see him.

Harry went down for him, and he was the cutest little puppy, but he was frightened. I went over to him and said, "Hello, Gandhi." And he kissed me. I wanted him, and W.R. said to buy him.

So he paid that old hotel bill because I was crazy about the dog. But it took a long time for Gandhi to get used to me. A dachshund is very sensitive. He'd take one look at me and run under the bed. But he was just a puppy.

I had a lot of trouble with him. Every time I'd go to Europe there was trouble. The time we got off the boat at Gibraltar they said, "We're sorry. You cannot bring the dog into English territory." The boat had already left and I raised hell. I was screaming that I wanted the boat to come back—I think it was the *Queen Mary*. I wouldn't get off the dock. They sent for the Mayor, and the only solution was for us to go to Algeciras, over the line, with a motor escort, to be sure that Gandhi would not pee on English territory.

We had reservations in Gibraltar, but I was screaming like a wild Indian, so we took the police escort and went to Algeciras. We stayed in the most beautiful hotel I've ever been in in my life, right opposite Africa. From there you can take the boat to Tetuan.

But the time we were at Bad Nauheim, Charlie thought that if he shaved his head, his hair would grow longer. So he shaved his head. He'd do anything for a joke, anyway. We were going out to a dinner party that night. I said, "I'm not going out with you. You're baldheaded."

Well, he had a Harpo Marx wig, with curls, but I called off the dinner date. We went downstairs to the bar and sang. There was a whole hotel filled with heart patients, and we were roaring at the tops of our lungs with

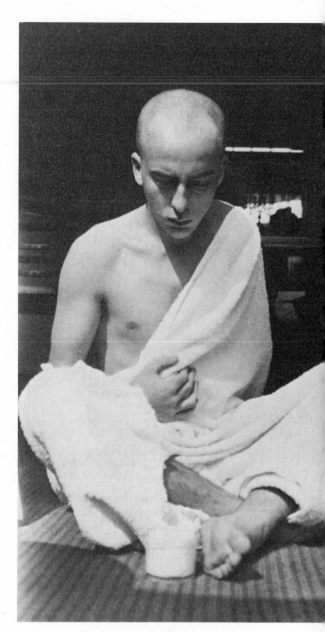

In Bad Nauheim, Marion found the dachshund that was to become her treasured companion and named him Gandhi. This inspired her nephew to play the part. *But then he got tonsillitis. It was a little cold and he didn't have any hair. Then he really was like a poor little puppy.*

Doris Duke. They were all after her, even Marion's dog Gandhi. *He followed her continually. I decided he was after her money; she was richer than I was.*

operas that we didn't know. The management was going crazy and we were singing: "O-O-O PAGLIA-A-A-CCI . . ."

The next day we went to Frankfurt, and Charlie wore his blond wig. He was the life of the party. And right in front of the police, he turned a somersault, and the wig came off, and they started to chase him. It was a funny thing. W.R. said, "What is he up to?"

I said, "He's just a funster. Let him alone."

But right away he came down with tonsillitis. It was a little cold, and he didn't have any hair. Then he was really like a poor little puppy.

Since we couldn't take Gandhi into England, he stayed in Paris when we went to London. I had a big suite for Gandhi at the Wagram, and he stayed with my maid and took advantage of the trees in the Tuileries. He practically ruined them all.

Harry d'Arrast, a French nobleman,* was walking in the gardens one day and saw Gandhi there. Harry said to my Swiss maid, Julie, "Why do you let this dog defecate . . . ?" She said I'd told her that Gandhi should have the trees to the city, and that was better for him than the keys.

Well, Gandhi behaved very nicely at San Simeon. He never did anything in the room—when I was watching him.

One day we were playing tennis. Normally, after the game Gandhi would retrieve all the balls and put them where they were supposed to be. But that day he forgot. He was following after Doris Duke, making love to her. He was a dirty little chiseler. He looked at me and then followed her, even though she was married to Jimmy Cromwell.*

I had thought Gandhi would never leave me. But he followed her continually. I decided he was after her money; she was richer than I was.

---

* Henri d'Abbadie d'Arrast had been Charles Chaplin's assistant in the making of the picture *A Woman of Paris,* and would become a director of comedy films.

* Businessman and diplomat James Henry Roberts Cromwell was married to Doris Duke in February 1935. They were divorced in 1948.

San Simeon. When W.R. left for the last time, his car paused halfway down the hill. It must have been an agonizing moment as he made his silent farewell. He ordered all work on the houses stopped, and they have remained as they were. This view of the Casa Grande shows a wing that was never finished. The windows were sealed permanently with cement.

Marion.

4

The Thomas Ince affair. Lindbergh returns triumphant. Mrs. Vanderbilt loses her guest of honor. A problem with taxes. The first of the
talkies. Marion makes a talkie. Mr. Hearst does a tap dance.

*T*homas Ince was a successful independent film producer
and former Broadway actor. He was forty-four years old
in November 1924 when he died.

*Stories surrounding his death often suggest a romantic link be-
tween Ince and Marion, ended at the murderous hands of W.R. and
covered up by Louella Parsons.*

*It happened during a pre-Thanksgiving cruise that year, aboard
the 201-foot steam yacht* Oneida. *Marion talks about some of the
guests aboard, but there were others along whom she doesn't mention: Charles Chaplin, Theodore Kosloff, and Dr. Daniel Carson Good-
man, a physician who was also W.R.'s film production manager.*

The Oneida *was then stationed in Wilmington, part of the Los
Angeles harbor west of the growing city of Long Beach. It was frequently transferred back and forth between Pacific and Atlantic waters via the Panama Canal.*

W.R. was the publisher of Motor Boating *magazine, and for his
yachting parties he was not restricted to use only of the* Oneida. *He
bought the Prince of Monaco's opulent* Hirondelle, *a vessel noted
for its indolent approach both to oceanography and to music. Push-
buttons exposed a glass section of the hull, and the keyboard of a
steam-powered organ.*

At the time of the sinking of the Maine *in Havana in 1898, Hearst
had offered the U.S. Navy the use of his yacht,* Buccaneer, *with himself as captain. W.R. further offered to fit the 138-foot steel-hulled*

Thomas H. Ince.

*steamer with the latest naval arma-
ments and to keep these weapons supplied with ammunition as needed. The
Navy accepted his offer of the vessel,
without W.R. as captain, and it sailed
under the flag. It was later returned,
with thanks.*

I was really furious about the Thomas
Ince story.

We had boarded the *Oneida* at Wilmington on a Friday for a short sail:
Seena Owen, a motion picture actress
who had been married to Raoul
Walsh's brother George, an actor; W.R.
and I, [W.R.'s secretary] Joe Willicombe, Elinor Glyn, my sisters Ethel
and Reine, Tom Ince, and the Barhams. I think there were thirteen
guests, plus thirty or forty crew members.

I had invited Tom and Nell Ince because I was very fond of Nell, but she
couldn't go because one of her boys
was having a birthday. "But will you
please let Tom go," she said, "because
he's been working awfully hard, and
drinking quite a bit. I think the rest will
do him good."

We got down to the harbor on Friday night. We had a quiet dinner together, and everybody retired early.
For dinner we had a lobster cocktail,
then turkey and a salad; nothing to
drink that I knew about, because anywhere Mr. Hearst was, no liquor was
served. And I remember that Tom Ince
said, "I would like to drink a toast to
my son's birthday." And Elinor Glyn
said, "Don't drink it in water; that's bad
luck." But I think we did.

The next morning, or maybe afternoon—because when I woke up it
was generally afternoon—Tom wasn't
around. I asked Willicombe where he
was. Willicombe told me that, the night
before, Tom had had an attack of
indigestion and had asked for some bi-
carbonate of soda. He had been belch-
ing and vomiting all night long, and he
had said he would like to go home.
Afterward, Nell said, "If he had been
drinking whiskey, that would have
done it." If he was, he brought his own
bottle along.

When we went into San Diego harbor, Willicombe sent for the launch
and put Tom ashore, and he went
home. A member of his family was a
Christian Scientist and didn't want a
doctor. Tom was sick for two days and
then died.

I went back to work on Monday
morning. I was working on *Zander the
Great* at the United Studios, where
Norma Talmadge was nice enough to
lend me her bungalow—her half of it,
that is; Connie Talmadge had the other
half. We couldn't work at MGM because we required an enormous stage,
and MGM didn't have much room.

Nell called me late Monday afternoon at the studio to tell me that Tom
had died. The doctors pronounced it
acute indigestion and said it had affected his heart. She was really in a bad
way when I went up to see her.

I went to the funeral with Nell and

The *Oneida* was built by the Harlan and Hollingsworth Company and launched in Wilmington, Delaware in 1897. Designed by A. S. Chesebrough, it displaced 396 tons. (Photo courtesy Morris Rosenfeld & Sons.)

Tom, Jr., and Dick and the other boy. I think he was buried in the Hollywood Cemetery.

When I read the story in the *New York Daily News* intimating that Tom had been shot, I was shocked. Who would shoot him? And why? The whole thing was so preposterous. There were no weapons aboard the *Oneida,* ever.* And he didn't die until late Monday. How long can one keep a bullet in his system?

The *News* also said that Margaret Livingston, who was married to Paul Whiteman, was on the boat. I didn't even know her. And she was supposed to be going around with Tom Ince.

There was one magazine piece about Louella Parsons getting her job as a result of seeing the shooting and not telling. Supposedly, out of gratitude, W.R. fixed her up on the papers. But she was not on board the yacht, and besides, she had been working for Mr. Hearst long before that.

But Joe Patterson started the thing

about W.R.'s being jealous. That was silly. I knew Nell Ince very well; in fact, I knew her better than I knew him. Tom wasn't staid, but there was nothing wolfy about him, not a bit. He wanted to be friendly with everybody, and he was jovial and very good-natured.

And then there was the story about thirteen at the table. I hadn't even realized there were thirteen at the table. But every little thing was picked up and made larger and larger.

One story had Tom buried at Forest Lawn and cremated the next day, before anyone could see him. That added to the mystery, of course.

They kept pestering Nell, and I told her just to make a statement if she wanted to, or to refuse to talk to anybody. She was really grief-stricken; she had been very much in love with Tom Ince.

How could a newspaper make up such a lie? I could have sued them, and I wanted to, but I had tried that once before—the "Marion Davies Murder" thing—and I had got nowhere.

---

* But rumors persist that W.R. would take along a gun to shoot at passing sea gulls.

W.R. said, "Never sue. That always enlarges a thing, keeps it going on and makes it worse. After all, newspapers are supposed to write good stories."

"Whether they are true or not?"

"Well, a retraction would be fine, but don't ask the *Daily News* for one. They won't do it."

Now, you can't blame the man who owns a newspaper. Very likely some smart reporter got hold of the story and said, "Here's a scoop." Maybe Joe Patterson didn't even see the story until it was printed. He couldn't be at the office all the time and watch and edit everything.

It was only the one article, and it drifted off to nothing. None of the other papers picked it up. It was just the *New York Daily News*. There was no evidence of any kind. When they investigated, they found out there was nothing to it.

But I kept on hearing about it. People will make a mountain out of a molehill even when nothing happens, and they'll build up a big story. If anything of the sort had really happened, everybody would have been in jail.

It was the most ridiculous story I ever heard in my life, but when you have an association with a very well known man like W.R., you are bound to get it.

But that Saturday we went on our way, not very far. And not fishing. I would not go fishing. I had caught one once and I felt so sorry I wanted to shoot myself.

He looked so pitiful, a 148-pounder. But the poor thing didn't want to be caught. And I got him on just a little thin line, a bass line. But it got hooked right on the side of the jaw. This was somewhere down in Mexico.

W.R. would never fish or hunt, and this was the first time I had ever been fishing. So everybody was telling me what to do. My line started running

and I couldn't hold on to it. I said, "Let me alone. I'll do it myself." I was big and brave.

Then my thumb got caught in the reel, turned all black. It took forty minutes, and the poor thing arrived and we didn't have a gaff. My brother-in-law George van Cleve took a shotgun. Wherever he got it from, I do not know. Maybe it was a pistol he had. And he shot it. I looked at it, and it was looking at me, and never, never, never again would I fish.

I thought, Get the hook out of its mouth and let it go. What's the use? We can live on bread and cheese and things like beer. You don't have to kill things to live.

W.R.'s yacht Oneida *was in New York harbor when Lindbergh returned a hero from Europe, after his solo flight across the Atlantic late in May 1927.*

The U.S. Navy had sailed Lindbergh to Washington, D.C., aboard the warship Memphis, *but to please the crowds Lindbergh entered New York harbor flying a seaplane.*

We were staying at the Warwick Hotel.* We went out on the *Oneida* with quite a few guests and took a motor launch and watched Lindbergh landing in the water. Then he switched over to the Mayor's boat—the *Macom,* I think it was.

We were following them, but we got ahead of their boat, and when we got to the dock my hair was all stringy and long—from the fog and the water.

When we arrived at the Battery, everything was roped off. The cars and the policemen were waiting for Lindbergh.

---

* W.R. owned the Warwick Hotel at Sixth Avenue (now Avenue of the Americas) and 54th Street in Manhattan. The hotel is still on site. The Mayor of New York City at that time was Jimmy Walker.

I didn't think we could get under the lines, but a *New York Evening Journal* reporter was there, and W.R. said to him, "Give me your card."

We were all ducking under the ropes when a policeman said, "Where do you think you're going?"

W.R. said, "I'm with the *New York Evening Journal*."

Then the policeman said, "What's your name?"

But W.R. forgot and said, "Hearst."

The policeman said, "Ahuh, get back there with the rest of the Hearsts." So we had to go back under the line, and we didn't know how to get out. Then W.R. saw the Mayor's car and took a dive for it. He left the rest of us flat.

I got into the fourth of the Mayor's cars, where I didn't belong at all, but I just snuggled in. My hair was soaking wet, and I had big goggles on.

The parade started. It was fortunate for me that the policemen were so busy with their horses and the crowds and the confetti coming down. They had little time to bother with me.

I was watching the policemen. They would take their horses and run them into the crowd. There were a lot of accidents that day. There were children everywhere; it was the most amazing sight I ever saw in my life. I think all of New York was there, along Fifth Avenue.

Just before we arrived at City Hall, where Lindbergh was to make a speech, I decided it was time for me to scram. I thought I'd get out of the car, if I could without being beheaded, and go over to the Warwick, get a good shower, curl my hair and then go to Cartier's and watch the parade. But just before we got to City Hall the others in the car started whispering, and I knew the questions were coming. They said, "Are you sure you're in the right car?" I said yes.

"Who are you?" I said that I was a reporter. They said, "You shouldn't be in this car. You've got to get out." I said I was getting out at City Hall. They said, "Be sure you do. And what paper do you work for?"

I said, "The *Mail*."*

Well, they made sure I got shunted out before we got to City Hall. And I had to push my way through that crowd to get to Sixth Avenue. There were no taxis in sight, just an elevated train. And I didn't have any money.

Anyway, I got on, and I was the only one on the train. Just myself and the man who was running it. He said, "Where's your fare?"

"I'm terribly sorry. If you'll give me your name I'll be sure you get the fare. I'm at the Warwick, and I have to get off before you go around the loop."

"That's all right. I was kind of lonesome, anyway."

I got off, went into the hotel and left word for the doorman to be sure to give the man his money the next time he came around the loop.

I jumped into the shower, then got my hair fixed; but instead of going down 57th Street, I got excited and found myself at Central Park. I was going along with the soldiers, marching. I had a few whistles, but not many.

I finally got to Cartier's, and I had been there just a second when the parade came along. Lindbergh was waving. W.R. was in the second car. I whistled at him and he looked up. He said, "Excuse me," and got out of the car and came into Cartier's. Everybody was so excited they didn't know what they were doing.

When Lindbergh got to Central Park they asked him if there was anything he wanted. He hadn't eaten anything, so he said, "I'd like a hot dog." And then he was supposed to go to the Vanderbilts', or to Long Island, to the Astors'.

_____

* Not a Hearst newspaper.

Marion in *Not So Dumb*.

I think he went there. Afterwards Mrs. Astor said that she couldn't get him interested in her guests. He had brought two men along: the one who had sold him the gasoline before he went overseas, and the one who had the maps. He spent all his time with those two men and wouldn't pay any attention to the other guests.

I called Jimmy Walker on the phone and said, "Tell Lindbergh to come over here."

The Mayor said, "Ask for anything, Marion. Ask for me to get the sun to come down and meet the moon. Ask me if I can do anything in the world, but don't ask me that."

Then I got Victor Watson* on the phone. He was at the banquet, and I

said to him, "Slide a note over to Lindbergh. Say, 'Could he come to the Warwick? Only for five or ten minutes. He could relax awhile with a few friends.'"

I expected a no, but in a few minutes he came back on the phone and said, "Yes. He'll be over in half an hour."

Quite a few people were there, and I said, "We're going to have Lindbergh." They didn't believe it.

But the telephone operator must have given the word, because in five minutes the whole place was surrounded. There were thousands of people, and we were on the twenty-sixth story, and I didn't know what was going on. I couldn't hear anything down on the ground.

Then the phone rang. It was the Mayor. Jimmy said, "You can't do this. Mrs. Vanderbilt is waiting at her house on Fifth Avenue, and she's got all the gold plate out. Little Gracie's there and the General, and they're waiting."

"I'm sorry . . ."

"She's got three hundred people waiting in the big ballroom. You cannot do this to her."

"Why don't you put the question to Colonel Lindbergh? Ask him what he wants to do."

"All right," he said, "I'll try."

I didn't want to be hanging around all night, so I got very independent. I said, "Call me back."

And he did. "I'm sending Esmond O'Brien up to see you."

So Esmond came, all dressed up. He said, "Look, Marion, I have to break the news to Mrs. Vanderbilt."

"What news?"

"That Lindbergh is coming here instead of going to her party."

"Oh?" I said. "Really? I didn't know anything about that."

"What am I going to say?"

Well, I didn't know, and that was his problem anyway. He said, "She'll kill me."

---
* He was managing editor of the *New York American*.

Mary Pickford was sitting next to Lindbergh. He was on my right and she was next. She sent me this note: "He won't talk." I wrote back: "Talk about airplanes."

I said, "I don't really know if he's coming here." And I didn't know how I could help him.

He said, "He certainly is. The Mayor told me to come over here and talk you out of this thing."

"Well, look. I can't talk Lindbergh out of what he wants to do."

After that you never heard such a racket in your life. It was like the whole hotel exploded. The sirens were going like mad. We went downstairs, but you couldn't beat your way through the lobby.

Then Lindbergh came in, in one of those little police cars. He had a white cap on and he was smiling. He was in a very good mood. People started crowding around, and I thought they were going to tear him to pieces. Finally we got him into the elevator, and we went up. Someone was playing the guitar, and after a while Lindbergh took the guitar and sat on the floor and played.

Ezzie O'Brien came back after a while. He said to me, "Well, I went in, and Mrs. Vanderbilt was standing with the General. I said I had some bad news for her. 'Don't . . . don't tell me,'

she said. 'He's not coming.' And she fainted dead away.

"When she came to, she said, 'You break the news to my guests. I haven't the strength.' "

So Ezzie had to face the whole room of people and say he was sorry that Lindbergh could not be there. He said, "You never heard such grunts and groans. And now can I join your party?"

"Certainly. Come on in."

Lindbergh stayed for two hours and played the guitar and sang. It was just a nice little intimate party. We also did acts and charades and games. George K. Arthur was there, and Harry Crocker and Maury Paul* and some friends I knew from New York. Carole Lombard was there, and I forget who else, but Lindbergh had a good time and didn't want to leave. Of course when he left, he still had to face the crowds. He had to fight his way through.

W.R. did a tap dance. He was the best tap dancer you ever saw. And he accompanied himself. He didn't need

---

* Arthur was an actor, and Paul the newspaperman who wrote the Cholly Knickerbocker society column.

any music, just one, two, three, bum—bum. He did this dance for Lindbergh. Whenever he felt the urge, he often used to get up and do a little tap dance.

It was very nice of Lindbergh to come. He didn't know who I was from Adam. But I guess he didn't want the stuffed-shirt business. We didn't talk much. Very little. But I could see that he wanted a bit of relaxation.

When Lindbergh was out in California, he came to MGM. And we were driving to the airport, and a potentate whose name I won't mention was taking all the bows from the schoolkids. The kids were bowing to Lindbergh, not Louis B. Mayer, but Lindbergh was sitting next to me, and he was laughing. He was very conservative, very quiet. Smiling, but not saying much.

Well, that was 1927, if I have to mention the date. The first thing you know, they are going to make me a hundred and five years old. They lie about Louella's age in *Who's Who*. If they can say she's sixty, then I'm ten.

And Tallulah never mentions any dates. They always make the older people younger and the younger people older. People said that Mary Pickford must be sixty-three, and I'd say, "Wait a minute. Now Mary can't be more than thirty-five." But why do they add on age to motion picture stars, while newspaper columnists can pull their own ages down?

Marion and W.R. made a point of taking time for travel. They made a trip a year to Europe, always stopping in New York.

In June 1927 Marion had rushed to New York to join W.R. for the celebration of Lindbergh's successful flight. They were again in New York when the public caught the enthusiasm for "talkies." Both events were spectacles of the times.

We had just come back from Europe when the signs were flashing, "See Al Jolson in 'Sit Upon My Knee, Sonny Boy'" or whatever it was. It really got me disturbed.

Maury Paul went with me to the Capitol Theatre to see the picture. When I heard the voice of Al Jolson, I thought, No. This can't be. There can't be talkies. I'm ruined. I'm wrecked.

When Jolson started singing, "When there are clear skies . . ." I started to cry. The mascara ran all over my face. He sang, "I'll think of you, Sonny Boy . . ."

Maury said, "What's the matter with you?"

The picture was really wonderful, but I kept thinking, I'm ruined. When we went back to the Ritz Towers, I couldn't stop crying. But I kept singing, "When there are clear skies, I'll think of youuuuu."

I was crying in the elevator, and when W.R. saw me he said, "What's the matter?"

Maury said, "Sonny Boy got her down."

I really thought I was finished. But the funny part of it was, I didn't have any trouble. No one thought I could talk, and I didn't think I could either. I stuttered. I was scared to death when I got word I had to make a test at MGM. I didn't know what to do. They sent me a script and said, "Memorize this."

I looked through the dialogue; it was very silly. So I called Irving Thalberg and said, "Do I have to play both parts?"

"No. We have George K. Arthur. We'll be ready in about half an hour."

"I can't memorize this in half an hour."

"Stage 2 in half an hour," he said.

So George K. Arthur came over, and he agreed it was the silliest dialogue he had ever heard. Like, "Do you think

In MARIANNE they asked me to do everything but stand on my head.
I danced, I sang, I did Chevalier imitations in a French accent.
I was dramatic and comic at the same time in my first talkie.

it's nice to be in a river with a cater-
pillar?" I tore it up and said we were
going to ad lib. He said, "But—what
about me?"

I said, "Just follow me. I'll lead you."
But he was English and he wasn't too
brave, so we had a glass of sherry before we went on the set.

There were others making tests, and
I was really cringing. When they said,
"Ready for Miss Davies," I was petri-
fied. I couldn't budge. But they found
me and we got on the set. They had a
camera with a big mirror on it so you
could see yourself while you were acting. I didn't care to look.

I'd had a little sherry, and you'd
think I knew what I was talking about.
I started a routine. I said, "This is a
dinner party where we are eating

ersters. From Brooklyn . . . ersters . . ."
And I went on from there, and I
wouldn't stop.

I said to George, "Sit down."

"There's no chair."

"Well . . . fall down. What's the difference?"

We went on ad-libbing lines until
Douglas said, "That's it. That's the
end."

That was Norma Shearer's brother,
the head of the sound department. He
was up in the booth. So thank God it
was over, and I went home and I talked
to Mr. Hearst and he asked how it went
and I said no. "I've decided I'm going
back to Europe; don't care for the climate out here. I like it better in Europe.
Much nicer. Better for me.

"As a matter of fact, this sound thing

73

is progressive, but I don't care for it. Get reservations tomorrow for me. The first plane, then a boat . . ." I went to the beach house and the whole family was there and I said, "Go away from me. Don't talk to me, please. I don't care for this idea at all. I'm going to sleep and I hope I never wake up . . ."

The next day Irving Thalberg called me to come to the studio immediately. I said to him, "I can't. I'm not feeling well."

"Look. I want to talk to you." He was very severe. He said, "I have some news for you which you're not going to like."

All right, I thought. So I got dressed and went over. He said, "What did you do?"

"I didn't do anything."

"You made a test last night. What did you do?"

"I didn't do anything."

"Well, whatever you did, you stunned the other people. You're the only one who's getting a new contract. Yours is the best; do you want to see it?"

I said, "NO!"

"You've got a new five-year contract," he said.

"You're lying to me, Irving."

"No," he said. "The others'll go. Gilbert, Haines, Arthur, Novarro . . . You're the only one. I want you to stay . . . Who wrote your dialogue?"

I said, "I don't know. He's the one you sent over."

"I'll have him promoted. Who was it?"

"He was a great writer. It was a wonderful script."

"But how did you memorize it so quickly?"

"Because it was such a marvelous script."

Then W.R. arrived. We looked at the test, and W.R. started to cry. He said, "My God, it's marvelous."

So they got me right into production immediately. In *Marianne*, they asked me to do everything but stand on my head. I danced, I sang, did Chevalier imitations in a French accent. I was dramatic and comic at the same time in my first talkie.*

Now I had to beat myself into talking. I didn't know anything about Christian Science then, but I thought, If you're going to do it, you do it. If you don't do it, you spank yourself. That was the idea. I tried talking with a pebble in my mouth, like Demosthenes. It might have worked for Demosthenes, but it didn't for me. I just swallowed the pebble.

Yet through all those takes, never once did I stammer. My leading man in *Marianne* was Lawrence Gray. He had a wonderful voice and a very good disposition. It was easy to work with him. Except one day he took off his uniform coat, because it was warm, and he put it on this curling thing the hairdresser had on the stage. He burned a hole in it.

He blew his top when they didn't have another coat his size in the wardrobe. But they whipped one up in a hurry, and the next day he did the same thing. He blamed it on the hairdresser, and there was a riot on the set. He was so mad, but he should have known the iron was there.

While we were making *Marianne*, Irving never lost his temper with me. He had plenty of reason to lose it, but he never did. He'd look at me and say, "Why did you do that?" He could give you a stare that made you feel just so high.

One time he said we could have an orchestra for three hours to do a number. We finished it in two hours. So I

---

* *Marianne* was not released until October 1929. The studio made both a silent and a sound version. It was reviewed favorably as a talkie, and the silent print was never shown.

suggested we throw in another number, and we did. He said, "Don't ever do that again." I thought Irving was really mad. He had never talked to me like that, and I choked up, but he left that number in the picture, and it was a big success.

Later he said he was sorry. He said, "You were right. I hate to admit it, but I like to give credit where it's due." The number I had added had already been written for the show, but he had said he didn't like it. It was "Hang on to me, hang on to me"; Benny Rubin and Cliff Edwards did it. My back was turned to the camera, because I didn't know how to sing very well. I was supposed to be weeping because my soldier was mad at me. I didn't sing the song. It was a good chance for them to do things behind my back.

Irving Thalberg was always very kind. If he was preparing a story for you, and you read it, he would ask, "Is there anything in this that you don't like?" He was terribly busy, but he would say, "Come to my office and we'll talk it over."

Everybody went to his office; I don't know how he ever got through his work. I'd go in and we'd argue a little bit, back and forth, and then he would say, "Is this entirely *your* thought?"

I knew what he meant. I'd say, "Yes. In a way." I had another honor; I was known as liar number one. But there were certain times when the truth would hop out of me before I'd realize it. So when I said, "In a way," he knew.

Irving said, "You don't understand what I'm trying to do. I'm trying to get you away from those namby-pamby pictures to do something with a little character. Mr. Hearst doesn't want you to do anything the slightest bit off-color, and I have no intention of doing that. I just want to strike a happy medium. I want you to do something that

Cover for the sheet music to *Marianne*. The music was by Fred E. Ahlert, and the lyrics for the title song were by Roy Turk. Joseph E. Weiss did the ukulele arrangement.

Norma Shearer, Will Hays, Marion and Irving Thalberg. *Irving loved parties; they were his way of relaxing. And everybody loved him too.*

75

isn't entirely gutless, something that means something. And I don't want to be told about these things by another person."

That was the only time that he got the hair up on his neck. He said, "Don't you have confidence in me? If you leave it to me, I'll see you through."

"All right," I said.

I was at a very bad disadvantage. Irving could talk me into anything, and he knew damn well he could. I didn't know as much as he knew. I thought you should reason things out, and if you were right, admit it; and if you were wrong, admit it. I didn't mean to be facetious; I just wanted him to know that I respected his opinion—which I did, and who didn't?

When *The Big Parade* was opening, I wanted to ask Irving something, so I went to his office. His assistant, Bernie Hyman, said, "Irving's home. He's very sick." But I heard him telling somebody else, "Send those reels of film over to Mr. Thalberg's house. He's going to work on them there."

So I went over to Irving's house. He was in bed with the flu. A screen was up, and the cutter was there, and they were working like mad. It was only four days to the opening, I think.

"Hello," I said.

"Sit down for a minute; I'm sort of working." He was saying, "Cut this here and cut that there and two inches here and . . ." On and on he went, until they finished the reel. "All right," he said, "what's griping you?"

"Nothing. I just wanted to come over and see how a sick person acts. And I've learned plenty."

His mother had said to me, "Please tell Irving not to work so hard. He's so sick." He wasn't yet married to Norma Shearer, but just after that, there was the lovely wedding. Again I was a bridesmaid, and Norma looked beauti-

ful in a gorgeous costume—the wedding dress, not exactly a costume.

W.R. was crazy about Thalberg. He said, "Ofttimes the word genius is misplaced, but in the case of Irving, it is a conceded fact." Look at all the wonderful pictures he made.

Irving loved parties; they were his way of relaxing. And everybody loved him.

He was always kind of frail looking. But he needn't have died so young. I think he ran his motor out, because all he had on his mind was work. Pictures and work.

Louis B. Mayer helped me out when I was called to Washington in the middle of making *Marianne*. I went by train. It was early morning when I arrived, and I wasn't feeling any too good, because I hadn't slept. I was worried because I didn't really know what they wanted.

The meeting was held in the Customs House, which looked like a jail. At the table were thirteen men, my unlucky number.

My New York lawyer who had made out my income tax was there, and a Commissioner Harris, who wanted to know what the deduction for an automobile for going on location was all about. I said, "If you go on location and use your own car, you have to buy gasoline and all, and that's the deduction."

Then it was powder, greasepaint and lipstick. I said, "Those are necessary for my work. Did you ever try to work on the screen without getting made up?"

That must have rubbed him the wrong way. The Commissioner said, "Don't be funny." And he threw out that deduction. Then he went on and on with the silliest things. Like hairpins, which anybody who's working would deduct.

My lawyer was looking at me as if he didn't know me, and those thirteen men were staring at me. At the end, the Commissioner said, "You have been defrauding the government. It will cost you exactly $950,000."

I went down to the bathroom there and started to cry. I was hungry. Even though I had had nothing to eat, I vomited.

One of the stenographers followed me in. She said, "This is awful. I've never heard anything like it before."

When I went back upstairs, the men had taken a different attitude. They even stood up, which was very nice; they hadn't done that before. I guess the secretary had told them I was very ill.

My New York lawyer turned out to be no help to me at all. I blamed him for the whole thing, anyway. When you are working, you cannot make out your income tax by yourself. You leave it to lawyers, and you pay them for it. If anything is wrong, it's not your fault.

I said to the Commissioner, "I'm sorry. I'm in the midst of a picture and I'm holding up the studio. What can I do?"

They wanted $950,000 in a certified check, and an extra $110,000. I said, "What is *that* for?" It was for dismissing the claim of defrauding the government.

As time passes, the government retires its records. While Marion's rounded numbers seem extraordinary, she did have tax liabilities for her film production company, her real estate investments and her personal income, and these figures may have covered several years.

During the thirties Marion continued to have tax problems. Newspapers reported that her tax for 1931—$100,292 —had been found deficient and that she was being charged an additional $52,044. Since the tax rates for that year were lower than they had been in the 1920s, it was the sign of a fantastic income. The total tax of $152,336 probably had to be less than five percent of her annual income.

I called Louis B. Mayer and got the money from him. He didn't want to stop the production, so he said, "Come back as quick as you can. Take a plane."

Of course I took the train back, and then I worked for two years for nothing.*

It was all a political thing. I don't want to mention his name, but he was the President of the United States, and he had been attacked by the Hearst papers for going to South America. He was getting even by using me.

---

* It was a studio practice to advance the stars money when they needed it—thus assuring cooperation and a continued flow of films.

Valentino tried to teach Marion to tango.

5

Chaplin makes a losing bet. A hole in the ice. Spurned by Garbo. Greasepaint, powder and lipstick. Crosby and Cooper and Gable: the nicest leading men. A film with Leslie Howard, who wasn't acting for a second.

One day there were thirty or forty of us at breakfast—we called it a "hunt breakfast." We asked Charlie Chaplin if he was going to become a citizen. Charlie said, "I doubt it."

"Why not?"

That started the argument.

Charlie had been here twenty years and had made a lot of money. So W.R. said, "You made your money in America. What's wrong with America? If you don't like it, why not go someplace else?"

"I will. However, I'm not going to have anybody tell me what to do." We let that one go, and then we got on the talkies subject.

I had just finished *Marianne,* my first talking picture, and I was a little nervous about the result.

Charlie Chaplin said, "I don't believe in talkies for myself, because I'm a pantomimist."

"I wouldn't say that entirely," W.R. said. "You can talk. You're talking now."

"I will never make a talkie," said Charlie.

"Why don't you want to try it?"

"I'm against the whole idea. And talkies won't last a year."

"I'd like to bet you they'll last a little bit longer."

"I'm telling you they won't."

"I'll bet you five thousand dollars."

"I'll bet you a hundred dollars they won't."

"All right."

Poolside at Marion's house at 1700 Lexington Road, Beverly Hills. Charles Chaplin is at left, followed by Louella Parsons; Larry Gray; Louella's husband, Dr. Harry Martin; Marion; Beltran Neasses; and Rudolph Valentino.

Charles Chaplin and Marion Davies. For different reasons, each preferred silent films to the talkies.

Then Charlie said, "I'm insulted. I'm leaving." And he left.

Harry d'Arrast said, "Look at the big genius. He knows all the answers."

"I don't know if he's right, but there should be no arguments at the table," W.R. said.

I said to him, "Why don't you go and apologize to him?"

"Why?"

"He's a guest, after all. Go and say you're sorry. Show him the other cheek."

"All right, I will." And W.R. went out with Harry d'Arrast and said, "Look, Charlie, I'm terribly sorry if I've hurt your feelings. I understand how you feel about talkies. You are purely a pantomimist. And this is out of your territory . . ."

"If I wanted to make a talkie, I would. But I'm telling you they will not last."

So they agreed that talkies wouldn't last, and W.R. said, "Won't you finish your breakfast?"

Charlie said, "No. I'm going anyway. Thank you." And he left in a huff.

It was a silly argument, but W.R. was big enough to go out and apologize. He liked Charlie, but Charlie was like a cat; he had to go and start a fight. I was glad he had left, and I decided we wouldn't allow him in the house anymore.

But W.R. said, "Oh yes we will."

"Oh no we won't."

"Charlie's all right. He's just a little nutty."

"You've apologized to him, and I think he should at least be gracious."

"Well, let's call him a genius."

Both Chaplin and Marion would make the transition into talking pictures. As theatres added sound equipment to their facilities, Chaplin expanded his talents to writing—both screenplays and music—and then to producing and directing. Gone were the days of vaudeville and one- or two-reel films. He made feature-length productions. And he moved to Switzerland.

Comedy moved from the kitchen to the drawing room, as romance moved from the parlor to the bedroom. But Marion still worked in costumes and wigs and furs.

In *The Red Mill* I had to go ice-skating in wooden shoes, which was ridiculous. I broke my arches. I had to skate alongside this Great Dane and fall through a hole in the ice.

When we rehearsed it, the dog wouldn't run, so they got a cat. Then he really started to run, and I was hanging on for dear life. I went down on all fours into this dirty pool over in the back lot. It was filthy water, and I got a frog in my throat, a real one. A little frog. And then they wanted to do the scene all over again.

But that Great Dane had caught the cat and broken its back. I went straight to my dressing room and called the Society for the Prevention of Cruelty to Animals.

I didn't mind falling in the water, but I didn't think they should have used a cat or let that dog get it. I didn't get any sense out of it. So I refused to work.*

That was the picture Fatty Arbuckle directed, but under a different name. After all the scandal, Nick Schenck felt sorry for him and gave him a job. They called him Will B. Good. That was his name as the director.**

But then they didn't like the rushes, so they put George Hill on. Then they didn't like George Hill's work, and they put Eddie Mannix on. And Eddie got fired.

That picture had so many directors I can't remember all their names. Every day I'd have a different director.

I went to the preview because I wanted to see the public's honest reaction. But where I thought I'd get laughs, I didn't. Nobody else cried at the drama, but I found myself in tears. I guess I was just sorry for myself. It laid a pancake. When I was ready to leave the theatre, my mother, who had come with me, had gone to the powder room, or so someone said.

But she hadn't. She was outside writing out preview cards. She knew my heart was broken, because I'd worked awfully hard on that picture, and now the reaction was null and void.

The next day there was a big stack of preview cards on Irving Thalberg's desk. "It was a great success," he said. All the cards were flattery; there was not a word of criticism.

---

* Was Marion thinking of her co-star, actor Karl Dane? The dog was a Saint Bernard.
** William Goodrich was credited on screen.

Marion with "Rover" in *The Red Mill*.

The Red Mill. A hole in the ice. *It was filthy water and I got a frog in my throat, a real one.*

I don't know how my mother managed to write all those cards, but Irving fell for them. Luckily he didn't know her handwriting. They said: "Marion is gorgeous—the best comedienne in the world." "Terrific." "She's marvelous."

Irving said, "They're wonderful cards. We've never gotten any better. You can't still think it laid a pancake?"

I said yes.

Then I went back to my bungalow and rang up my mother. I said, "What did you do that for?"

Now I had to figure out how to get those cards away from Irving before he found out. So I called his secretary and I said I wanted the preview cards.

"What do you want them for?"

"I want to show them to my mother. She doesn't think I'm any good on the screen. I'm having a hard time convincing her that the reaction was good."

Well, she gave me the cards. And I destroyed them.

I used to go to Europe for three months every summer, then I'd come back and do about three pictures a year.

Once I was doing two pictures at the same time. On one set I would work from nine in the morning until six. Then at seven I'd go to work on the other set and work until four in the morning. I'd sleep in between. I did that for about six weeks. There were two different crews, because the crews wouldn't work that long. And two different casts.

I could take it then; it didn't bother me at all. I even liked doing it, working day and night. I wasn't on union time, but I was getting paid a high salary. W.R. wasn't in Los Angeles then, and I didn't tell him about it. The moment they knew he was away, they asked me to do the work. I don't know whether the studio was going broke, or whether they just needed an extra picture.

When I had a choice, I liked working at night better than in the daytime. I didn't like the cold early mornings with the cold greasepaint on my face. I had my chauffeur drive me and my maid to the studio. If I had been driving I'd never have gotten there. I didn't know one street from another. I wasn't sure where Santa Monica was, much less Burbank.

Though Marion was surrounded by wealth and the glamour of Hollywood stardom, still she retained a sense of humor and compassion for those who worked for her or with her. Marion is still remembered for her kindliness and great generosity. She was never a snob.

The best way to get along with directors is not to be the star. Just be under direction, which is the proper thing to do. That's what they're there for; they're supposed to direct you— you're not supposed to direct the director.

If you say, "I don't like the way you're doing this scene," it humiliates him. You should take orders. Otherwise you wouldn't need a director. Most stars don't realize that. And every director has a different approach.

Actors may think they know it all, but they don't see the outside view. You have to rely on the director to tell you where you're wrong. The person who's observing knows more than the person who's actually doing it. I learned that at the Empire School.*

Most directors are very sympathetic. They'll say, "Look, you're a

---

* The Empire Theatre Dramatic School was located on the southeast corner of Broadway and 40th Street in Manhattan.

Marie Dressler, Marion and Jane Winton in *The Patsy*.

little bit underbalanced in this scene,"
or ". . . a little overemotional in that."
You should take the cue and measure
it down.

The kind of director you need will
just come up and say, "Now, look, you
can do better. You're nervous. Take
it easy. You know what the scene is—
just pretend there's nobody looking
at you, and give it all you've got."

That's if you have anything to give.
If you make a mistake, then he'll tell
you. Bob Leonard and Richard Bole-
slavsky* were that way. But Boley had
a heart attack and died after making
a picture with Joan Crawford. He was
very sensitive.

Right after *Marianne*, which was a
talkie, I made *The Patsy*, a silent film,
in fourteen days. It was a very funny

picture and it did very well.* Marie
Dressler and Larry Gray were in it, and
King Vidor directed.

I was the patsy, the youngest one
in the family, who everybody hated.
They'd say, "Run and do this, or do
that, and take your elbows off the
table, and blow your nose."

I saw Garbo only once, when she
decided she wasn't going on the set.
On a very warm day I happened to
go by in time to hear her say, "Why
should I work? It's so silly and I'm hot.
. . . Goodbye."

"Hello," I said.

She said, "It is very silly for people

* The author of *Acting: The First Six Lessons*, a
classic for aspiring thespians.

* Released in 1928, it grossed $617,000, and MGM
reported a profit of $155,000. They also reported
that it took twenty-seven days to make.

to work in this heat. Look at this hot dressing room; and not even a toilet."

"You can use mine if you want to."

"No, I've got mine." She had one of those pots. "It's very good for this reason—you can dump it out on top of the directors."

"Aw, you wouldn't."

"I wouldn't, eh?"

She really had a wonderful sense of humor.

Then she said, "I don't feel good. I don't why people work like this, under these conditions. It's perfectly preposterous. Now I have a leading man who seems to think he can be a little bit salacious."

"Who's that?"

"Jack Gilbert."

"Oh! But he's very nice. I've seen him," I said, "but I don't know him."

"You don't? Don't!" Then she said, "Come and see me sometime on the set." Now that sounded very funny, because everyone knew she wouldn't allow anybody to see her on the set.

I was doing my picture right on the same stage. Her half was all blocked off, but mine wasn't, and one day she came over. I thought, This is flattery, that she'd come over to see me act; I must be great. When she went back to her set, I said to the director, Pop Leonard, "Have you got a scene you can do without me? I'd like to go over and repay the compliment."

"I'll give you about five minutes."

I went into a maze of flats, which she had planned. She was in the middle of a scene, with Fred Niblo directing, but the moment she heard me walking along she said, "Stop the camera. . . . Who's there?"

Fred Niblo saw me and said, "Miss Garbo does not want anybody on the set."

I said, "I know. But Miss Garbo came on my set, and I thought I'd repay the compliment."

Greta said, "I've got to get my hair done—I'm terribly sorry."

I said, "Can I go and help you get your hair done?"

She said no. "I have my own hairdresser." Well, she had this little bit of a dressing room with the flats around it, and she told the hairdresser, "Push the hair anyplace; it annoys me." To me she said, "Why don't you go back to your set?"

"Well," I said, "I thought I'd like to come over and see you. I understand you're a wonderful actress. You were nice enough to come to my set. I thought I'd repay the courtesy." I was dying to see how she worked.

"You're very funny. You make me laugh," she said. "I didn't come over to see you—I came over to see a great actress, Miss Goudal." Jetta Goudal was doing a scene in French.* "She's a very good actress, but she's stealing my stuff, and I don't like it." Then she said, "They're calling you on your set."

"I don't hear any call."

"You're wasting my time. Get off before I have to kick you off. Go back to your set. I won't act. I don't like anybody watching me."

I said, "Well, that goes both ways. Don't you come on my set, either."

"You're very funny, but it's very peculiar. To me, you are null and void—is that the word?"

I said, "Uh huh."

"I don't care about your acting. I just like to visit."

"Well, so do I. And I'm going to stay here."

"Oh no you don't. It's going to cost the company money, and you're going to be blamed for it. They'll put it on your production."

"Then I'll leave."

Once Arthur Brisbane wanted to

---

* The action of *Her Cardboard Lover* takes place in Monte Carlo. Jetta Goudal, a celebrated European actress, co-starred with Marion.

watch Garbo work, and one of the studio heads took him up to the sound booth, way up above. Suddenly she said, "I will not go on any further. There is a man up in the booth whom I do not know. He's watching me, and I will not perform till he gets out."

How could she see, with the lights on her face? But she would not move, and Brisbane had to leave.

She might have smelled him. Anybody could.

I always maintained that if you're so shy about visitors, why wouldn't you be shy about the electricians or the property boys? There's always an audience. You might have hundreds of people looking at you while you're doing a scene. What difference does a few visitors make?

I would be at the studio early to get my makeup on, but I didn't go on the set. I'd slop the makeup on and read the paper and take it easy. The dialogue didn't mean anything to me. There was some old-fashioned theory that you could remember it if you slept on it, so I used to put it on my pillow at night. But that didn't work; when I got on the set, I didn't know one line of it. Anyway, why learn it at night when they were going to change it in the morning anyway?

I'd be in the bungalow and I'd be wanted on the set. I'd say, "Just a second, and don't give me those three horns. Not even one."

One horn meant they were waiting for the star; two horns, the rest of the cast; and three horns, the stragglers. After that, the assistant director would come over and very politely say, "Will you kindly come on the set?"

I'd say no; I was trying to learn the dialogue. Bing [Crosby] got mad at me

every once in a while, but W.R. never did. He used to coax us not to work. I think he thought it was a waste of time.

Sometimes I would get to the set around eleven. Sometimes ten—sometimes noon. Then at luncheon we had banquets at the bungalow, and we'd sit around and talk about things. We wouldn't talk about pictures.

We would get back on the set around three, do a scene or so, and then have tea about four-thirty. They would blow the whistle at five, and everybody'd whisk off. So we'd only get a few scenes done all day.

But W.R. didn't worry about the budget. He'd even call the set at about a quarter to five and say it was time to quit. He'd be lonesome. He'd say, "You've been working all day"—not knowing we'd done only one scene.

When I first started making movies, I was on the legitimate stage at the same time. On matinee days, Wednesdays and Saturdays, I didn't work in the films. To make up for those days, I'd work very late, and I'd work Sundays. There weren't any regular hours.

W.R. never demanded regular hours from anybody. It was not at all like it is now, like a machine, with a time clock. In those days you'd go on the set when you were ready, then you'd rehearse and think a scene over, discuss it, make little changes here and there, and then try it again.

When I was working at MGM, I'd leave the beach house early and do my makeup in the automobile. I used very little; just the greasepaint, the powder and the lipstick. The eyelashes were hard to do while the car was going.

It took exactly fifteen minutes from my house to MGM, and I'd be all made up when we got there. Only my hair would need to be fixed, and I'd be on the set right at nine, all ready, and we'd talk the scenes over. Then we'd get a normal amount of work done.

Marion's makeup for *Going Hollywood* made her look like Greta Garbo.

Marion disguised as Jetta Goudal for a scene of mistaken identities in *Her Cardboard Lover*.

Jetta Goudal, Nils Asther and Marion Davies in *Her Cardboard Lover*.

Football star Red Grange wanted Marion's autograph.

I didn't want to quit at five, but some of the other actors would blow their whistles and go off the set. I would stay and do close-ups. That was kind of smart of me anyway.

Then I'd look at the rushes and talk with the director and the writer, and I wouldn't get home before ten or eleven. Then I'd go over my dialogue for about two hours and still be up early the next morning.

That was at MGM, but Warners was different. There you weren't allowed to make yourself up. No matter how early you were, there was always a delay waiting for the makeup man. Then they fixed your hair over and gave you a big mouth. That was the Joan Crawford mouth idea. By the time they got finished, I was bound to be late on the set. We used to call them the wrecking crew, but you didn't want to blame anybody. I'd just say, "It was my fault."

It made no difference. The time that was lost was always made up in some way.

Marion was indeed a unique movie star. With the support of W.R., she had financing and promotional opportunities that transformed the make-believe stories of the film into the real events of the day. She could be precocious and powerful. She had the support of her fans among the public. She could pay for extra scenes in her films and for the extra niceties of life. And she did.

In 1926, her "bungalow" was completed on the MGM lot. Decorated in

The makeup men fixed your hair over and gave you a mouth. That was the Joan Crawford big mouth idea.

Interiors of the dressing room
in Marion's bungalow.

ornate Spanish castle style, it was situated in Davies Square facing the administration building and served as more than just a dressing room.

It was a fourteen-room mansion which cost $75,000 then, and it frequently was used for lavish luncheons. After serving at the MGM lot, it was dismantled and moved to the Warner Brothers Studio when Marion moved there. Finally it was moved to Benedict Canyon in Beverly Hills and sold as a private house.

We used to have big luncheons in my bungalow. There was always some potentate arriving from Washington or Europe. The studio didn't mind, because they sort of liked the publicity. And we'd make up the time. We'd work a little bit overtime.

I would invite the whole cast to the luncheons, and the studio executives, and maybe some other stars who were working on other sets—Norma Shearer and Joan Crawford and the rest of them. Not Garbo, because she wouldn't go anywhere; she'd just stay in her dressing room and eat salad.

When they'd tell me that so and so was coming for luncheon, it was hard to keep my mind on the work. When people were on the stage and you had to talk to them, say "How do you do and blah, blah," and then you had to get right back into the character again, it wasn't very easy.

I thought I had a more difficult job to do than Garbo had. She could relax between scenes, while I had other things to do. But she didn't agree.

W.R. was after me all the time about my acting. He used to say, "I don't mean to criticize, but if you'll do it this way . . ." And he'd explain it. "You don't put enough drama into it. Your comedy is all right, but your voice is too high-pitched."

He would coach me, and we'd go over the scripts line by line. When I'd see him with a pencil, I'd say, "Oh, Lord, don't change it. I've got it memorized."

He'd say, "This little change won't bother you."

We'd rehearse it, and it would throw me off a bit. Lots of times he'd sit on the set, which would make me a little nervous. He'd say, "You've got to do that over. You can do better." He had a very good sense of the dramatic, and of comedy, too.

Once I was doing a scene with Louise Fazenda. The dialogue wasn't very good. W.R. wanted to change it, and he said, "You're supposed to be a secretary, so when you apply for a job, Louise should ask you, 'Are you an amanuensis?'" I didn't know what it meant, but he wanted to change it to that.

I said, "Well, she probably has it rehearsed already."

"But we should change it anyway, if she knows what it means . . ."

I said, "She does. She's very intelligent." When we went on the set, I was almost afraid to give the new dialogue to the director.*

When I told him, he said, "Oh, for Christ's sake, do you know what amanuensis means?" I didn't know. Louise looked at me and winked, and then they had a discussion about that line. Hal Wallis was the supervisor,** and he asked if anybody knew what amanuensis meant.

"Well," said the director, "that fixes it; let's go back to the old dialogue. This is a lot of crap."

Louise and I let them go on with their little act, and then I said, "Now wait a minute. I don't know how to pronounce it, but Louise does, I think."

---

* Lloyd Bacon was directing *Ever Since Eve* for Warner Brothers, and this was to be Marion's last film.
** Supervisor was an early Hollywood term for producer.

91

8

On the set of *Ever Since Eve*. From the left, cameraman George Barnes, the camera operator, director Lloyd Bacon, and stars Robert Montgomery, Louise Fazenda and Marion Davies. This was Marion's last film.

Facing page: Marion with Gary Cooper in *Operator 13*. *There was never anything naughty about any pictures I made.*

Right: Mary Pickford, Gary Cooper and Marion. *I tried my best to follow in their tracks, but an imitator is always a poor example.*

She said yes, then she added, "It means, are you qualified to be a secretary?"

The director called up the studio librarian, who told him it was okay. "All right," he said, "if you want to say a crap line like that, it's all right with me, but I don't want any part of it."

Louise said, "Well, after all, I've memorized it that way." Now she hadn't, but she was quick, and since W.R. had changed it, I wanted it in.

Usually they had to admit that W.R. was right. But when we'd go over the scripts after dinner, I'd think, Oh, here we go again.

I'd say, "Don't change too much. You're driving me crazy. I won't be able to do anything tomorrow." But he'd usually insist, because he took a keen interest in our work.

But I was the one who had to face the director in the morning. I'd say, "Let's give it a little more life, be a little more literate and give it more intelligence."

W.R. would never allow the director to shoot a kiss on the mouth; the side was all right. He said that kissing on the mouth was unhealthy. Maybe he was right. I had read that there were more germs on the mouth than anywhere else, and I thought, How awful for lovers.

Besides, W.R. said, children do not like kissing. I didn't believe it until one time we were looking at a movie, and John Hearst's little boy Bunky, who was then eleven years old, was sitting alongside me. The hero grabbed the heroine and gave one of those luscious kisses, and Bunky hit his head and said, "Ughhh. That makes me sick."

Kissing embarrasses youngsters. W.R.

knew that. He said, "That's why Mary Pickford is such a great sucess. Remember this: play to the youth. Teach them a lesson about the beautiful in life, and do not do anything to make even one mother say, 'I do not want my child to look at that picture.' If you play to the younger audience, the older ones will take care of themselves."

Mary Pickford never made anything that was the slightest bit sexy. Neither did Shirley Temple. But I couldn't compare with them. I tried my best to follow in their tracks, but an imitator is always a poor example.

There was never anything naughty about any pictures I made. W.R. would not allow it, and he was in on every bit of cutting. We managed to strike an intermediate path.

I was very, very lucky that I always had—I won't say leading men; I have to call them stars. Bing and Clark and Gary Cooper and Bob Montgomery, Leslie Howard and Ray Milland were stars in their own right, and I was very fortunate. I had no prejudices at all. They were all very fine people to work with.

Bob Montgomery was especially nice. He would take my part when I felt I was being a little bit kicked around by a director. He'd stand up for me. I liked Bob because he had a striking character which said, "All right, I'll be your defender. I'll help you with your problem." A good, honest citizen with a sense of security.

Bing Crosby was always a million laughs, and Gary Cooper was a wonderful, silent sort of sage. He always gave very good advice. And he liked to eat just as much as I did.

We'd eat enormous luncheons, and he'd tell me about horses. He knew I was afraid of them, but he adored horses. He said, "If you love a horse, a horse loves you."

I said, "That doesn't prevent a horse

from getting mad and biting me on the toe."

But he'd tell me how faithful horses were, and little things like that. Between scenes we'd go into these dissertations about horses and golf and various animals and ranch life. He was a good, wholesome person.

Bing liked to talk about his wife a lot. He was full of fun and liked to play pranks. I loved it too, if I knew who the prank was on. Invariably it was on me.

There was an old gag I should have known. You walked in and they said, "You do this dialogue." And you'd get started and you'd find out that the camera wasn't going and the sound wasn't on. Little laughs like that. I don't think that in all the time I was working I ever had any fights with any members of the cast.

Raoul Walsh was the main prankster. He used to egg Bing on. They even had a record made that went, "We'd sit on the set, we'd work all day, we'd go over to Davies's bungalow, we'd have a little drink . . ." The whole studio heard that.

I was making *Bachelor Father* with Ray Milland and Big Boy Williams, who was the big lover in it. C. Aubrey Smith was my father.

We had to do a scene where I rush in a doorway and the rug slips and I am supposed to do a fall. But the rug wouldn't slip. The director said I didn't run fast enough, but the rug was practically glued down: there was rubber underneath. Bob Leonard said, "I'm not trying to protect you. I'm trying to do a scene."

But the property man, Jimmy, had been working with me for quite a while and he didn't want me to break my neck. They fixed it, so my magic carpet and I made one big entrance, my legs went up in the air and that scene was finished with. I was a little bit sore,

but I wasn't really hurt. I had to take a lot of falls and I got used to them. I'd take it easy and go limp.

Ray Milland used to talk about England and Ireland. He was very pleasant. We never had any trouble at all.

Though Marion made three or four pictures a year, whenever one was finished she found time to travel. Before the next production, she would return to San Simeon and invite the cast and crew to come up. Leisurely and rather luxuriously, they would rehearse and get into their roles.

I had seen Leslie Howard in *Berkeley Square* in New York and I was set on having him for a leading man. He was a very fine actor. Maybe I had an audience crush on him, but I thought he was perfect. And he did do a picture with me, called *Five and Ten*. It was supposed to be the story of Barbara Hutton.

When he arrived at San Simeon for the rehearsals of *Five and Ten,* I looked at him and said to the butler, "Who's that?"

Bob Leonard, who was to direct the picture, said, "That's Leslie Howard, I think. I'm not sure." I didn't think it could be, but sure enough it was.

He had looked taller on the stage, I think because I had watched him from the front row. He was introduced all around, and I was very effusive. But I kept looking at him and thinking, That is not the same man I saw on the stage.

Later Leslie asked me why I had looked at him the way I had, the first time we met. He said, "Didn't I live up to your expectations?"

"No. I thought you were Puff Asquith."*

"Good Lord, no. I'm about half an inch taller than he."

---

* Anthony Asquith was a film director and the son of a British statesman.

Leslie Howard was like a naughty boy and his wife would yell at him. Ruth was forty and rather fat, and she treated him like a child.

"I didn't have my measuring rod with me."

I said to Bob Leonard, "Don't you think you could have a lift put in his heels?" I had worked with lots of leading men who were not quite tall enough, but if you suggested they use a little platform, they would get furious. But Leslie didn't mind. He stood on a platform for me.*

It's just a trick of the trade that a man should grab a girl, look down at her and say, "I think you're divine," and that she should look up and say, "Do you really?"

We had a regular theatre at San Simeon, and we rehearsed for about two or three weeks. After rehearsals we would go swimming. Leslie was like a naughty boy, and his wife would yell at him. Ruth was forty and rather fat, and she treated him like a child. She would say, "Now don't go in the swimming pool. You might catch cold." Just to tease her, he would jump in the pool and lose his trunks.

She'd yell, "Stop that! Come out of there!" I hoped W.R. wouldn't come down to the pool and see him. He was too grand for that.

Leslie wanted to be jolly and gay, but I don't think he went to many parties, because his wife was always around. And that is a kind of a handicap to any man.

Leslie was a great actor, yet he wasn't the type to throw himself forward. He would always try to give the scene to his leading lady, but he couldn't: he was too good. He was not a ham, and he was not pretentious. He was such an easy actor that the things he did didn't seem to be an effort at all. The lines would flow out of his mouth, exactly as if he were carrying on an ordinary conversation. He wasn't acting for one second.

Finally we finished the picture, *Five and Ten.* Everything was wonderful. But when I looked at the rushes, I noticed something peculiar: my face was always at the wrong angle. I found the answer: the cameraman was in love with Mary Duncan, and all the lighting had been to flatter her.* Mary was absolutely unconscious of that fact, which made it very funny. I was half in the shadows, and she didn't even know he was in love with her!

There was only one way to defeat that. Working at night with another cameraman, I got close-ups of myself and pushed them in.

---

* Marion was 5 feet 4 inches tall, weighed 120 pounds, and had blue eyes and natural blond hair—which was lightened to platinum, though she often wore wigs.

* George Barnes was the cameraman and Mary Duncan a supporting actress in *Five and Ten.* The high society plot had Mary and Marion competing for the love of Leslie Howard.

I made only the one picture with Leslie. After that, he did a picture with Norma Shearer* and then went back to England. Many years later there was the airplane accident and the ad in the newspaper.

On June 2, 1943, during the war, a British Overseas Airways Corporation flight from Lisbon, Portugal, to England was attacked by enemy aircraft. It crashed into the Bay of Biscay. Leslie Howard was among the thirteen passengers and four crew members who were never found and are presumed to have died.

He had made a lecture tour of Spain and Portugal for the British Council, a government cultural office. The tour was seen as a way for him to relax. He had been ill during the previous winter; he had just turned fifty and was acutely aware of the aging process. He had taken up spiritualism and was obsessed by the privileges of youth.

I had a friend in London who knew them very well, and she wrote me about the ad. It appeared in the *Daily Express* just before he died. It said, "In case anything happens to me, get in touch with . . ." It was his secretary's telephone number. It looked to me like a suicide note.

It was all hushed up, and by the time I got to England again, I had forgotten about it. But at the time, I was mystified. Would he have killed himself—and the pilot too? They never found him. It was too bad. He was such a kind person.

Before we made *Five and Ten*, they wanted me to have Clark Gable; I wanted Leslie Howard. The part required a society man. A test was made

with Gable. I looked at the test and said, "No. No, Irving. He looks like Jack Dempsey, and you can't possibly put him in a role like that."

Irving said, "You'll be sorry. Gable is going to be the biggest sensation in the world."

Well, the lights went on and there was Clark Gable, sitting in the back. He'd heard the whole thing. He didn't say anything. He just looked.

I said to Irving, "Did you know he was in here?"

"No," he said. "But he wants the part."

"It's nothing against him," I said. "It's just that I don't think he's suited for that part." Well, a few days later I was walking on the lot and Clark Gable came up and said, "I'm the pug, remember me? I'm Jack Dempsey."

In *Polly of the Circus* I wanted Clark Gable for the part of a minister. Irving said, "He's no good for society; you said that yourself. Now you want him to play a minister!"

I said, "Irving, I just realized you were right."

I wanted Clark Gable for the part of a minister. Gable and Marion in Polly of the Circus.

* Romeo and Juliet.

He did play it, but he was not very willing. He'd come in and say, "Do I still look like a prizefighter?"

I'd say no. "You're just like a minister." He was very good as a minister, but Irving thought it was the wrong casting. After that we did another movie, *Cain and Mabel*, over at Warners.

In CAIN AND MABEL, Gable played the part of a down-and-out heavyweight fighter. Marion played the part of a down-and-out musical comedy star. They wound up together in New Jersey.

Neither got any good reviews for their efforts. The critics thought they were miscast.

The night Gable and Lombard got married I was working and couldn't go to their wedding. I was very happy for them. It was too bad it ended so suddenly.

Gable was making GONE WITH THE WIND when, on March 29, 1939, he married Carole Lombard, a popular top Hollywood star. But their life together ended on January 16, 1942, when Carole was returning from Indiana. She had appeared at a rally in her hometown, selling war bonds, and had boarded Trans World Airlines Flight 3 in Chicago. The plane stopped for fuel in Las Vegas, Nevada, took off for Los Angeles, and crashed into Table Rock Mountain. Carole, her mother and all aboard the plane died.

I visited Norma Shearer on *The Barretts of Wimpole Street* set, but I was shushed right off. And once I went on Joan Crawford's set. She was doing *Within the Law.** I just went in for one

second, and she said, "Well, come on in, Marion."

I knew, when she said that, that I shouldn't be there, so I just watched for a second, then took off. It's not supposed to be the proper thing for a star to go and visit another star; apparently they get nervous. But it didn't matter to me. Anybody could come on my set. It was open season, and I didn't charge admission. I guess I didn't figure myself as a star. I thought of myself as a poor, unfortunate creature who was trying to make a career of herself. The President of the United States could come on the set and it made no difference to me.

When Calvin Coolidge and his wife, Grace, were Mr. Hearst's guests up at San Simeon, she got stuck in the elevator one night. There were bad storms and all the lights and everything went out and you could never tell when the electricity would go back on. Fortunately it was only ten minutes. But then another thing happened that I think was very amusing.

Calvin Coolidge never drank anything, but the first night he was at San Simeon we had some Tokay, and he said to me, "What is that?"

I said that's *Tokay.*

He said, "What is it?"

I said, "Non-alcoholic."

I gave him a glass, and then he said he'd have another. I gave him another. This was some Tokay that W.R. had kept in his wine cellar for years. It had belonged to his mother. Dinner was announced and I said, "I'll go with you."

But he said, "I'd like to have another drink. It's good. Best darned non-alcoholic drink I ever drank in my life."

He started talking at dinner, and kept on drinking the Tokay. I said, "What would you like to do tomorrow? Would you like to go down to the zoo?"

---

* The Broadway play by Bayard Veillier was released as a film under the title *Paid.*

"No. I can see all the zoo I want in Washington."

He smiled a lot—he was in a very good humor—and Grace said to me, "You know, Calvin is usually sort of austere, sort of an apple-cracker. But he's really had a good time here."

At that time Coolidge was no longer saddled with the pressures of the presidency. He had been succeeded by Herbert Hoover.

Mrs. Coolidge said they'd like to see the studio, so then we went down to MGM. I was doing *The Floradora Girl,* a musical.

Of course, when we got to the studio, Louis B. Mayer wanted to take over. He had a big banquet for the Coolidges, and then they went back to Washington.

I really had a good time at MGM. I liked it there. I was very fond of Irving and of L.B. And we had no quarrels, much, except that once in a while I'd go up to the front office and say I thought I should be doing something big, like washing elephants.

On the left, Marion in *The Floradora Girl*.

The back lot of the MGM studio.

W.R.

6

The beach house. Howard Hughes, who loved ice cream and never drank or smoked. Gloria Swanson invents a game. Death takes an old friend. Mother's perfume was gardenia. Mr. Hearst, who was no different from anybody else.

On September 9, 1926, Louella Parsons wrote: "Marion Davies will soon move into her beach house at Santa Monica. It is the largest house on any southern California beach. While being shown around, I counted fifteen bathrooms, and even Marion doesn't know how many other rooms there are. When she tires of it, she plans to convert it into a beach club."

We had plenty of space in Santa Monica. I owned property on both sides of the house. I had bought some from Will Rogers, so there was my house and then another guest house and then a lawn of about sixty feet, on the right. On the left-hand side were two extra houses and the staff house.

We had ten guest rooms and a living room with each, so that was twenty rooms. There were twelve staff rooms, and another little house on the side had four more staff rooms. We had more staff than we had guests.

W.R. liked the beach house, but that was when the architects came in again. More additions were added on. It almost got to be as big as the White House. Bigger, maybe. Just like you build with little blocks, he added on and on. But little blocks wouldn't have cost the money.

There was a big pool with a Venetian marble bridge over it. The bridge had to be removed after we sold the house. They claimed there was a law against a bridge being in the middle of a swimming pool that was open for the public. But the pool was ten feet deep in the middle, and I think it was absolutely wrong for them to remove it. I don't know what they did with the bridge. I guess it was sold or chopped up.

I was awfully disappointed when I went down and saw that. Most people just don't have any appreciation for the value of a thing like that.

Vincent Astor used to come out to California quite a bit. And the last time I saw him he wanted me to come down to the beach house. It had been made into a hotel and he thought he was staying in my room. But he wasn't. Mine was up on the third story, on the top deck. He wanted me to explain exactly what had been in the house before we sold it.

They had done the house beautifully, then. It had been refurnished and carpeted. It was all modern art, but the wood paneling and the ceilings were still there, and the Gibbons carvings.* But not the Oriental rugs.

Now it's all changed. Three or four houses have been built on the tennis courts, and that changed the whole architecture on the right side. When I saw it, I didn't even recognize it. I dreaded to go by. It had been so beautiful inside, and when I last saw it, it needed paint.

In January 1960 Ocean House would be reduced to a parking lot. Marion then told reporters that she had spent over seven million dollars on the place during the fifteen years she had used it.

She had sold the property in 1945 for only $600,000. And that was just about the cost of the thirty-seven fireplaces that had been installed.

There had been a little disagreement

about property taxes. Los Angeles had assessed Ocean House at $220,000 in 1939, and Marion had filed for relief. She wanted $50,000 in relief, but E. K. Potter, the chief county appraiser, resisted her appeal. She then described the house as a "white elephant."

Between 1945 and 1960 Ocean House was a private beach club, and then a hotel. But its thirty bedrooms were not enough for profitability. So there was an auction. And then the wrecking crew moved in.

Today, some of the old servants' quarters still stand. They are used as a private club. And the sign at the gate still remembers when it was known as Beach Palisades Road. But most people, thinking only of the traffic as they roar past on the Pacific Coast Highway, do not know of the times that were had at Ocean House.

---

* Grinling Gibbons's carvings originally came from England, and other examples may be seen today at Petworth Castle, when it is open to the public, south of London near Horsham.

Marion's beach house in Santa Monica, California.

The beach house. *There was a big pool with a Venetian marble bridge over it.*

Marion posing on the beach in front of the house. From a postcard.

Jack Gilbert was very nice, but he was extremely nervous and sensitive. Sort of unpredictable. He used to go into very sordid moods, and say he didn't like anybody. One night at the beach house we had gotten tired of sitting around the swimming pool and had gone out on the sand. There were thirty or forty of us. There was a group of writers around Jack, and I could hear an argument. I heard Jack say, "I'm going to commit suicide."

And they said, "Dare you to."

Well, that was not the thing to say to a man who was in that mood, but they were teasing him. They said, "Prove it. You've talked about suicide so much, prove it to us. If you've got the guts to do it, show us."

And Jack said, "All right, I will."

I thought, "Uh, oh."

While everyone was chattering away, he went out and walked into the waves. And he kept on walking until I thought, This is not funny. I said, "Somebody stop him."

But they said, "Let him alone. He'll stop himself. Just watch him. He won't do it." They thought it was a big joke.

Maybe their voices carried across. Whatever, he suddenly threw himself down, and then he came wading in and went down on the sand. He burst into sobs and beat the sand and cried his heart out. He couldn't do it; he had been challenged and he couldn't do it.

I got mad. I said, "I think that's the rottenest thing I've seen anybody do to anybody."

I felt awfully sorry for Jack Gilbert. He was in love with Greta Garbo, and she would have no part of him at all. That was why he was blue.

He was very much the artist type, with flashing black eyes and nervous, emotional moods. Those writers didn't understand it. They were just watching and pushing him. And imagine the emotions going on inside him. He felt

he had to do it, and he didn't have the guts to do it. It was a hell of a position to be put in.

One night Greta Garbo came to the beach house with Jack. She walked in the door saying, "Hullo. I'm tired," then the first thing she did was to take off her high heels and throw them in the hall. She said, "You got a pair of bedroom slippers?"

I said yes.

I was getting them for her when I heard sounds. I found her jumping on my four-poster bed, testing the mattress. She was jumping so hard, her head was hitting the canopy. She said, "Good mattress."

When she got the slippers she said to me, "Get me a knife." She slit the backs off my slippers and put elastic bands around them. "Thank you," she said and went downstairs.

She didn't dance at all. She just sat in one corner with Jack Gilbert. Everybody was looking at her, saying hello and all that, and it sort of annoyed her. She was terrifically shy; she didn't want to mingle with anybody. It wasn't snobbishness, just shyness. I never saw the like of it in anybody else.

Once Greta had an argument with Louis B. Mayer. Mayer was very good to work for, but when anything went wrong, you'd have to go up to his red-carpeted office. Greta had refused to do some picture, and Mayer had sent for her.

The picture was ANNA CHRISTIE, Garbo's first talkie. Though the star had threatened to go home to Sweden, she lost her savings in the failure of the Beverly Hills First National Bank. So she played the part of a waterfront girl in Eugene O'Neill's story, though maintaining that she disliked the play and the portrayals of Swedish characters. This film would be advertised with the famous slogan: "Garbo Talks."

Jack Gilbert was very much the artist type, with flashing black eyes and nervous, emotional moods. (Photo by Ruth Harriet Louise.)

L.B. probably gave her his long, emotional talk. Everything was from the heart. He should have been an actor. He'd bring out a little bottle of pills and say, "I'm faint." That was what he did when you didn't do what he asked.

Mayer was telling Greta why she should do the picture. He had gone to all the trouble to pick her out of everybody in Sweden and make her the great actress she was, so why did she turn him down at this moment, when he needed her cooperation on a picture he was positive would be the greatest thing? The act went on and on and she didn't say a word.

When he was finished, she looked at him and said, "Maybe *ja* and maybe *no*. But I don't think so." And she left.

I knew Howard Hughes for a long time, and I always liked him. But I've heard that people who worked for him said he was kind of a hard taskmaster.

He was just a big, awkward, overgrown country boy, always very shy, very polite. He was a little hard of hearing. He was kind, he really was, and smart, but he didn't show it.

He came to many of our parties and

Immortalized in commercial art. Marion and friends at the beach: an artist's concept from one of the popular fan magazines. The man sitting is almost certainly meant to be Gable.

At that time Howard was having a problem with the seaplane. I didn't think he'd ever get it off the ground. He offered pilots all kinds of money to take it up. W.R.'s pilot told me he was offered a million dollars to fly it. Howard took it up once or twice himself. He was very brave; he knew no fear, even after that accident he had. How he got out of that one nobody knows. He was awfully smashed up, but he would still fly, because he had great confidence and was not afraid of anything.

The gigantic seaplane, a two-hundred-ton wooden boat with many engines, was nicknamed the Spruce Goose. *Ordered by the government for service in World War II, it was not finished in time and was anchored in Los Angeles Harbor until it was scrapped. It was flown only once, by Hughes, in an unannounced flight that reached an altitude of twelve feet. It was then declared a menace to navigation.*

Hughes would also crash an amphibian into Lake Mead, but he retrieved it, repaired it for flight and then put it in storage.

But Marion is referring to a different accident Hughes suffered, in July 1946. Another plane had been ordered for service in World War II, the XF-11, a reconnaissance craft, but it had not been delivered in time.

Hughes piloted the first test flight, and shortly after take-off he crashed on Alpine Drive in the residential district of Beverly Hills. His chest was crushed, nine ribs were broken, his left lung collapsed, his left shoulder was broken, his nose was broken, his skull was fractured, and he had third-degree burns. These damages were repaired in a five-week stay in a hospital, but the government canceled the contract for the XF-11.

was very nice and affable. He was good company, because he didn't talk too much. I don't know what he thought about San Simeon, because he didn't say.

He was also a good friend. I remember a time when W.R. wasn't feeling well and wanted to go to Seattle to see a doctor. Howard worked all night long on one of his airplanes, having the seats removed and beds put in, all for W.R.

Howard Hughes was just a big, awkward, overgrown country boy, always very shy, very polite.
He poses here with Pauline Gallagher, Lois Wilson and Skeets Gallagher at the Tyrolean party.

The movies were more or less a sideline with him. An amusement, like playing solitaire. But every movie he made was a success. The one with Jane Russell and Walter Huston, the western, was very good. He directed it himself, every scene. It got a lot of publicity because they said it was naughty or something. That was *The Outlaw*.

Howard went around with Billie Dove. I think he went with her longer than with any other girl. The other girls were more or less just ice cream.

He loved ice cream, you know. He never drank or smoked, but he was an ice cream addict. He ate it by the quart. At one time I too was an ice cream fiend, and we used to have ice cream races at night. I always ate the most, so I always won. I'd start with four big scoops of orange ice and pineapple ice and ice cream, then I'd take four more, and if anybody would challenge me, I'd take four more. Then they would have to do the same. One man said he had once won a prize for eating ice cream. He said to me, "Nobody can outdo me." Well! He was green when I got through with him. I could never get enough.

Gloria Swanson was at the beach house one night. She was a little prankster at heart; she loved to have fun. She said, "Here's what we're going to do. Let's not look at a picture tonight; let's play a game." It was a little like playing Post Office. You would say to a man, like Harry Crocker or Lawrence Stallings, "Who would you like to marry?"

They would look around. It was just a game, but still their true feelings came out. They would say, "That one." Eleanor Boardman or somebody else.

We would say to both of them, "Come into the next room and seal the ceremony."

Then we would go into the Marine Room, next to the library, and they wouldn't know exactly what was happening, but we had it all planned. We had a pillow there and they were supposed to kneel. I would say, "Do you take this woman to be your lawful wedded wife?"

The man would say, "I do."

I'd say, "Seal the pact with a kiss." As they reached forward, Gloria would take a bag with ice in it and bang them in the face. They would fall backward. We wouldn't let them out of the room until we pulled that gag.

It sounds silly, but it was really fun. That night, we noticed that all of the writers were picking out Aileen Pringle.* She had to work overtime being the wife in the gag.

Joe Hergesheimer was taking it very seriously. He really did want her, and when we got them in there and I said, "Seal the pact with a kiss," Gloria Swanson gave him a double sock in the face.

He got up, but instead of taking it in fun, he said, "This is outrageous. This is what I've heard about Hollywood parties. I'm going to write a book about this. And I'll denounce you all. All of you." Then he left the house.

He did write about it. But he didn't mention any names. He just said how crazy the people in Hollywood were.

Joseph Hergesheimer had already written several novels about the elegant, refined and decadent world of those people he would term "the international leisure class." Hergesheimer worked at writing for twenty years, retiring in 1934 to spend twenty years

---

* An actress who worked in the movies from 1923 to 1939.

more in silent observation. He was quoted, later in his life, as saying, *"It was the dullness of pleasure that drove me to the pleasure of dullness."*

We are uncertain what piece Marion thinks Hergesheimer may have written to expose Hollywood. But Samuel Goldwyn had made Hergesheimer's novel CYTHEREA into a film in 1924, assuring the author a footnote in movie history, not for the story, but for the first use, in the dream sequences, of the Technicolor process.

After he left, Gloria said, "I have another idea. Let's get the men with mustaches. We'll put down a piece of paper, and blindfold them the moment they walk into the room."

We showed them the piece of paper on the floor and said, "Can you pick it up, blindfolded, with your mouth?" They would think it was easy, and we'd blindfold them. Then Gloria would shove in a big bowl of molasses, and they would kneel down and go right into it, getting molasses all over their mustaches. It was just prank stuff, kid stuff, but it was fun. We both loved it, but some of the men didn't like it.

Bebe Daniels and I were very good friends. She said, "I can sew." And I could sew, too. So she said, "I'll bet you can't sew a dress."

I said, "I certainly can."

She said, "I'm going out the night after tomorrow, and I'd like to have a white satin dress with some sort of a long fringe. Something that looks graceful."

I said, "Have you got a pattern?"

"Don't tell me you work by pattern? I thought you could make dresses."

"I used to, when I was a youngster. I used to make my dolls' dresses."

"Well, that was very good training. If you can make a doll's dress, you can make anything." So I really worked on it, like mad. I got it all ready for her

and I sent it down. I didn't know if she wore it or not, but the very next day a dress arrived from her with a note. It said, "Thanks very much for the white satin dress. I wore it and it was a great success. So here's one I made for you last night, when I came back from the party."

It was the most spectacular gown, with rhinestones sewn all over it. I thought she must have stayed up all night. Then I saw a label: I. MAGNIN AND COMPANY.

I called her up and said, "I hope you feel all right after working so hard after the party."

She said, "Well, I came home from the party at one o'clock."

"What happened? Did the dress I made you fall apart?"

She said no. She said, "I worked on yours from two until the wee small hours of the morning."

I said, "I'm sure. You sewed all those spangles on by hand?"

She said yes.

I said, "Did you sew the I. Magnin label on, too?"

She said, "What??!! I've been loused up."

Alec Moore, whom I had known fairly well, was staying with his niece in New York. She told me that he wasn't well, that he wanted to go to California to get some sunshine.

I talked to his doctor and learned he was very sick, although he himself didn't know it. He had tuberculosis of the throat, which was a very bad thing. So he came out with us on the train. He coughed a lot. One night when we were playing cards on the train, he had an awful spell.

The doctors came to the beach house where we were staying and said, "He's got to get to a warm climate." I was working—just finishing *The Floradora Girl* and doing some retakes on another picture. Alec went to Palm Springs.

One night W.R. and I went to see him in Palm Springs. He looked to me like he was failing. He seemed all right at the moment, but I asked my sister Reine to stay with him. He had two or three nurses, but Reine stayed for two or three days, and then she came back. She felt that she was in the way. She said, "When somebody's not feeling right, they don't want anybody hovering over them."

The next day the doctor called and said the Ambassador would have to go to Monrovia.

I said, "Is it serious?"

He said, "You can't tell. Monrovia might help him; Palm Springs hasn't."

So he moved to Monrovia, and one night we went down there to see him. I could hear frogs croaking.

I said, "My God, that's no good. It must be damp here."

I called his doctor and said I'd heard frogs croaking. The doctor thought it was all right, but I said it wasn't. I would have had him at the beach house, but that was also near the water, so it wouldn't have been any good, either.

Two days later he was in Los Angeles at the Good Samaritan Hospital. He didn't want to go back to Palm Springs, so they'd brought him there. I phoned him. Alec said, "I have no relatives, not even cousins."

"Why are you telling me this?"

He said that he just wanted me to know.

Well, I was working that day, and about one o'clock the next day, I was on my set and there was a phone call. They said, "Get down to the hospital right away. He's dying."

So I rushed down, in costume, my hair all done up and very blond. When I went in he looked up at me and said, "I'm all right, Lillian."

He thought I was his wife, Lillian Russell. But she had been dead for fifteen or twenty years. Then he said, "Will you kiss me, Lillian?" So I bent forward and kissed him on the cheek.

Well, my God, they hurled me into the next room and they gargled me and they sprayed me, and they said I shouldn't have done that, because he had the most awful tuberculosis.

There was nothing that could be done for Alec, so I decided it was better for me to go back to the studio. They called me about six that night and said if I wanted to come back, it was just a matter of minutes. So I went again, and by the time I got there he was dead. A lot of people were outside his door—ten or fifteen, maybe. When I walked in, he was covered up. The doctor said, "Everybody out there wants this suitcase. They say they are his cousins and in-laws . . ."

I said, "He told me he had no relatives. But Lillian Russell had a daughter by her first marriage to a man called Solomon, who was an orchestra leader. That would be the only one who has any connection with him."

So they had lawyers investigate, and Dorothy Russell got the suitcase. I don't know what was in it—probably just his clothes and maybe some jewelry.

Miss Russell had a child by her first husband, music conductor Harry Braham. She had no other children.

Her second husband, Edward Solomon, was an orchestra conductor. John Chatterton, her third, was an opera singer, a tenor. Alec Moore was her last spouse, and he had been a widower for eight years.

Known to her fans as the American Beauty Rose, Miss Russell died June 6,

W.R. with Arthur Brisbane. *Nobody ever got the best of W.R. in an argument. He had debates with Arthur Brisbane quite often, on various different topics.*

She was a soprano, famous for her stage performances and for a long relationship with Diamond Jim Brady, a gambler now remembered for his penchant for red plush and prime ribs.

My mother died about four one morning after a big party we had at the beach house. The watchman—Maine was his name—come for me, with my sister Rose. He said, "Your mother's ill."

So I said, "Wait a minute—I'll just get a coat."

Rose and I went, and as we were going by Sawtelle Boulevard I said, "Rose, that's Mother's perfume." She used gardenia.

When we got to the house, my sister Ethel was there and my mother was dead. I had heard about self-control, but it doesn't always work. I just went crazy.

Then the telephone rang. It was W.R., calling from the beach house. He said, "I'm awfully sorry."

I said, "It's all right . . ."

He said, "May I be a mother to you?"

That was the sweetest thing. He said, "I'll try my best." She died of angina pectoris. Sudden death. She was quite young when she died.

Rose Reilly Douras (Mama Rose) died in 1928, at age sixty-six. The gardenia smell could have come from the nurseries the Japanese gardeners had established along Sawtelle Boulevard. The flowerful Oriental community still exists in West Los Angeles, though now threatened by new projects to widen the roads.

It seems Marion had a strong sensitivity to odors. She mentioned the smell of Arthur Brisbane on page 86, and as she recorded these notes, apparently the gardenia smell triggered another recollection of Brisbane. So it follows.

Nobody ever got the best of W.R. in an argument. He had debates with Arthur Brisbane quite often, on various different topics. Arthur had a great mind. Maybe he picked some of W.R.'s brains. But when they were having a discussion, if Arthur stopped standing up straight, and bent lower and lower, you knew he was wrong.

Once a very wealthy society woman said to W.R., "I wish your newspapers would keep my son's name out of print."

W.R. stopped her. He said, "If you can keep your son out of the divorce courts, his name will be out of the papers." She couldn't say another word.

W.R. never got angry, but when he looked at you with those piercing eyes, you'd think he was looking right through you. He would wait a long time and then say something. He was right and you couldn't argue. Some people said, "I'm afraid of him . . . the way he looks at me. He doesn't like me."

I'd ask him why he looked at so and so like that, and he'd say, "Like what?"

I'd say, "They think you don't like them."

He'd say, "Do I look like a villain?"

I'd say no. But perhaps he was a little austere. He didn't mean to be, at all. When he was looking at somebody and saying something, he might be thinking of something else more important.

Well, there were always debates, and he wouldn't say anything; he'd just listen. He didn't want to be bothered with any nonsensical confrontations.

If he got mad at bridge, he'd just say he wasn't going to play anymore, and he'd get up and walk away. He didn't like bridge anyway, and I had to coax him into a game. Then I'd start nagging him, "Why did you play that card?"

When he'd walk into a room, no

matter how many people were there, he sort of awed them. Maybe it was his height. They would almost be fawning, and he didn't like that at all. He was very unpretentious.

I'd tell him it was just respect for him, but he didn't like it. "Why don't you treat me like an ordinary person? Which I am. I'm no different from anybody else," he'd say. "Matter of fact, I'm worse." But when he was present, the conversation would be immediately censored. Everyone would try to be very elegant, and there'd be no cattiness. It didn't matter what was said, anyway; he wasn't listening. His mind would be way off, thinking of something else.

He'd come down and play tennis once in a while, and then he'd beat everybody on the courts, except the professionals. You had to look out for his right-hand drive, and his serve. He didn't seem to move much, but no matter where you put a ball, he'd send it back. He'd play for two or three hours and then go back to work. He had tremendous vitality.

In Europe he'd take us to museum after museum, and we'd be exhausted, while he'd be fresh as anything. I wanted roller skates so I could do the Louvre, but W.R. wouldn't be a bit tired. All day long, he'd want to go on to another place, while we'd want to go back to the hotel.

Then he was never tired at night, at dinner. He'd want to dance, and everybody else would be dying on the vine. Then he'd be up the first thing in the morning and be downstairs waiting, trying to get us going.

We'd go too far ahead of the others, and sometimes we would have to sit and wait for them.

Summers in Europe. A black eye. A $6,000 Renault. Marion buys a painting. Suspected of espionage, and guilty too. A scoop for Mr. Hearst. The cold shoulder in Paris. St. Donat's. A snake in the Thames. Millions of dollars in antiques.

We went to Europe every summer—for at least eight summers in a row. Of course I had been there before, when I was a youngster.

We generally had from twelve to twenty-two guests, and it got to be a routine. We would leave about the first of May or June. We'd get on the boat, and we always followed the same route. We'd come back in September or October.

Except for one diversion: we went to Spain one time. But generally it was the same route: London, then France, then Germany, then Italy; then we would go to St. Donat's Castle, which is in Wales. Sometimes we went to Scotland. But I never went to Ireland. It was a general routine, and I got to know it so well.

I used to like to wander around by myself. You take a Baedeker or you hire an old guide who really knows the place and you say, "Take me to some places that people haven't seen." Then you go and enjoy yourself, and you can say, "I've seen where Michelangelo is buried." You can only do that by yourself.

With a party of twenty, it was different. My maid would sit in the front of the car with the chauffeur, and we would sit in the back. We'd go ahead of the others, and sometimes we'd have to sit and wait an hour for the rest. We'd look around, and then we'd go on and leave word. W.R. would say, "I'm not going to sit here waiting for the delinquents."

It was awfully hard with a big party. There'd always be argu-

115

We went to Europe every summer, at least for eight summers in a row. Here W.R. leads the way up Mount Vesuvius.

ments. Some guests wouldn't like each other, and they'd want to change cars; we had that all the time. I would be dead tired, and the bickering would go on and on until I'd go crazy.

We'd leave Paris and go to the Châteaux district, and then our guests would all go off to Deauville to gamble. They'd leave a note behind. Then W.R. would say, "I don't know how to control people like that." The only way was not to take them along. But that was his constant annoyance. The only one in the parties we had traveling with us who wanted to see everything was Harry Crocker.

W.R. always maintained that if people wanted to go to Cannes or Biarritz or places in Paris to have fun, they could just as well do it in New York or any restaurant. He thought that if you went to Europe, you had to see Europe and understand educationally what the history was. There was no time for any jollities or frivolities in Europe.

If anybody wanted to go to a night-club, he'd say, "This is an educational tour. If you don't appreciate it now, you never will." So everybody would pretend to be on their toes, but I'd know they weren't listening.

W.R. would be saying, "This is a wonderful fresco by Filippo Lippi, painted in the fifteenth century. Notice the colors . . ." And such and such. I couldn't blame him for being impatient with people. He was trying to teach us something, and we didn't want to learn. He might as well have been hitting his head up against a stone wall.

He took the trips to Europe very seriously. He was intrigued with Versailles, but mainly he liked the little villages. Like Rotenburg, a big decaying wall around a little bit of a city. There was a little hovel of a hotel and a tiny restaurant. Nothing there but a cathedral with loud bells at night. Plain, but solid, and with history behind it. W.R. thought that was enchanting.

He was crazy about Florence. We'd

116

I always liked Venice: it was fascinating. And the pigeons liked Marion.

plan to stay three days, and it would turn into three weeks. There was so much to see.

Rome is the most wonderful place in the whole of the European continent. I even found the little church where Fra Angelico was buried. I just accidentally hit on it when I was walking around by myself. It was on a side street. I went in, and next to the altar was a gray slab. It said, *Fra Angelico.* He was an artist, one of the greatest we ever had. And I saw where Michelangelo was buried, in some little church that they don't have in the guidebooks.

Fra Giovanni Angelico da Fiesole is buried in the large Gothic-style church of the Dominican friars, Santa Maria Sopra Minerva, in Via dei Cestari, at the Piazza della Minerva, behind the Pantheon in Rome. The memorial is in the first chapel to the left of the entrance.

Michelagniolo Buonarroti (Michelangelo) died in Rome but was buried in Florence in the Church of the Holy Cross (Chiesa di Santa Croce) in the Piazza of the same name near the center of the city. The floor of that Franciscan sanctuary is paved with the tombstones of Dante, Machiavelli, Rossini, Galileo, and the wife of Joseph Bonaparte. The decor is by Donatello and Giotto.

We'd stay at Claridge's in London and at the Excelsior in Venice. I always liked Venice; it was fascinating. No automobiles there, or anything like that. You arrive at a party at night in a gondola, and you don't know whether the tide is up high or not. Usually you land on a level with the main entrance. The steps are underneath the water, and the whole first floor is usually vacant. The people live above.

It is a lovely place. Every once in a while you do see dead rats floating around. But in all the little houses the people sing. They sing like mad. The Italians love to sing.

Princess Jane San Faustina, an American married to an Italian prince, was a very good friend. She was the social hostess in Venice for everybody. She was a widow and very outspoken; she would say whatever she wanted to say. She didn't like the Italians at all.

She was about seventy, and everybody looked up to her. They thought she was just marvelous and everything. But she would snap them back into line if she thought they weren't doing right.

One time I was supposed to go to a party over in Venice at the Grand Hotel. But I went swimming in the afternoon, and then I was starting up on one of those athletic bars and this thing hit my eye. It gave me a black eye, which I did not know how to explain.

I had to go to the dinner, so I wore a black veil over my face and made up my other eye in black. My new way of going out. And they all said, "My, what a new innovation. A wonderful idea."

I said, "Well, I'm just playing the black ghost. It's a new idea I got from Paris."

It was always the beach in the morning, then luncheon on the beach. The Excelsior has an enormous restaurant right on the Lido. Then after luncheon we'd go into Venice and look at the various historical places. The Bridge of Sighs and all that sort of thing. And antique shops, of course. Then tea in the evening, around six, and a dinner party at night. It was a very restful place, I must say.

Once we were driving in France. There were about twelve cars. W.R. had a chauffeur named Hall who got a little drunk that day over the wine at lunch. We were passing through a small out-of-the-way village near the coastline when he hit a goose.

Mr. Hearst said, "You're fired. But first take the goose and go back to the house and say that it was killed. Then I'll drive." Well, I would rather drive

with Hall drunk than W.R. sober, because W.R. was a wild driver. But we waited and watched, and when a woman answered the door of the farmhouse, W.R. got out of the car and went over. I was left waiting. The others had stopped and were wondering what was happening.

I said, "We ran over a goose."

They said, "Well, how silly. This is the road, and if the goose comes down from the house . . ."

Well, I refused to argue that. When they came back, Hall rode in another car, and W.R. drove to Bordeaux.

I didn't find out until we got back to Paris that W.R. had arranged for that woman to have a new car, a Renault. He had it delivered to her with a goose inside.

I only found out because they called him to ask what kind of goose to put in the car. He looked at me kind of sheepishly. But that was what was done. It was his way of making the poor woman feel better about her goose. He didn't even send his card, just a new car, a $6,000 [sic!] Renault. That was his way.

In Paris we stayed generally at the George V. Once in a while at the Hotel Crillon, but usually at the George V. It was the more modern. It was very nice there.

I had to lay out the rooms every time. Joe Willicombe and Harry Crocker would help a great deal, and it was a hard job. Believe me, laying place cards is a hard job. We'd try to keep everybody in a good mood when they were tired from traveling.

When we were in Paris, they had a habit of serving orange juice after dinner. You could have all the wine you wanted at dinner, but afterwards they would serve only orange juice. They still do it.

We were in the living room of Count Barney de Castillene's home and they were having some entertainment. The Duke of Manchester and Mrs. Otis Belmont were there.*

Now the Duke was supposed to be a dissolute sort of character, but because he was the Duke, everybody showed him respect. He said, "You know, I'm roaring thirsty."

"I am, too," I said.

But there was only orange juice, so he said, "I know where the pantry is. Would you like to go with me? We'll crack up a bottle of champagne."

"Don't you think you should ask your host?"

"Why should I? I'm not obligated to him in any way. I merely came here because I thought he was an interesting old dodo, and he has a crazy bulldog who tries to bite but has no teeth." Then the butler came around with more orange juice, and the Duke said, "Never mind that, just bring out a bottle of champagne, and I'll open it myself." He got one, and we went into the pantry, and he popped the cork and poured it out.

I couldn't stand to drink very much; I just wanted one glass. But he kept pouring and pouring, and finally Barney de Castillene came in and said, "I thought I sort of missed you. And you know, if you had asked me for champagne, I could have given it to you. I don't think that's very nice of you."

So the Duke of Manchester said, "I say there. You've taken my money without asking me, so why can't I take your champagne without asking you?"

The next day we went to Joseph Duveen's place, a very nice place. He had a house on a large farm estate and it was beautiful. I was looking at various different things and I was interested in one picture.

* Mrs. Belmont was the former Mrs. William R. Vanderbilt. In August 1923 she sold her New York townhouse at Madison Avenue and 51st Street to Arthur Brisbane for an estimated $500,000.

Duveen was an art dealer, and I liked the Lawrence painting of the boy called Arthur Atherley. I knew it was beautiful, but he was asking more than I thought I could afford to pay. He said, "Mrs. Horace Dodge wants that picture."

So we were leaving, going down the stairs, and in came Count Barney de Castillene with his old bulldog, who was almost as old as Barney. The dog went, "Growwlll," at Joe Duveen.

Duveen said, "But your dog knows me."

Barney said, "He knows all of the art dealers in Europe." They had gone to every shop, and as Barney and his wife [Anna Gould] learned art, the bulldog also learned.

The next day Joe Duveen had gone to London with the painting, and later I saw him there. He said, "Mrs. Dodge is still following me around. She's offered me much more money than you. And that painting is worth at least six hundred thousand dollars."

I said, "Has Mrs. Dodge the love for that painting that I have?" So we got very artistic. "You know, there's something about me. . . . I'm really so much in love with that painting. I'll just die if I don't get it.

"Mr. Hearst will be so sorry," I said. "I don't think he'll ever buy anything here anymore . . . but that'll be all right."

So then he said, "You've got me."

You see how smart I was?

"How much do you want to pay?" he said.

I said I'd pay a hundred thousand.

He said, "You're torturing me. I can't do it."

I said, "Think it over." I thought he was putting on an act. And he called me the next day.

"One hundred fifty," he said. "I'll just take a big loss on it." Well, we started to bargain. I offered a hundred

119

PORTRAIT OF ARTHUR ATHERLEY AS AN ETONIAN, Sir Thomas Lawrence. Oil on canvas. A gift of Hearst Magazines, Inc., it is part of the permanent collection of the Los Angeles County Museum of art. (Courtesy William Randolph Hearst Collection.)

forty. I knew I was going to win, and finally he said, "All right."

I wanted to see the painting again, but when I got over there, he was quite upset. He said there had been an accident. "Mrs. Dodge came over, and when I told her the painting was sold, she was so amazed that she started to run down the stairs, and she fell and broke her leg."

I said, "Oh, oh. That painting's bad luck." Then he was very nice. We had made a bargain, and he said, "Someday that painting will be worth much more than even six hundred thousand dollars. It will go into the *Pinky* class; it will be priceless." So that was the painting that I gave to a museum.

The Los Angeles County Museum of Art now has the painting, a gift of Hearst Magazines, Inc. It was done in 1790 by Thomas Lawrence, who was later knighted and became president of the Royal Academy.

The Lawrence painting Pinky, *a portrait of Miss Mary Moulton Barrett, is now in the Henry E. Huntington Museum in San Marino, California. Duveen paid $377,000 for* Pinky *at a 1925 auction at Christie's in London, before the California pioneer family acquired it.*

Another time W.R. and I went into the Duveens' shop in New York. Somebody I'd never seen before was there; it was Joseph Duveen's uncle [Henry] or his brother [Benjamin], and I had a book under my arm when we said hello. He said, "I have many things to show you, and your daughter." Well, did I feel small. And W.R. didn't quite like it, either. It didn't really mean anything. It was the sort of thing that happens lots of times.

I was having some hats made at Le Monseigneur's when Harry Crocker and W.R. arrived and said they had been asked to leave France.

W.R. said, "But there's no reason why everybody else has to go."

"What happened?" I asked.

I found out later, in the newspapers. It was so terribly involved. W.R. had discovered something no one was supposed to know. There was to be an international pact. It had been an official French secret. At first, I didn't realize how much I'd had to do with it.

W.R. said, "I'm really the only one asked to leave. You can all stay behind."

He left within half an hour. He said to me, "You stay. It would only be decent for you to get your fittings." I'd ordered twelve thousand dollars' worth of clothes. "It wouldn't be nice if you walked out."

I thought that was very kind of him, after he had been asked to leave. I would have said, "To hell with them," but they had the most wonderful hats there, and so I stayed behind with Maury Paul and my sisters. Everybody else left, going right to London.

Maury and I had booked some engagements for one full week in advance. I was surprised at how many people phoned and said, "Very sorry, but the party's off."

I got the cold shoulder from people who had known me very well just a few days earlier. I said to Maury, "The air's getting very cold. Frigidaire. I can't stand the atmosphere around Paris." I was trying to get my fittings done in a hurry, and everywhere I went there were gendarmes following. I had gendarmes outside my door, and so did my sisters. It turned out that Harold Horan had been arrested.* We were all under suspicion. They thought we must

---

* The Hearst Newspapers' Paris correspondent.

I was having some hats made. This hat was made by MGM.

know something, and they wanted to find out where we were.

The only two who didn't snub us were Mrs. Otis H. P. Belmont and Mrs. Abraham Lehr. I only went to Mrs. Lehr's party. She was supposed to be one of the social leaders of Paris, and her husband was quite fabulous. They were very wealthy.

Mrs. Belmont really stuck with me. She even stayed in the apartment with me and tried to get the gendarmes away from the door.

Every place I went I was followed, so we stayed in the hotel for a week and waited—Rose and Ethel and Maury and myself. I decided that I would have the dressmakers come to the hotel for my fittings. I finally said, "Here's my money. Send the stuff to America."

Mrs. Belmont got me out of Paris on a plane. My sisters came right over to England after me, but they had an awful time dodging those gendarmes.

We never went back to France.

W.R. got the most wonderful reception when he arrived in London. There was a big dinner party for him; I think Winston Churchill was there. The English weren't angry with W.R.; they agreed with him. They thought he was just one hundred percent for discovering the pact.

I didn't know what it was. I was just one of those silly, giggly idiots who don't pay much attention to politics. But it was some sort of a pact.

It was a French proposal for a pact between France and England. The secret design to strengthen the navies of those two countries was a violation of agreements signed at the end of World War I. But with the rising threat of another confrontation with Germany, this was viewed as a necessary step for the welfare of France.

There were rumors that the foreign minister of France even set up the leak of the secret memorandum, which would have been a double-double on Marion, and on the police. Still, its publication was a clear journalistic scoop for W.R.

They flew to Ensenada to avoid a tax problem. The San Francisco *Examiner*'s plane was pressed into service.

The cool English reaction to the memo reflected their traditional desire to be aloof from Europe, uninvolved in its wars and specifically unattached to France. The English had enough problems maintaining their empire.

While it seems likely that W.R. was asked to leave France in September 1928, as Marion says, it was not a binding order. W.R. was again in Europe, taking the baths in Germany, and passed through France in August and September 1930. This time, the French government cited his "hostile action" of 1928, and he was formally expelled. The order was delivered to his apartment at the Hotel Crillon in Paris, and he left the country immediately, to return again only once—by chance.

The pact was between France and England. It was very important and definitely detrimental to the United States. The French were frantic to find out who had released the news. They put Horan in jail, and all kinds of strings were pulled, but nobody could get him out. They wouldn't believe he hadn't done anything. He was held for months, although he was just one of the correspondents there.

Horan had not gotten the pact anyway. I knew that, but the police looked down the whole list of people we had gone out with. They figured it must have come from the American embassy. I didn't pay much attention at the time, but, looking back on it, I could really have been in trouble.

It had happened at a luncheon at the Elysées Palace in Paris. Ganna Walska, the opera singer, who was married to Harold McCormick, was there. And Dolores del Rio [a film star] and her director, Edwin Carewe,* along with several counts and others.

As I remember it, I was having a conversation with a person whose name I do not wish to mention. We were in the dining room, and I noticed a half-opened door. I wanted to see what was behind that door.

_____

* Carewe was also Dolores del Rio's husband.

I opened the door. There was a huge safe behind it. One of the doors of the safe was open, and I just happened to look through. I saw something written in French, and I thought: Just for fun, I'll sneak this thing.

I know I shouldn't have stolen it, but I was in a gay mood and I was curious.

I put it in my sissy-britches. I was too smart to put it in my bag, and I didn't want to be caught with it. I knew it was thievery, that if I got caught I would be thrown in the Bastille.

I thought it might be fun to read it. Then I'd mail it back anonymously. I'd say, "You left this hanging around."

We left and went back to the hotel. I had forgotten about it until I started to take a bath and the darn thing fell out. I thought: Oh, what a nuisance.

When I saw W.R. I said, "Look, I stole something. What am I going to do with it?"

"What did you do that for?"

"You know me, curiosity."

I was no kleptomaniac, but this had intrigued me. I had a great urge to learn French as it is written, not as it is spoken, but I'm darned if I could understand one word of it. I left it with W.R. and went over to get my hats fitted.

The next thing we heard was that the document was missing. W.R. was told to leave; the French thought he'd taken it.

They said to him, "Did you take any documents?" Of course they searched his apartment like mad; they looked every place. He took it very nicely. Then they said, "We will give you exactly one hour to leave."

He had it, but what he had done with it, I do not know.

W.R. never said a word about it afterwards, and I didn't either. When anyone would ask him how he got hold of it, W.R. would say, "I haven't the slightest idea." He'd give them a pale stare and he would shut up, like a clam.

He did say to me, "Thanks for the scoop." A newspaperman loves that kind of thing, and the means was justified for the fact that the pact was against America. W.R. was astonished by it. He did explain it to me in full detail, but I do not remember any of it.

Marion said a lot about her travels, as well she could. She traveled a lot, and a lot of people traveled with her. But travel is a hard experience to define.

They say it broadens the mind. But most people travel only when they have business or when they want pleasure. Some travel not at all. They say the word travel is derived from trouble.

Mary Carlisle went with us one year. Buster Collier and some of the other Hollywood people did. Otherwise most of them would be family or some guests from New York. We would pick them up as we went along. We'd meet somebody going the same place and we would all go together.

We always traveled by car. Once in a while by airplane. The last trip by airplane, we got caught in an awful storm between Madrid and London. We landed about five hundred miles outside of London, in a hay-field. They had signaled [from Croydon], "Would you like to land with rockets around?" We didn't. Who would like to land with rockets going up through the fog? We went on our merry way and we were miles from London and it was raining like mad.

We had to walk for hours and finally we managed to get some cars and then we stopped at a little inn.

The landing was less than 60 miles from London, near Lympne, a seaport near Dover. The New York Times *re-*

ported the adventure on June 21, 1934. The plane was registered in Holland, chartered by W.R. for the trip.

In the meantime there was a newspaper story, "Plane crashes with party aboard." And all our names were in it and everybody was in a dither. When we arrived in London about eight in the morning, were they glad to see us. They thought certainly we had crashed.

Eileen Percy was on that trip, and so was Harry Ruby, but she wasn't married then. To him, at least. It was right after her divorce from Busch, of the Anheuser-Busches. She married Harry Ruby after that trip, and she was just as frightened as I was. When I get frightened, I can't say anything.

Unless I get really frightened. Then I let out a tremendous roar. But on that plane, everybody was frightened. One time you could reach your hand out and touch the English Channel waters and the cliffs of Dover. I thought we were sure going to crash into them a few times, and once would have been plenty.

That was the year that we didn't want to land in France. The year before, we had that problem about the French pact and we were going to fly to England by the ocean. But we did land in France, at Bordeaux, to refuel. We didn't get out of the plane.

The trips to Europe invariably ended with a visit to England and a stop at W.R.'s largest house, the 135-room castle of St. Donat's in southern Glamorganshire County, Wales, seven miles southwest of Cowbridge. St. Donat's was named for a man of Irish birth who had made a pilgrimage to Rome in the ninth century. He became the Bishop of Fiesole and was later canonized.

St. Donat's was way out in the country, about fifty miles from Cardiff, which is a coal-mining town. It is a beautiful place, right on the Bristol Channel. It was built in the eleventh century and was terrifically big.

W.R. added two tennis courts and a new, modern swimming pool about two hundred feet long and a hundred wide. We'd go there at the end of our trips, and we'd stay as long as we possibly could—take life easy after the tour. That constant routine of getting up early, motoring all day long, resting at night and seeing the town the next day was really hard on the system.

When we arrived at St. Donat's, about forty Welsh singers, wearing high silk hats and lace dresses, sang for us.

Alice Head helped W.R. find and buy St. Donat's Castle in Wales. She was in charge of the corporation's British publications, but often visited San Simeon—where this picture was taken in 1933.

St. Donat's was built in the eleventh century and was terrifically big. (Photo courtesy Atlantic College.)

Floor plan of St. Donat's Castle. (Courtesy Atlantic College.)

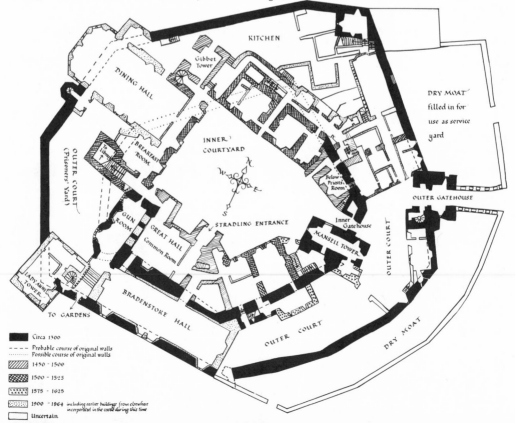

KITCHEN

Gibbet
Tower

DINING HALL

DRY MOAT
filled in for
use as service
yard

INNER
COURTYARD

OUTER
COURT
(Prisoners' Yard)

BREAKFAST
ROOM

N
W   E
S

Below
Priests'
Room

OUTER GATEHOUSE

GUN
ROOM

GREAT HALL

Common Room

STRADLING ENTRANCE

Inner
Gatehouse

MANSELL TOWER

OUTER COURT

LADY ANNE
TOWER

BRADENSTOKE HALL

TO GARDENS

OUTER COURT

DRY MOAT

▓ Circa 1300
--- Probable course of original walls
⋯⋯ Possible course of original walls
▨ 1450 - 1500
▧ 1500 - 1525
▨ 1575 - 1625
▨ 1900 - 1964 *including earlier buildings from elsewhere incorporated in the castle during this time*
☐ Uncertain

The front door was built in the fourteenth century. (Courtesy Atlantic College.)

St. Donat's is now the home of the United World College of the Atlantic. (Courtesy Atlantic College.)

W.R. added two tennis courts and a new, modern swimming pool. In all, W.R. occupied the castle for only four months and put it up for sale in 1938. Before it could be sold, the British Army requisitioned it for officer training during World War II. No sale was recorded until 1960, when M. Antonin Besse bought and donated the property to the school. (Courtesy Atlantic College.)

W.R. kept St. Donat's open all year round. There were numerous guest apartments. We used to have visitors from London, and there was a staff of about thirty or forty.

While W.R. went to St. Donat's, I sometimes spent the weekend at the Sutherlands' house in Kent. On one such occasion we were supposed to play golf in the morning—Harry Crocker and I and Eddie Kane and Leonora Bushman. And Eddie Clark was to play with the Prince of Wales and Prince George.

Harry had one room and I had another, with a bath between. I had a very beautiful bedroom. But on the other side were Leonora Bushman and Eddie Kane. Instead of putting two girls together, they put a man and a girl together. They wanted you to have a nice, happy weekend. But it was not for me. Harry was always in the bathroom reading the *Daily Express*.

The hostess, the Duchess of Sutherland, didn't realize that we don't do that in America. They only do it in England. It's a habit there. They want you to have a nice weekend, so if you'd brought a friend along, you were together. It sounds very salacious, but they mean it right.

We'd been up late the night before. We'd had a wonderful party. We were playing Pyramids and were having a lot of fun, but we had to be off at eight in the morning. I tried to get in the bathroom, but Harry Crocker was in there again. He'd locked both doors and was reading the paper; I could hear the pages rattling.

They had one of those little washbasin things, so I used it. Then I washed my hands and I thought, If I ring for the chambermaid, this will not look so good. I thought: I'll throw the water out the window.

I got ready—and then I heard voices below. It was the Prince of Wales and

Prince George, right under my window. If I'd thrown it down, I'd have drowned them.

I didn't play golf. I went punting in Geordie Sutherland's launch. He said it was a new boat, but it wasn't. We went down the river about ten miles past the locks and got stuck.

Geordie said, "I think the motor's gone out."

I said, "Maybe it's some weeds in the propeller."

He said, "I'll see." He reached underneath and said, "Yes, that's what it is."

When we arrived at St. Donat's, about forty Welsh singers, wearing high hats and lace dresses, sang for us.

I said, "Lean over. I'll hold your feet." And he pulled the weeds out. We started out again. The wind was fine, but there were no sails. And the boat stopped again. I said, "Is something radically wrong?"

"Well, this happens all the time. I can't understand it."

"If this happens all the time, why do you run it?"

"Well, the only thing we can do now is row. You take one . . ."

"Look," I said, "we're miles away and it's getting late."

The Thames at that point wasn't very wide. There were all kinds of weeds over at one side, and we jumped out, into the weeds. Something stung me on the foot. It felt like a snake.

We had to walk two miles to find an inn. By the time we got to the inn, I didn't feel any too good. I said, "Call up Arlene* and tell her to send a car over here so we can ride back. My foot hurts. And get me two double whiskeys."

I got them down, and it saved my life, I think. When we got back to the

_____

* The Duchess of Sutherland.

129

house, they were all waiting. The Prince of Wales said, "Well, what a happy holiday! Where have you two been?"

As if we could do anything in a little boat.

I was limping, but I put on an evening gown and we had dinner. Everything was fine when I went to bed, and then suddenly I had needles and pins all over. I called for Harry Crocker, in the next room. I said, "Get me back to London. I'm terribly sick. I think I've been bitten by a snake." My foot was all swollen and pus was running out.

He said, "I don't know how we can get out of here. We're supposed to spend the weekend."

The Duchess came in and looked at my leg and said, "Marion, that's pretty bad."

"I'm terribly sorry, Arlene, but I think I'd better go back to London. I think a snake bit me."

"No," she said. "There are no snakes in England."

"There are none in Ireland either. St. Patrick drove them out. But something bit my leg." It was getting bigger and bigger.

She got the car for me, with a chauffeur, and Harry and I made the long drive to London.

We got to the Savoy Hotel about four in the morning. I said to Harry, "Call up Sir Thomas Hoarde immediately and tell him to come over and see me." He was the Prince of Wales's doctor. Well, he wouldn't answer the phone.

So I said, "Get me a plane. I've got to get back to St. Donat's. There's a good doctor there. And my foot's getting worse."

Well, he only pretended to call. Then he said there were no planes that night. But I saw him; he had the receiver down. I knew he was skunking

me, and that he didn't want me to get on a plane with a leg like that. So I said, "Send for Leonora."

Leonora was Francis X. Bushman's daughter, who was very nice. She came in, and we got a car and went to Sir Thomas Hoarde's house and woke him up.

He said, "You've been bitten by a snake."

I said, "A water moccasin?"

"I don't know. Where've you been?"

I said I'd been in the river.

He treated my leg. It hurt a bit, but I didn't mind. I had some brandy. He said, "The best thing for you to do is stay in bed for at least three weeks. And keep your leg lifted up."

I said, "There's a Dr. Wilson down at St. Donat's."

He said, "You don't attempt to go there with that leg. You stay in London, and I'll look after it."

I said, "All right." But I wanted to go home, and home was St. Donat's. You get that feeling when you're sick. In the morning I said, "Get me reservations on the train." I knew Harry Crocker wouldn't let me fly, because W.R. had told him not to let me fly, but when his back was turned, I'd asked the operator about the trains. I knew there was a train at five-fifty, and we took it.

I was in bed for three weeks, with Dr. Wilson taking care of me. My leg was hanging up high.

So that disproves the theory that there are no snakes in England.

Afterwards, when we went to Germany, to Rotenburg, I was in the stable grounds, and I suddenly had the most awful pain in my leg. A big horsefly that had been eating horse manure had banged me on that wound. It got infected again, and I was back in bed for three more weeks.

I had a miserable time in Europe.

Later the Duchess said to me, "You

know, Marion, I should have warned you beforehand. I must tell you something funny. Geordie always does that trick with his boat. It's just a gag of his."

I said, "Yeah?"

Anyway, everything else was pleasant. We always had a good time at St. Donat's.

There was an oubliette in the castle. It was way up high, and there was a tower, and the oubliette went way down beneath the house. It went right into the Bristol Channel.

That was where they put the criminals. Down the oubliette they went and right out to sea. That was the eleventh century. A magnificent place, and we had a lot of fun there.

W.R. had remodeled St. Donat's, but with all the old things.

The dining room was the largest room in the house. It looked like Henry the Eighth's dining room. It was enormous.

It had one of the finest ceilings I had ever seen. W.R. had gotten that ceiling from the Boston Museum and had it sent to England. Of course I think the Boston Museum had bought it in England first, but the museum didn't have room enough for it, so W.R. got it and built the whole dining room around the ceiling.

He bought Bradenstoke Abbey and had it moved and put in. And everything in there was old. Old brick, for instance. Nothing modern. And the English people liked that.

Bradenstoke Abbey cost five hundred thousand dollars, and that only made one room. If they had stopped to realize it, W.R. knew more about

English antiques than they did. They should have appreciated his gesture. That castle had to be taken from Scotland to Wales, a long trip.* And it was an enormous big banquet room— made, I think, of gray stone. Every brick was from the twelfth century, and they were all brought to St. Donat's and added to it.

W.R. was very clever doing that. This was something he enjoyed doing. He was very immersed in antiques and old things.

Of course the bathrooms were different. They were all done over in marble. They couldn't possibly complain about it being modern; it was all old stuff.

But he was always on an even keel. He was very interested in the newspapers. That came first. Maybe I came first, but he used to work very hard on the newspapers.

And he was very concerned about his antiques. If anyone was a little careless, like they knocked over a lamp or something, he'd say, "I don't think it's very nice for people to come in and break things in your house when they don't even know the value. It shows discourtesy."

About everything else, he was very generous. You could have all you wanted, the horses, anything to eat or drink, but the moment you broke something, he really wouldn't like that. His mother gave him that feeling for antiques when he was a little boy. She took him to Paris and she used to take him to all the shops and he never lost that feeling. He bought millions of dollars' worth of antiques. He would go into a shop like Charles of London

---

* Bradenstoke-cum-Clacke was in Wiltshire County, not Scotland, and was less than fifty miles away. The abbey served as the assembly room at St. Donat's. And the castle now serves as the campus for the Atlantic College.

and they would say, "Here is a beautiful table from the sixteenth century."

He would look, and say that it had
been restored. They'd say, "Where?"
He would show them something way
down underneath, in a corner, and
they would be amazed. He didn't like
paintings so much. It was antique furni-
ture, then armor, then tapestries, and
then paintings last.

He had difficulty in getting a lot of
his things. But he was persistent. A
Frenchman, Comte de something or
other, said, "You are the man who
comes to countries and takes the ceilings away from the people and leaves
them roofless."

But if W.R. had his heart set on
something, he'd get it; it didn't matter
how much it cost. He bought a cloister
in France, and it ended up at San Simeon in the warehouse; it was never un-
packed. He wanted to give it to San
Francisco, but I don't think they took
it; they were afraid it would cost too
much to put up.

He had so many things, we had them
catalogued. He had volumes catalogu-
ing the many priceless things he
owned.

There was quite a bit of difficulty
about one room. It was done by
Charles of London and was simply
beautiful. It was an English room, and
W.R. had it on show in New York. The
English wanted it returned to them for
their museum. They created quite a bit
of fuss, but he was determined they
were not going to get it. I don't know
what became of it.

Everybody always wanted things
back. The French wanted him to return
the Gobelin tapestries so they could
hang them in the Louvre. All four of
them, together.

In the last few years, W.R. could
hardly buy anything in England. They
said they didn't want anything more to
go to America. He would buy things,

and not only would they not have them
delivered, but they wouldn't return his
money, which amounted to thousands
of dollars. They seized his things *and*
his money, which I didn't think was
quite fair.

When he didn't have any more
warehouse space to hold things, he
sold some stuff at Gimbel's. They got
rid of the debris, and they had a hard
enough time talking him into doing
that. He finally consented to it, but
then he insisted on picking out the
things himself.

He knew every piece he'd bought
since he started buying antiques. He
told them what could go. It was all

132

W.R. cleared out some of his warehouses and put things up for sale. This was the scene of one sale—which included his collection of arms and armor—at Gimbel's department store in New York in 1941.

right if the museums wanted things, but when something was going to be sold to somebody else, he would say no. He wanted everybody to have a chance to look at the things and to acquire an education and a feeling for things.

There must be five or ten rooms full of his things in the Metropolitan Museum. And he gave millions away to museums in the United States and England. Probably he gave away much more than even Mellon did. He spent all his time browsing for antiques, and W.R. knew the best when he saw it.

There were so many dealers that to find anything, you had to stay in London or Paris. There was nothing left in the little towns. They had picked it all up.

Well, we always traveled in Europe in a group. There were always people around. I guess I had more than one duenna. There was never any chance to be alone.

That was my impression of Europe. Like when you're hit on the head with a hammer. It feels so good when it stops. I liked coming back and seeing the Statue of Liberty. Home sweet home meant an awful lot. I could rest and relax and I always liked a pause.

Marion.

8

Chez Marion. Terrified by a horse. False teeth for the King of Spain. A shrewd young lady meets George Bernard Shaw. Doris Duke attacked by a monkey. Churchill throws rocks at the swans. Eluded by Adolf Hitler. The Queen's Garden Party.

arion and W.R. traveled frequently and far, and wherever they went they were entertained in a manner befitting their own style of hospitality. An endless procession of royalty, heads of state, leaders of industry, authors, artists, film stars and celebrities of every kind passed through their lives, either as hosts on their travels or as guests at San Simeon, Ocean House, Wyntoon or St. Donat's. Marion remembers some of them now, along with the parties and other occasions at which they met.

The longest time W.R. and I were separated was for two weeks in 1937. I was doing *Cain and Mabel* and got held over for more scenes. W.R. went to New York and got a houseboat. It was the middle of summer and very hot in the city, so he went to stay on the water up at New Rochelle. I got there only for the last two days, and then we went to Europe.

When we came back from the European trips, we'd have a party. They were usually wonderful parties.

One was at the Ambassador Hotel. It was planned to be a surprise party. After all the excitement I'd had in Europe and New York, I was supposed to be taken out by my sister Ethel to a quiet dinner.

Arthur Brisbane was along. And W.R. They said, "We'll just stop at the Ambassador and have a quiet dinner."

Nobody was even at the station. Only Ethel.

When we got to the hotel she said, "Let's go upstairs and wash up."

"What's the reason?"

"You've been traveling, and I think you should put a dress on. I brought some things from the beach."

We went upstairs and got dressed in evening things. I thought it was silly, if there were only four of us going to have dinner.

When we went downstairs, W.R. and Arthur Brisbane were waiting. I thought it was funny that they were wearing tuxedos. I also thought it was ridiculous.

Then I saw a sign, CHEZ MARION. I said, "What's that? A new restaurant?"

They'd taken over the big ballroom —not the Cocoanut Grove, but the Embassy Room—and it was a wonderful party. Joe Schenck, L. B. Mayer and all the producers were there. A lot of the stars, too.

Another time when I arrived back from Europe there was another surprise party. I was a little bit wise to that one, but I was surprised at one thing: at the bar they had a big white horse.

Everybody knew I was afraid of horses. I took one look and let out a scream. I ran like mad and hid, and I wouldn't go back in until they'd gotten rid of the horse.

That was a western party. I was afraid of horses because when I was about twelve I'd had an accident. The horse started to run and I let go and landed on some logs and broke the end of my spine. I was in a plaster cast for about three months.

I loved horses, but I didn't want to ride them. I was always afraid they were going to rear or turn around and bite my foot.

I used to have Harry Crocker as my master of ceremonies. When I was working, he'd take care of my guests. There were numerous guests. Like Secretary Swanson and Secretary Kellogg.

Claude Augustus Swanson had been a U.S. Congressman and Senator from Virginia as well as Governor of that state. He was appointed Secretary of the Navy in Roosevelt's 1933 cabinet.

Frank Billings Kellogg was the Secretary of State during Calvin Coolidge's administration in the late 1920s. He had been a U.S. Senator representing Minnesota, and an American Ambassador to the Court of St. James in London, before winning the Nobel Peace Prize in 1929. A student of law, he was later appointed to the Permanent Court of International Justice, which meets at the Hague.

[Winston] Churchill was my houseguest. He came with his son Randolph and Randolph's cousin John, who liked to play the piano. They arrived in Charlie Schwab's private car, the railroad car, and they stayed at the beach house.

Charles Michael Schwab had started his career as a stake driver at the Edgar Thomson Steel Works. He became president of the Carnegie Steel Company, then moved to become president of the United States Steel Company for six years, before buying the majority of the stock and being elected a member of the board of directors of the Bethlehem Steel Company.

MGM gave a big reception for Churchill. And he had a sort of lisp, but it didn't come out over the microphone. He couldn't figure it out and I couldn't figure it out, but a lisp just does not register.

We went to the opening of *Grand Hotel*, and afterwards there was a big party at the Roosevelt Hotel. I was working then, so I didn't see much of Churchill. He was a very good guest because he had so many things to do that he didn't become a nuisance. And he stayed quite a while, maybe three or four weeks. Then he went back to England.

He liked his Scotch and his cigars. They were what kept him alive.

The Duke and Duchess of Sutherland were guests and also Secretary Forrestal. I think Edwina Mountbatten was there. Louis Mountbatten arrived afterwards. He had been at Malta.

James Forrestal was an executive of a New York City investment banking firm until World War II. He was then named Undersecretary of the Navy with special responsibility for procurement and production. He became the Secretary of the Navy in May 1944 and for five years held that position and worked for the unification of many functions of the military services. He resigned in March 1949 and entered the naval hospital at Bethesda, Maryland, for treatment of severe depression. Two months later he jumped out a window to his death. The Navy would later commission a nuclear-powered aircraft carrier in his honor.

Louis, the first Earl Mountbatten of Burma, was married to Edwina Ashley, and would follow his father into the British admiralty. The Mountbatten family had renounced their German title, Battenberg, at the outset of World War I, but other members of the family had married into the Greek and Swedish monarchies, and this would allow Philip, a Mountbatten, son of Prince Andrew of Greece, to marry Princess Elizabeth, a Windsor, who is now Queen of England.

Well, Harry Crocker took care of them when I was working. And every year that we went to Europe, he went with us.

I also went to St. James Palace and Windsor Castle. And I had met Sir Ernest Cassel, who was the father of Edwina Mountbatten.*

The Mountbattens had a gorgeous house on Brook Street with all the walls done in lapis lazuli. She had an enormous big suite for herself in front, and in the back Louis had a room about a tenth the size. He had a hammock to sleep in.

He was a sailor and he wanted it that way. Just like they have on boats, there were two portholes in his room. You could look out one and see Malta. You could see water in the other one. It made him feel at home.

Edwina was giving a party for the King of Spain* when we were in London. The party was at Le Monseigneur's, the same name as my hat shop in Paris. But there was a funny story there, sort of a secret.

The King was at the dentist's. After that revolution in Spain they had kicked him out and he had to leave without a thing. When he got to England he wrote and asked for his false teeth. They sent them to him in an envelope, but they were all cracked up. Just like little pieces of salt. He had to get a new set of teeth.

I thought it was pretty lousy for them to do that; but he had just forgotten them when he left. He handed his teeth around and showed us they were all cracked into little pieces. He couldn't speak very much English and he was practically in hiding.

After all, a diamond ring may be important to you to wear on your hand, but false teeth are awfully hard to get.

Well, we went to one of those nightclubs where you go in and you walk

came an international financier, reorganizing the government of Uruguay's treasury and acquiring the Royal Swedish railroads. He raised loans for Mexico, China and Egypt, and died in 1921, bequeathing ten million dollars for medical and educational purposes.

* Alphonso XIII left but never abdicated the Bourbon throne of Spain.

---

* Sir Ernest Joseph Cassel was Lady Mountbatten's grandfather. An emigrant from Germany, he be-

downstairs. Now who wants a bomb shelter? But the place was jammed.

I had on a white lace dress that I had brought from Bergdorf's in New York City and it had a little train on it. This Hapsburg character, also from Spain, said, "Darling, would you like to dance?"

I said yes. Well, instead of him going ahead, which is quite proper, I went ahead. He stepped on my train and tore the whole back of my dress out. I was left with a slip in the back.

I picked up the lace and said, "That was nice. Thank you." Then I went to the ladies room and asked for some pins. But this was in England. There was not one pin. They did have some black hairpins, and I fastened the train back on.

Of course he didn't mean to do it. It wasn't really his fault. But I was thinking I should have a long coat. That night I was just wearing one of those short things. I went back and was sitting there and every time I moved, something pinched me in the back. I didn't care for the lobster. I didn't care for the salad. I was so mad at him I said, "You'll pay for this."

He said, "I don't understand."

That was nonsense. It was a white lace dress and very expensive and I was naked in the back, practically. A man might not be mad, because he doesn't wear a dress, but any woman would be furious.

W.R. was there, but he was way off. He didn't see that.

Prince George came to the beach house once. He was the Duke of Kent, also, and the eldest of the boys. His brother was the Prince of Wales who became the King, because George died in an airplane accident during the war.

Sir Thomas Lipton* was a guest, and the Lindberghs came up to Wyntoon. Henry Ford never came out. We saw him in Detroit. We had luncheon with him one day and then went to his factory. It was quite amazing to see how they built those cars, all in a row.

Sir Thomas Lipton was a very good friend of my mother's. When we lived in New York, my mother used to invite him for dinner every once in a while. Sir Thomas Lipton had one trick that I always remembered. He would have dinner for my mother and father and champagne for everybody. I thought he too was drinking champagne, but then I noticed that he would bring out a special bottle—it looked just exactly like a champagne bottle—with the same label on it. One night I said, "May I take a taste of that?"

It was ginger ale. I said, "I caught you that time."

He said, "The reason I do this is because I don't want people to think I'm ungracious. But I do not drink." I thought that was sweet. I've often thought, I could do that myself. But I certainly would not put ginger ale in the bottle.

He had amazing stories to tell. He was very much like George Bernard Shaw, although he didn't have all of the wit. He had that same sense of humor. Even if he was Irish, he was a very fine man. And he was very much the same in looks.

Shaw had that caustic Irish wit which is very detestable, and Sir Thomas Lipton had quite an amount of it. It is very, very annoying, because it is one of those wits that stabs. And nobody likes to be stabbed. Not these days. The mutiny's over.

---

* Thomas Johnstone Lipton left Ireland in 1865 and, after a decade in America, settled in Scotland. He prospered by merchandising cocoa, coffee and the world-famous Lipton tea, and he was made a member of the peerage.

George Bernard Shaw came out to California [in 1932] when I was doing *Peg o' My Heart* at MGM. There must have been fifty or sixty people waiting in line to see him. It was raining, and a lot of them didn't have umbrellas. He said, "Can't you get the property department to give them umbrellas?"

We let them in, and he walked up and down asking them questions. He was trying to be nice. When someone said, "Now, Mr. Shaw, what do you think of your picture . . . ?" he'd say, "Now what do *you* think of my picture?" He was interviewing them, and he was very funny.

Shaw was always caustic. On the set, he said, "I don't think anybody knows what they're doing. . . . They're all stupid."

We went up to San Simeon with quite a big party. All the young girls would sit around him and listen, and I did, too.

At dinner the first night he was sitting on my right. I hadn't had a chance to get acquainted with him, because I had been working when he was on the set. I said, "I have two great heroes—as far as writing is concerned."

"Who are they?"

"You and Shakespeare."

"Why mention me in the same breath with Shakespeare?"

I said, "Well—*Androcles and the Lion.*"

"Did you read that?"

I said yes.

He said, "I didn't think you had the intelligence."

"I have the intelligence to read it, but I haven't got the intelligence to understand it. Now you can explain it to me."

"Pretty shrewd you are, young lady."

"Thanks for calling me young lady." We started an argument, and I said, "I'll bite you for every clever word."

He said, "I'll bite you."

The next day he wanted to sit by the fireplace. All oldish men like to sit by fireplaces. The girls were all around him.

I said to Shaw, "Would you like to see the zoo?"

He looked around at all the girls. "This is enough zoo for me." Finally he said, "But I do like to walk."

Katharine Menjou* and Constance Talmadge went along with us. I had to shoo the others away. Katharine had a camera and was dying to get a picture of him, but he had said, "I will not have myself photographed. I don't like people who do things like that."

Katharine hid in a bush, but he said, "After I've seen the animals, I will walk backwards until you tell your friend to put that camera in her pocket and walk behind me. She'll never see the front of my face."

He was pretty smart. I told her to come out of the bush. She said, "I'm sorry, Mr. Shaw . . ."

He said, "Just your type. Blondes are always dumb." We were all three blondes.

He was so witty that nobody could ever match him. He'd come back with something twice as witty and make you feel the size of a worm. You'd decide there was no use talking to him any longer.

He got along very well with W.R. Shaw realized he was up against a strong mentality, so he didn't try any tricks. W.R. would never try to outdo anybody; he'd just look at them, and that would be it. They'd fade.

I never saw anybody in any conversation ever beat Mr. Hearst. They were up against a wall when they got to him.

Shaw and his wife stayed about a week and then started down to the studio by airplane. They got stuck in a fog and landed at Malibu Beach. We

---

* The wife of actor Adolphe Menjou.

Shaw was always caustic. On the set, he said, "I don't think anybody knows what they're doing. . . . They're all stupid." Shaw poses with actor Lee Tracy.

At a luncheon in Marion's bungalow in 1933. George Bernard Shaw sits on Marion's right. To her left are Louis B. Mayer, Clark Gable and George Hearst. Across the table, in front of Marion, Eileen Percy looks at the camera while J.W. Considine, Jr., to Miss Percy's left, looks at Mrs. Shaw. Partially hidden by the lamp are Una Merkel, Robert Z. Leonard, O. P. Heggie and Charles Chaplin.

We left the bungalow and went onto the set.
A crowd followed and Shaw said, "I don't like this."
We dodged into an alleyway.

were waiting at MGM—Louis B. Mayer and John Barrymore and Clark Gable were there. It was raining and we were worried. When they were an hour and a half late, I said to W.R., "You'd better phone."

They had had to shoot through a hole in the fog and land right on the beach and wait for a car. Mrs. Shaw [Charlotte], a little bit of a Scotch-woman, was covered with mud and sand.

Hundreds of reporters had gathered outside the bungalow.

By the time they arrived I was already an hour late getting back on the set. I was thinking about work, not the big luncheon.

Mrs. Shaw came, and I got the maid to get her cleaned up. She asked for a little bit of Scotch. It was her little secret, because he never drank anything. I gave her a little noggin, and we washed her off.

At lunch Shaw sat next to me. I said, "Why aren't you eating?"

"I don't like your food."

"Well, I didn't cook it."

"I'm a vegetarian," he said. That's how it went.

When John Barrymore said, "Mr. Shaw, would you sign a little album for my son?" Shaw said, "And how old is your son?"

"Six months old," he said.

Shaw said no. "He's too young to appreciate it."

Barrymore got sore and left. He went out into the rain and ruined his costume. He was making *Reunion in Vienna* and they had to get another costume for him.

We let the newspapermen come in, all of them soaking wet. But instead of them asking him questions, he asked them questions. He wouldn't let them say a word.

We left the bungalow and went onto the set. A crowd followed us. He said,

"I don't like this." We dodged into an alleyway and were met by a makeup man, Cecil Holland, in a big cowboy hat.

He said, "Would you sign my hat?"

Shaw said to me, "Who is he?"

"He's an artist—a portrait artist." He was only the makeup man, but when Shaw thought he was an artist he signed his cowboy hat, and we went on.

Ann Harding was working with Bob Montgomery and Alice Brady in a play called *When Ladies Meet*. Shaw was standing there, with his long whiskers, watching.

Alice Brady said, "Well, how do you do?"

And Shaw said, "I can recognize you by your Irish accent, but I don't know your face."

Ann Harding came up and said to him, "Don't you remember me?"

"No."

"I did *Androcles and the Lion*."

"It must have been a pirated version."

Well, she ran to her dressing room, and we got word that Shaw was to be removed from the set. She went into hysterics and said she wouldn't work any longer.

The next day the *Times* had a story, "George Bernard Shaw Insults Ann Harding." The reporters had been all over the place, and they'd gotten the story quickly. Shaw was furious. He said to me, "What kind of a country is this?"

I said, "It's not quite as bad as Ireland—but I've never been there."

"Then how do you express an opinion?"

"Well, you don't know about Hollywood—you only just came here."

"We'll have no fights."

When they left, they took a boat from San Pedro and through the Panama Canal. Both Shaw and his wife wanted me to go with them, but I was in the middle of the picture and I couldn't do it.

He didn't think making films mattered anyway. He said, "It will never last. It's no good. It's phony."

We wrote occasionally, but I never saw them again.

I guess as long as I knew Mr. Hearst, I'd just sit and listen. Unfortunately the conversations conveyed nothing to me. I always had my mind on something else. I had a one-track mind and that stopped me short. It didn't do me any good.

I wasn't good in pictures, either. I just liked to dabble in this or dabble in that. Of course, I was no genius.

At another luncheon, Mary Pickford was sitting next to Lindbergh. He was on my right and Mary was next to him and she sent me a note: "He won't talk."

I wrote her back, "Talk about airplanes." Lindbergh had a one-track mind—airplanes. She did, and then he talked freely. If you talked about things he wasn't interested in, he wouldn't answer. Up to that time his mouth had been closed. It opened to say "No" to the photographers and "No" to the autographers—just like Shaw.

Everybody was very enthusiastic about Lindbergh and thought he was a great person for making the attempt to go to Europe alone. It *was* a great feat; it took great courage and a lot of stamina and a lot of stubbornness. And those are things that are quite close together.

He had a straight face, but lots went on behind it. He wasted no conversation on idiosyncrasies.

He was then a big success, but that didn't go to his head. He was a per-

fectly independent person, but an introvert.

At San Simeon, we enjoyed having a lot of people visit. Yet W.R. would stay primarily to himself. When the spirit moved him, he'd come down and join them.

His mind was always working. You could tell by looking. He had a great broad forehead, and there were so many things going on in there that he had very little time for relaxation.

Over the years thousands of people must have come to San Simeon. But W.R. didn't really select them; I think most of the guests selected him. We'd get a little message, "I'm arriving . . ." But he never mentioned any feeling against sharing San Simeon.

Between my pictures he'd say it would be nice to kind of relax and just have a few people. We'd have about ten guests, and it would be really quiet. The place is huge and you would only feel about so big. When he wanted quiet, I wouldn't invite the ones who wanted constant merriment.

We were never concerned with the service or the food. There was the housekeeper and three butlers, two cooks, two chefs and a third chef for the staff.

W.R. wanted the animals around because it was picturesque. And he thought the zoo might entertain the guests.

He couldn't inspect the animals, because a lot of them wouldn't let anyone near. There were thousands of animals, and I don't know how many cowboys and managers, but the men took care of everything. It just went like clockwork.

Yet W.R. was the clock that made it tick. And it went fine, except for the day a lion got mad and clawed David

Hearst's leg. He got a scar from it. But there weren't any bad accidents.

A woman from San Francisco, a very good friend of Eddie Kane, said she knew all about the honey bears. She put her hand in the cage, and the bear nipped off the tip of her finger. And she had gloves on. We went for the doctor, and they sewed the end of her finger back. Still, you couldn't keep the people from getting where they weren't supposed to be.

And I was a culprit, too. I used to tease the ape. Doris Duke had no fear of animals until a spider monkey went after her. We were walking around, and this tiny little monkey got hold of her slacks—she was wearing beautiful gray corduroy slacks—and she let out the most awful scream. I think the monkey was mad at her because she was fascinated by the black panther, which was really a raging animal. She went over and was cooing to the panther. All the panther would have had to do was *whap*, and she would've had no face left. But she was fascinated, hypnotized, by those big yellow eyes and that coal-black face. Maybe she thought the little monkey was the panther because we were walking around and it was so unexpected.

W.R. asked me what he should do with San Simeon, but I wouldn't discuss it. I said, "If you're talking about fifty or sixty years from now, I'll give you an honest answer. You should give it to California, as a museum." Someone else had suggested it for the state capitol or the California White House, but I didn't think that was a good idea, because the people were taxed enough. I never saw W.R.'s will, so I never knew what he planned for San Simeon or Wyntoon.

San Simeon was presented to the State of California in 1958 by the Hearst Corporation "in memory of William Randolph Hearst, who created the enchanted hill, and of his mother, Phoebe Apperson Hearst, who inspired it."

Tours are conducted seven days a week all year, except for Thanksgiving and Christmas, and tickets are sold out weeks in advance. Jobs as tour guides are hotly contested among students, for guides are allowed to live at the castle in the summer.

If the state was reluctant to accept the gift and to undertake costs of maintenance and operation, the public was not unwilling to reward the effort. The historical landmark is the only one in the state to show a profit—which goes to the California general fund.

Wyntoon is still privately held by the Hearst families.

David Lloyd George, the liberal anti-imperialist member of the British Parliament, was first elected in 1890 and served for fifty-four years.

Prime Minister of England from 1916 through 1922, he became the first Earl of Dwyfor in the last three months of his life (1863–1945).

He was married to Margaret Owen in 1888, and two years after her death in 1941 he married Francis Louise Stevenson, whom Marion met.

We got to know Lloyd George very well, and he invited us down to his house. He was really one of the finest men I ever met in my life. I used to call him Santa Claus because he looked a bit like him.

He had a very nice secretary, whom he married. Once she and I were at luncheon with Alice Head* and the presidents of Oxford and Eton and

---

* Ms. Head was the director of the Hearst British publications and had assisted W.R. in the purchase of St. Donat's Castle.

Cambridge. We were the only women. We sat at a long table. The windows were open, and there were no screens. They were talking and making speeches about the colleges and education when suddenly I let out a yell like a Comanche Indian. A bee was buzzing around my feet.

We had mead, which was made from honey. It was supposed to be a cordial, but I didn't have a chance to taste it. Everybody else had mead, but the bee was all around *my* feet. I broke up the whole meeting. I screamed at the top of my lungs, "Get the bee out."

Lloyd George said to me, "Don't touch him. If you don't touch him, he'll go away."

I said, "Heck, he's stung me already!"

Well, right after the luncheon we left, and when I got back I missed one glove. I rang about it, and his secretary said, "Mr. Lloyd George would like to keep it, if you don't mind, as a souvenir."

I was so flattered. But it was the only pair of white gloves I had brought from America. But he was a sweetheart. She sent me the glove, and I autographed it for him and sent it back.

He had been retired then, and he was the kindest man. W.R. thought he was just magnificent. He loved life in the raw; nothing phased him. He never had a word of criticism about anybody. He was really a great man. I wondered why he had been dislodged. England would have done very well if they'd kept him on.

He said to me, "Your name is Davies. Are you Welsh?"

I said yes.

"There is a Davies Lumber Company in Wales and there's a Davies Street in London."

I acknowledged that—but I didn't tell him my real name was Douras.

Lloyd George came to St. Donat's once on the Fourth of July. The English don't think too much of the Fourth of July, but W.R. had bought thousands of dollars' worth of fireworks and the villagers were there and Lloyd George came down to make the first speech. The skyrockets were going high, and we had wine and supper for all the village. Such a thing had never been known in England: an American acknowledging the Fourth of July while he's there.*

Lloyd George made a beautiful speech. It wasn't quoted from anything; it came right from his heart. He said that George Washington was a great man.

He said, "We will concede the fact that he was born in England, but let us remember that he did quite a lot for America." There were three cheers.

An American flag flew at St. Donat's, and it was a little larger than the English flag. The Welsh people didn't complain about it, but the English did. They wanted the two flags to be the same size.

The question was brought up: What can you do about it? W.R. said, "Are we to cut out the stars?" He could have taken down the English flag and kept the American flag up. Maybe they wouldn't have allowed that. But what an issue to make! It was just a little bit bigger.

I could understand their viewpoint, but they failed to consider that they were up against a terrific American who wanted his flag, and nobody was going to talk him out of it.

Churchill asked us to come down for the weekend at his house. But it was a customary thing with me not to spend

---

* The Coast Guards objected. The fireworks were disturbing the shipping in the Bristol Channel.

weekends at anybody's house, if I could help it. I always had a strange feeling, even in a hotel, and I had that longing to get back to my own territory.

But we went down to his house. He had a place outside of London, and he had this huge brick wall which he had built all by himself. And he built a brick garage. He was quite an artist. He painted apples and oranges and occasionally a bottle of gin or something like that—but very artistically. And he had a big pond with swans, white swans and black swans. And this one day, they were fighting. One grabs the other by the throat and it was horrifying. Churchill was picking up stones and throwing at them. He said, "Oh, you bally bloaters!" And one swan was undoubtedly going to kill the other one. But he couldn't stop it. He kept throwing rocks and stones and I decided that I didn't want to look any longer. I was chicken-hearted.

I went up to the house with his son Randolph, and we sat before the fireplace. It was always cold in England. When he came back he said, "One is dead, naturally."

I said, "Why do you have swans that fight?" Dumb Dora.

Churchill said, "Just show me one that doesn't fight." I didn't know anything about swans; I didn't even know what the swans know. I only knew Gloria Swanson.

One night the Aga Khan had a big party at Claridge's for Aly Khan and Thelma Furness. George Hearst insisted that I go downstairs to see the big boy, the old Aga Khan.

He was so fat he couldn't walk. He was seated in a chair and everybody was standing around, bowing, before him. He got paid in diamonds for what he weighed, but I wouldn't bow before a fat load of diamonds, so I just walked by.

He muttered something to me. He wanted me to come back, but I wouldn't go. I danced twice with George and went upstairs. By that time, they'd all gone home. I had no right to leave my party upstairs, and they were disgusted with me.

On another trip Charlie Munn* met the boat at Southampton. He said, "I'm entertaining the King of Spain tonight."

I said, "I'm sorry; we have an engagement to go down to Sunnydale." That was the Prince of Wales's house, and Prince George was going to be there.

He said, "Would you trade two princes for a king?"

I said, "I'll try to divide them up." We went to Sunnydale, then back to the embassy, where Charlie was having his party. When I walked in he said, "I think you're the rudest person who ever lived. I had the King of Spain here, and now it's almost one o'clock, and you promised to be here at eleven."

I said, "I took two princes instead of a king." It was the truth, but he was furious with me.

I met H. G. Wells when I was in London. Lady Sybil Colfax was having a tea party at the Chelsea Embankment, which was where all the artists lived. She would have tea parties every Thursday, with the artists and writers mixed in with the society. It was all right, but it was kind of boring.

She called me and said, "Now, you

---

* Munn, known as Mr. Palm Beach, was visiting his daughter—The Countess of Bessborough.

Marion was intrigued with Hitler but missed a meeting with him. Nazi flags fly from the buildings in this picture, taken when Marion and W.R. visited Germany before World War II.

have not come to any of my teas, and next week I'm having Mr. H. G. Wells."

She must have known that he was a great idol to me. I had read his story of the other world and everything, and I said, "Of course I'll be there."

Elsie Mendl had just been married and was still on her honeymoon when she arrived with white hair and a purple suit and scarlet shoes and her old husband—no, I think she was older than her husband.

I had visualized H. G. Wells as a big, virile man with a great deal of character. I thought he was a great writer. When the butler finally announced him, I was one of those who sprang right to the front. I wanted to see him first.

He was a little man, about five feet four, with a high voice. He said, "Hello, Elsie." And he said to me, "How do you do? So glad to see you."

I just went to pieces. I said, "Oh, Mr.

Wells, I've read your stories, and I think you're wonderful."

He said, "Ohhh—thank you very much. That's quite divine of you."

I got my coat and went home. I had him built up as a big man, but big men don't always have brains, and brains don't always have a bass voice.

I didn't meet Hitler. I wish to God I had, but I got skunked out of that one, too. When I was in Germany and everybody was saying, "Heil Hitler!" I wanted to see what that character was like.

There was an aide of Hitler's, a Dr. Hanfstaengl,* who used to play the piano for him. His nickname was Putzi.

---

* Ernst Hanfstaengl was the press officer for the Third Reich, a Harvard graduate and a friend and advisor to the Chancellor.

He was kicked out after a while. When he came to Bad Nauheim, W.R. refused to see him. W.R. said, "If he's anything to do with Hitler, I don't want any part of him."

I said, "Well, I'll see him."

And I talked to Putzi. He said, "The Führer wants to see Mr. Hearst. He will be glad to come here."

I said, "Wait a minute—wait a minute. Mr. Hearst has no desire to meet Mr. Hitler. But I have."

"Yes?"

"I'll tell you why. When I was in Munich I went with my niece when I heard that he was arriving at the Brown House.* He wasn't at the Brown House. Then we went to the airfield, and he wasn't there either. From there we went to the Munich Opera and waited. Eventually we went back to the Brown House. I got back to the hotel at three in the morning. I didn't get to see what he looks like."

"You want to see him?"

I said, "Do I!" I didn't tell him why I wanted to see Hitler. The reason was that I'd heard his voice and I wanted to see how he performed, to see what kind of a character he was. At least I could go home and say I'd seen him, just to show off.

I'd missed Mussolini, and I thought I was going to edge in on this one. But every time I found out where he was going to be, I'd go there, and there was no Hitler. He was supposed to be at Frankfurt to see a presentation of *Joan of Arc*. He was going to make a speech beforehand, and then they were going to have the play. I hopped into a car by myself and went there. *Joan of Arc* was there, but not Hitler. I got so intrigued I had to see that man. If it killed me, I had to see him.

Putzi tried to set it up, but Hitler didn't want to meet me. He wanted to see Mr. Hearst. I worked on W.R. for three days, and I even got Harry Crocker to work on him, but Harry didn't get anywhere either. Finally I said to W.R., "Have a heart. I've gone every place to see this man . . ." You know a woman can talk a man into anything.

Harry and Putzi and W.R. and I flew to Berlin. I hated to fly, but I wanted to see that man. When we got there, only W.R. and I were to go in. I understood that Hitler didn't understand a word of English. So we had wanted Putzi to be the interpreter.

Ruth Selwyn was at the airport, and she said, "Marion! My God, I can't get out of the hotel. Could you come over to the Statler?"

I said, "Look, I have a date."

Harry Crocker said, "Go ahead. We'll go on and then meet you at the hotel."

She said, "I've called up Nicky,* but he won't give me a cent to get out of here. The housemaids won't help me pack my things, and I can't get out."

I said to her, "I'll fix it. How much do you owe?"

It was about seven hundred dollars. We started packing her things. In the meantime I was waiting to get over to see Hitler. He looked like Chaplin, I imagined. Possibly worse.

I was throwing her things into the trunk. The phone rang about twenty minutes later, and W.R. said, "We're in the lobby, waiting."

I said, "I'll be right down." Then I said to her, "Come on. I paid your bill. You can send the trunks to America and come to Nauheim with us." I didn't even know her very well, but I thought the routine must be planned. I got downstairs and said, "I'm ready to go."

W.R. said, "The plane's waiting."

---

*Hitler's office on the Briennerstrasse in Munich.

* Her sister Pansy was married to Nick Schenck, the president of Loews, Inc., which owned MGM.

I said, "What about Hitler?"

He said, "I just went in for five minutes and then I left."

I said, "What about me? Harry, you promised."

Harry said, "I couldn't help it. We only had five minutes with an interpreter and then we left."

"Thanks," I said.

I didn't talk to anybody for two days, I was so mad. I just wanted to see the guy. I think it was planned. Harry had wanted to take my place, and he did.

W.R. said, "I didn't understand a word Hitler was saying, and I didn't understand his interpreter either." He was cold on the whole subject.

W.R. was not impressed by him. He wanted to talk about the persecution of the Jews, but Hitler's answer was this: "There is no persecution of any sort." Hitler said that the Jews should not have taken over the industries that were supposed to be for Germans.

W.R. answered back, "I should think industries would belong to every nationality." Then he said goodbye.

W.R.'s answer came not only from his head but from his heart. He didn't approve of Hitler's theory whatsoever. He said he didn't like it at all, that it wasn't fair. He said that created hatred and war.

It was a very clever answer; and he meant it. W.R. never said anything just to be clever. Whatever he said was just him, because he knew what he was talking about. He had a great brain.

Those *Jude verboten* signs were all I saw. I thought that was a very bad mistake. I think anybody who is equal to a job is entitled to one. If they do their work properly, they're entitled to as much as anybody else.

We were gone before the camps and the violence.

W.R. didn't like Hitler at all. I don't think he cared for Mussolini any too much, either. He did say one thing, though. He said, "Mussolini can be credited for the new roads."

I met Chamberlain that same year. I think we had luncheon one day at their embassy, Number 10 Downing Street.* I didn't pay much attention, because I'd been out the night before.

I thought Chamberlain was very nice. He was sort of a placid man. But when they talked politics, it was way out of my cycle, entirely. I was thoroughly motion pictures, and I was not even good at that. The politics would just go in one ear and out the other.

When our guests would hear we were invited to a dinner party by the Duke of Windsor or the Mountbattens, they'd try to get in on it. There were loads of things to see in London—the Tower, the Bridge, the Cheshire Cheese thing—but when you mentioned a duke or some lord, then their ears would perk up. If you mentioned a collection at some museum, they were tired; they couldn't be bothered.

I think W.R. was very patient and very charitable.

When we were in London I used to have an excuse for leaving a party. I would say, "I'm sorry, I have to go back to the hotel. I have to write one of Mr. Hearst's editorials."

That was a joke, but the English can't take a joke. The first thing I heard was that they were saying, "Marion Davies writes the editorials." They really believed that. They said, "Isn't it amazing that Marion actually writes his editorials? How amazing. How brilliant she is."

I shouldn't have said it, but I didn't know they had no sense of humor. Nobody ever wrote Mr. Hearst's editorials but himself.

Now I did not have a nose for news, but I could appreciate it when I got it.

---

* Number 10 is the Prime Minister's residence and office in London.

149

Marion dressed for riding, at San Simeon.

Everybody was talking about Wally Simpson in the fall [of 1936]. I was at Phillip Sassoon's house the night I got the word, by the grapevine.

I went back to St. Donat's and told W.R. the story. I said, "They're going to get married." As you see, I was a little ahead of things. He immediately called New York. The operator at St. Donat's said, "What number?" and

W.R. said, "New York—the daily *Mirror*." The operator fainted. She couldn't conceive of anybody calling New York from Wales. But W.R. got the call through all right, and afterwards we sailed.

He said, "I think it's a good idea for every member of the party to keep in hiding." And that was the story that broke in the New York *Mirror*.

The paper said they were going to be married, and they got married about a week or two afterwards. The King wouldn't talk to me any longer.

By the time we arrived in New York, we heard the speech over the radio [December 11, 1936]. I must say I did cry. I couldn't help it. I almost made a river. "The woman I love." It was so wonderful.

The King was charming. He had a great mind, and he should have been king. No doubt of it. He had great intelligence, but I wouldn't call him a politician. I think he would have been the greatest king of England.

I had gotten the information one night at a very stately party. Prince George was there. He was a very nice boy, too. Afterwards he became the Duke of Kent. His mother was Queen Mary and his brothers were Prince Henry and Prince George. I think she had five, but one died.*

Prince George had already married a countess who was after him.**

Another summer I went to the Queen's Garden Party. It was amazing to see. Everybody was imprisoned in Buckingham Palace. The men and girls

---

* King George V and Queen (Victoria) Mary had six children. Edward was king for less than a year in 1936; his brother Albert Frederick Arthur George, the Duke of York, became King George VI. There was Princess Mary, the only sister; Prince Henry, the Duke of Gloucester; Prince George, the Duke of Kent, who died in World War II action; and Prince John, who had died in 1919 at age 14.
** Lady Elizabeth Bowes-Lyon, the daughter of the Earl of Strathmore and Kinghorne.

Marion on horseback.

arrived and had to sit in their cars for hours, twiddling their thumbs, wondering when they were going to get into the Palace just to bow before the King and Queen. It was a lovely, lovely way to spend one's time.

The Duke of Kent wanted me to go. I said, "I want a personal invitation." I really didn't want to go, and W.R. wouldn't go to anything of the sort.

I didn't have the clothes anyway. You had to wear white gloves, a garden dress and a big hat. So Prince George went out and got the clothes for me. Of course they didn't fit.

I said, "Don't you dare send me a bill for those. They don't fit." I had to have safety pins in the back. But I went, and it was a very nice garden party, I must admit that. I wore my white gloves and a foulard print dress, in very good taste, and a big straw hat. The hat was so big I thought it would hide me.

We sat there, and finally everybody stood up. The Queen had arrived. The Prince wanted a drink very badly. He had left me two or three times to have one.

I didn't know you were supposed to kiss the Queen's hand. She went around to everybody with her hand out. She went right by my nose. I was horrified. They always say, "When in Rome, do as the Romans do." But I don't believe in that theory, and I wouldn't do it anyway.

You were supposed to stand up, and I didn't. I was sitting with the Prince. He had come back from the bar, and I was afraid he was going to get plastered. Well, the hand went by and everybody was awed. She had on white gloves, too, and she went right by me. I said to him, "Who's that?"

"That was my mother."

Oh God, I thought, I'm ruined; I had better leave England immediately.

He said, "That's all right."

"I don't think so. I'm ashamed of myself."

"She didn't even notice you."

Thank God for that. So I never really met the Queen.

When we were in Rome, W.R. was invited to see Mussolini, and when you're invited you have to go. If you're in a country and you want to learn about it, it's a good idea to go and find out what they have to say for themselves; you might want to write a good story about it, when they're not looking.

He told me that Mussolini had this huge room—almost as big as Louis B. Mayer's office at MGM.

Contessa Dorothy di Frasso asked us to a party to meet Ciano and Mussolini's daughter.* She had a house high up on a hill in Rome, called the "Villa Madama."

I never met Mussolini. He wasn't at the party. W.R. was sitting on Dorothy's right, and I was way at the other end. Ciano was at the head of the table. I was on his right, and Arthur Brisbane was alongside of me. Ciano did not speak a word of English, and I couldn't speak Italian.

Then I made the famous remark which everybody at the table heard. I said, in French, "Why do you tease the Abyssinians?" I just meant it as a joke. I meant the Ethiopians.

---

* The eldest of Mussolini's six children, Edda, had married Count Galeazzo Ciano, who had negotiated the Axis agreement, politically linking Italy with Germany, in the fall of 1936. At the party Marion recalls there were thirteen at the table. The Hearst correspondent in Rome, Frank Gervasi, reports that W.R. was upset by the unlucky number, and annoyed with Gervasi for causing the situation. He had rushed the missing guest, his wife, to a hospital, and the next day, July 24, 1937, their son Tom was born. Later he would become the managing editor of Bobbs-Merrill, and responsible for this book.

Ciano just looked at me with a kind of funny look. Brisbane left the table and went down to W.R.'s end, and then a note came to me: "I have been informed that you are telling American secrets. Do not talk about American secrets."

It really annoyed me. If I'd known any American politics or secrets, I wouldn't have told them. I didn't even know how to speak Italian, much less French, but Brisbane had told W.R. that I was giving away military secrets.

Brisbane was mad because he couldn't get Ciano's ear. I sensed that immediately. When Brisbane came back with that note, I read it and said, "Put this in your pocket. You might use it for posterity." The only thing I did understand Ciano saying was, "Hollywood. Hollywood."

Brisbane said, "Why don't you give me a break? We're leaving in the morning, and I have to get an interview with this character—for my column."

I said, "I'll see that you get it, all right."

I knew he had sold me down the line, and I was darned if he'd get a chance to see Ciano. I was determined to keep Ciano away from Brisbane; I could do it by a wink of the eye.

The music started playing when we were having coffee. We danced, Ciano and I. Brisbane the wallflower watched, waiting for his chance to get at him. When the music stopped, I'd say, "Encore." My feet were sore, but I was determined. Finally I got the word from W.R. that it was time to go. I left very hurriedly, and Brisbane didn't want to come with us. I said, "Come on! Come on! We're supposed to go home, and you have to leave early in the morning." All the way down the hill he never spoke to me. He was furious that he didn't get his interview. But if he'd been decent to me I would have said, "Move right in. Take my seat."

Marion on the merry-go-round.

9

A t the slightest drop of a hat, any occasion at all, we would say, "Let's make a costume party." Then the telephones would start ringing and we'd get costumes sent up from Los Angeles. Carloads of people would arrive, and musicians, extra chefs and all that sort of thing. It was really fun.

W.R. loved the costume parties.

We had one at the beach house where he was President Madison and looked very handsome. I was a character from *Little Old New York.*

Norma Shearer came in her *Marie Antoinette* costume, even though it was supposed to be an all-American party. She came down from her own house, which was four or five blocks away, and her dress was so huge that the back seat had to be taken out of the car for her to get in. She had on a wig that weighed tons.

Merle Oberon was one of the ladies-in-waiting. Hedy Lamarr was there, and Charles Boyer was made up as an ambassador. Ouida Bergere, who was married to Basil Rathbone, came; Basil arrived as the French ambassador.

When they got to the library, they found there was only one door, and they wanted to take it down to let Norma Shearer through. I said, "No, no. She'll have to take her dress off. I'm not going to take the door down."

Hedda Hopper was in the hall and saw this amazing entrance. She said to Norma, "How dare you come as Marie Antoinette, with

At the slightest drop of a hat, any occasion at all, we would say, "Let's make a costume party." Then the telephones would start ringing and we'd get costumes sent up from L.A. Carloads of people would arrive, and musicians, extra chefs and all that sort of thing. It was really fun.

Left: W.R. loved the costume parties.

Right: W.R. was President Madison. Norma Shearer came in her Marie Antoinette costume, even though it was supposed to be an all-American party.

Bottom right: Film director John Farrow with his wife, actress Maureen O'Sullivan, and Norma Shearer, who *had a headache all night because that white wig weighed about 25 pounds, but she wouldn't take it off.*

Liz Whitney was lying on the floor posing, and W.R. got mad and said, "If you want your picture taken, stand up."

There was a Tyrolean party after Norma and Irving and W.R. and I had gotten back from Bad Nauheim. Marion with Irving Thalberg and Norma Shearer.

Gloria Swanson, Marion, Constance Bennett and Jean Harlow at the Tyrolean party at Ocean House in 1934.

Marion, Clark Gable and Eileen Percy at the baby party.

a French court, when you know that Mr. Hearst has been chased out of France? How dare you? You should turn around and go back."

They had a fight in the hall, and Hedda wrote about it.

The butler came to me. I said, "Take them around the ballroom way. You can open both doors there to let them through." Norma had a headache all night because that white wig weighed about twenty-five pounds, but she didn't take it off.

We had photographs made, and Liz Whitney was made up as a squaw, and she was lying on the floor, posing. W.R. got mad and said, "If you want to have your picture taken, stand up."

Finally we went in to eat, and Norma's gown was so big she had to have four chairs.

Now I knew that she didn't mean it as an insult, but it was supposed to be an all-American party. And she knew that Mr. Hearst had been kicked out of France. She might have had a little quirk in the back of her head. Irving [Thalberg] always said she had a little something funny back there. But that was how she arrived. I don't remember Irving being there. It might have been after he was dead.*

There was a Tyrolean party, after Norma and Irving and W.R. and I had gotten back from Nauheim. We had a brass band. That was also at the beach house and everybody was in German costumes.

At San Simeon we had a covered wagon party, and a paper wedding anniversary party for Connie Talmadge and Townsend Netcher. We had another cowboy party there and also a big masquerade party. Anybody could be whatever they wanted to be.

At the Lexington Road house we had

a baby party, and people you didn't know could get in. A character with a big head and a mask came in wearing a diaper. He was wandering around all night long, and everybody was wondering who he was. By the time we really got curious, we couldn't find him. We thought he was a prowler, but nothing was missing. In fact, something was added. There was a gun left in the hall.

W.R. didn't dress for that party. He wore an evening jacket with long striped pants. I told him that he should wear a ruffled waist, but he wouldn't. He put a stocking cap on and I said, "You should put a hat on—a real hat." He said no.

Louella Parsons had written about an earlier costume party at the Lexington Road house in August 1926: "Marion Davies was the hostess at a brilliant costume ball given at her home. . . . A Russian dining room and a new swimming pool were built for the occasion to take care of the 200 guests who accepted her invitations. The Biltmore and the Ambassador [Hotel] orchestras played."

There were many parties, but the circus party [in 1937] intrigued me so much I had to have another party within a month. The merry-go-round was brought back, and the hall wall torn down and put up again. We put it on the tennis courts, and they tore that wall down and put it back twice, to get it in and out of there. W.R. didn't care about the expense at all. He said, "Have the merry-go-round again."

I said, "Let's leave it here." But we couldn't; it belonged to Warner Brothers.

We had the *Midsummer Night's Dream* party at the beach house, and that was Jack Warner's party. He had a huge orchestra, about 125 pieces,

---

* The party took place in April 1938, two years after Thalberg had died.

160

The merry-go-round intrigued Marion so much that she had a second circus party at the beach house. *The wall had to be torn down and put back again, in order to make room for it. W.R. didn't care about the expense at all. He said, "Have the merry-go-round again." I said, "Let's leave it here." But we couldn't; it belonged to Warner Brothers.*

Clark Gable and Carole Lombard at the circus party with W.R. and Marion.

Director Mervyn LeRoy was table-hopping.

Marion outfeathering Claudette Colbert.

From the left, Irene Dunne, her host, Bette Davis,
Louella Parsons and Mary Brian.

seated in front of a blue ship decorated with orchids. He put carpets all around, except for the dance floor, and he supplied the food and decorations. I think I supplied the liquor, but it cost him a fortune. It was an enormous party.

It was after the opening of the movie,* and the picture didn't end until two in the morning, and everybody was so tired that only half of them came to the party. We expected five or six hundred, so that didn't make it any too merry.

The beach house was a lot of fun. We had a bar downstairs that was called the Rathskeller. It was underneath, where the dressing rooms were, by the bath-house. There was an enormous room, kind of a lounge, with a wonderful oak bar that had been brought from England. The wine cellars were behind it.**

We used that until Aimee Semple McPherson attacked me over the radio. She said, "Marion Davies has a bar in her house." Everybody had a bar in their house. Why did she have to pick on me? We had used it only once, I think. But then I turned it into a nice little soda fountain. We put in ice cream and stuff, and, needless to say, only children used it.

Every weekend we would have an orchestra in the ballroom, and supper —a buffet—for everybody. We would have only a hundred or a hundred and fifty people in on a weekend, and we'd look at movies after dinner.

We'd have a full show. A short and a newsreel and a feature picture. We had a screen that used to come up from the

ground. One night we got to playing around with it, and Princess Marie de Bourbon* fell down and busted the screen.

It took about two hours to get the screen fixed so we could see the picture. It was just one of those tricks. We were just jokesters. Anything for a laugh.

*Harpo Marx went to many of these parties, and he writes about them:** "My initiation [to the 'Hearst Crowd'] was a costume ball, to which I went, uninvited, as Kaiser Wilhelm. I won second prize. Nobody knew who I was except Charlie [Lederer], who had smuggled me in.*

"It was fun for a while, playing Mystery Man to the hundred most famous people in Hollywood. But I had to cut out early, before I keeled over from suffocation and exhaustion. I must have been wearing fifty pounds of disguise: spiked steel helmet, bald wig, mustachios, nose and chin putty, uniform with medals and epaulets, knee-high boots, studded sword-belt and a three-foot ceremonial sword. When I got tired of going around goosing everybody with the sword, I could only keep it from dragging on the floor by walking on tiptoe. Even more tiring was holding the monocle in my eyes. My face hurt more than my feet did."

Harpo tells of his exit from the party, with a ride toward home that developed into a family dispute between his benefactors, and abruptly ended with his abandonment on Sunset Boulevard, three miles short of his destination. Hitchhiking for the Garden of Allah Hotel, he was able, as Kaiser Wilhelm, only to stop traffic, but not to procure

---

* A gala premiere of the film *Midsummer Night's Dream,* starring Dick Powell, Olivia de Haviland, Anita Louise and James Cagney and directed by Max Reinhardt, was held at the Beverly Hills Theatre, Wilshire Boulevard at Cañon Drive, on October 16, 1935.
** The Rathskeller was constructed in England in 1560. Despite the Germanic name, the room had belonged to an inn in Surrey and seated fifty.

---

* The Princess was an actress who had played Marie Antoinette in Marion's 1924 epic drama *Janice Meredith.*
** From *Harpo Speaks!* by Harpo Marx with Rowland Barber (Bernard Geis Associates, 1961).

A bearded Bette Davis with friend.

Dolores del Rio and Cedric Gibbons.

The costumes were provided by W.R. He got them from the studios. Trying them on for size became part of the entertainment. Henry Fonda and his wife made do with these outfits.

David Niven, dressed as a pickpocket, with his wife.

William Paley and his wife Dorothy.

Sonja Henie and Tyrone Power.

a ride home. He went to the police station.

And later to San Simeon, many times:

"One thing we had in common was a knack for gymnastics. One rainy weekend, Marion and I practiced acrobatic stunts in the main library, after pushing a lot of junk out of the way.... Marion's diamond necklaces and bracelets kept falling off, and we kept picking them up, but as far as she knew she didn't think she lost any."

I remembered reading about the party that Earl Carroll had in New York, with the champagne. It was held in the theatre, I think, after the show. A girl [Evelyn Nesbit] was supposed to have been nude in the champagne. It was a party just for the bachelors and the married men who didn't want to be married for the time being.

There was a big scandal about that, and I think Earl was convicted and jailed. I'm not sure, though I was in New York at the time. The papers had it every day, for quite a while.

I don't think he meant to do any harm, but when you have a big party at your house it's very hard for the host or hostess to keep control. Most of the guests behave themselves, but some don't. It's still that way.

We went to the opening of *Gone with the Wind* with Raoul Walsh and his wife and Clark Gable and Carole Lombard. It was at Grauman's Chinese Theatre, I think.*

I guess Raoul Walsh's wife was bored. She disappeared. As it was a long picture [220 minutes], Clark said, "Let's go into the lobby." We asked

where the office was, so we could sit in there.

Phones were ringing, and we answered them. People would say, "Can we have reservations for next Tuesday?" We'd say, "Very sorry, no reservations. We're very busy; no reservations for at least six months." The manager didn't know what we were up to. We had just asked if we could sit in his office, quietly.

But Clark had said, "You answer that phone, I'll answer this one." Carole got another one, and we had a good time. They were always joking.

I was doing a picture* with Clark then, and after work we used to go down to the beach house and have dinner and then go to Venice for the rollercoasters.

Carole took over the pier at Venice one time. She engaged the Fun House with all the jingly things and games with things that go down from the top. Katharine Menjou, Adolphe's second wife, was there, and she went down one of those chutes and hit the bottom of her spine, which is the coccyx. After that we used to call her Coccyx Katie.

We used to drive those little cars that crashed into one another. Charlie Chaplin, Harry Crocker, and all of us went regularly, every night, no matter how late or how much work there was.

There was a man with a straw hat who would drive up and bonk us, and we would roll back and forth. You could get black and blue.

I don't know if Chaplin ever went on those—he was too conservative. But Carole and Clark and Eddie Kane and Harry Crocker and Polly Moran and various other guests who were at the beach house always went.

_____

* On Hollywood Boulevard, which, in December, was also known as Santa Claus Lane.

_____

* *Cain and Mabel* was the last picture Marion made with Clark Gable, but it was not in production in December 1939, when *Gone with the Wind* was released.

166

Constance Moore.

George Jessel loved to wear uniforms.

W.R. and Hedda Hopper.

Actor Fred Stone came as an onion, his beard and mustache made of scallions. With him are his daughters Paula, at left, and Dorothy.

Walter Winchell shows Gable how to do it, while the actor takes notes.

Jean Harlow with Harpo Marx.

Polly Moran was an actress who made more than thirty films in California. She was also a rather flamboyant and unpredictable lady. The titles of some of her films perfectly match her offscreen personality: TELLING THE WORLD, WHILE THE CITY SLEEPS, SHOW PEOPLE, THE UNHOLY NIGHT, WAY OUT WEST, HOLLYWOOD PARTY, and CHASING RAINBOWS.

She was also in Marion's film IT'S A WISE CHILD.

The amusement parks were built on the municipal fishing piers at Santa Monica and Ocean Park and Venice beaches, south of Marion's Ocean House. Marion and her friends could have walked, ridden down Ocean Front Walk in a tram, or been chauffeured to these entertainments.

One night someone was yelling, "Come on in. Come on in and see the naked woman dancing . . ." It was Polly Moran yelling. We tried to get her away, but there was a crowd around, and they knew who she was. She was yelling, "Come on in, all you crazy folks without any mentality. Come on in and see a crazy show." We decided we would pretend we didn't know her, so we went to a shooting gallery. That was the way to get Polly off.

Lots of nights in the winter I went alone to the pier. I had decided that the rollercoaster was not going to defeat me. I wanted to show them I wouldn't scream even when it went down—whoop! W.R. didn't like the rollercoaster and didn't want me to go. He said there were an awful lot of accidents on them, and he would beg me not to go. I'd say, "I'll be seeing you," and he would stay behind. I think he went with me once.

I got on that rollercoaster one night and didn't get off until seven in the morning. I kept paying the man, and I sat in the front seat, the middle seat and the back, and I stood up with my arms folded. I even sat backwards. Then I said, "I have it controlled."

That was fine until the next time we went. A sailor in front of me lifted up his head at the wrong time. His head went right off into the ocean.

That cured me. No more rollercoaster.

To me, Venice and Ocean Park were gaiety. I had not been allowed to go to those things as a youngster.

I liked the hamburgers and the hot dogs and the airplanes. To me the ferris wheel was just divine, though everybody thought I was nuts. I would go on the ferris wheel to memorize my dialogue.

Lili Damita and Errol Flynn came one night. Once there was a drunk who dropped his hat among the dodgem cars, and when he saw Clark Gable and Carole Lombard and Charlie Chaplin, he was too shy to take his hat back. They were passing it around, back and forth, and he was running for it.

W.R. went as many times as he could stand it. Not frequently. He was afraid I might get hurt because I was so exuberant. One time we got caught way up on the top of the ferris wheel. I think it was a gag pulled to scare people. Once we went down in the diving bell. We went to the bottom of the ocean, and you could see the fish. It was a beautiful thing until the man said, "I think the cable is broken."

My sister Ethel was with me, and she was a bit of a scaredy cat. There was a telephone and I said to him, "How far down are we?" He said we were about three miles under the sea.

I said, "What's wrong?"

He said, "The cable broke."

Then I thought I recognized George Hearst's voice and I said, "You pull this thing up." Well, he had thought it was a good gag.

Cary Grant, Lionel Atwill, Leslie Howard, Walter Hampden, Ernst Lubitsch, Randolph Scott and Guinn (Big Boy) Williams stand, while Johnny Mack Brown kneels. The lady is Mary Carlisle.

Marion, at left, with Norma Shearer and Merle Oberon.

After FDR defeated Landon,* we went to Washington and Cissy Patterson gave a big party. W.R. stopped at the White House, and he was the first to stay for a weekend after Roosevelt had been inaugurated.

We arrived on a Friday, the night of the party. Saturday morning at eight, W.R. arrived at Cissy Patterson's house. I was there with Harry Crocker and some other guests. W.R. wanted to go right back to Los Angeles.

* The Governor of Kansas, Alfred Mossman Landon, was the Republican Party's presidential candidate in 1936.

W.R. cuts the cake. The circus party celebrated his seventy-fourth birthday, in 1937.

Sons Randolph and George have to wait for Bill to get the first bite of the Independence Hall cake at W.R.'s birthday in 1938.

Marion cuts the cake at W.R.'s seventy-third birthday party.

Of course I had an awful hangover from Cissy Patterson's party. So did Harry Crocker. I had just gotten to sleep at eight, and at eight-fifteen I got the word that I had to get up.

Cissy sashayed in in a long robe and said, "He's downstairs." W.R. was way down at the other end of the house, and we had to go and catch an eleven o'clock train.

He had had a talk with the President. It was very affable and everything was fine except that the President had asked him if he wanted a cocktail and W.R. had said no.

I said, "Why did you let the President take one alone? You could have taken it and thrown it in the wastebasket. That was a terrible insult."

He said that F.D.R. had only one. I said, "He might have taken two if you had taken one. That was no way to be." Well, they had a very nice talk, but then W.R. decided that the White House was a little cold and he couldn't sleep. He was nervous. He was supposed to have another conference in the afternoon, but he had gotten a little tired, and he decided he wanted to go back to Los Angeles. He told me this on the train.

I think W.R. and the President may have had some little disagreement—I do not know what. I do know that W.R. would never spend a weekend at somebody else's house, whether it was the White House or Buckingham Palace. He always wanted to be in his own place.

I could understand that feeling, and I got used to it. I got to be the same way. I was miserable even overnight at somebody else's house. I couldn't sleep. I wanted my own bed, no matter how ancient it was. And I had an eighteenth-century bed and I was almost as old as it was.

W.R. didn't say much about his conversation. He just said that the President was charming. We had met him in California, but I couldn't talk to him very much. It was at the Electric Parade at the Coliseum, and all the stars were supposed to ride around in the ring and get out and meet the President and say, "How do you do?"

Mrs. Roosevelt was really charming. I adored Anna, and the boys were nice. At one time Elliott had worked for Mr. Hearst, in the radio station in Texas. He was in charge, and he did very well. Anna had worked for W.R. also. She and John Boettiger worked on the Seattle newspaper. John was supposed to be the publisher, and Anna was the managing publisher, in charge of the women's page.

I don't think W.R. agreed with all of the President's policies, but he liked the Roosevelts personally. After all, W.R. had the right to express his own opinion, the same way he had done with Hoover. When he didn't like something, he would attack. Like the Pearl Harbor thing and this lending money all the time.*

He was definitely against a third term for Roosevelt. I might say I think it may be better to give a president a longer term, because four years go by so quickly. We could use it like a monarchy, like in England, where it goes on forever. If they were in for life, why would they try to graft? When you only have four years, there's a temptation to say, I'll get everything I can.

If the public doesn't like the president, they should have a vote and say they don't want him in. But that isn't so simple.

Mr. Hearst had an editorial writer in New York who wrote the general edi-

---

* And W.R. opposed a plan to license the press—part of the National Recovery Act in 1933.

torials. He was called Mr. Tompkins.

Any extra ones that were in the papers were written by W.R. He would notify Mr. Tompkins to write about such and such a thing, just as a suggestion, and Mr. Tompkins would write it and send it to W.R., who would okay it or make some changes. You couldn't tell the difference from his own editorials. Mr. Tompkins was very used to W.R.'s style of writing.

The editorials were never signed, so you never knew which was written by whom.

I would talk to W.R. about some of the editorials. I maintained that some women might know about politics, even if I didn't. However, I used to put in my two cents every once in a while.

W.R. would write them in his own handwriting. He might ask me what I thought about something, like the antivivisection thing or the Roosevelts. I usually agreed with him.

Among the other writers, he liked Winchell, but the one he adored was Bill Curley. There was Baskerville from Baltimore, and Walter Howey was always the little white-haired boy. W.R. met [Westbrook] Pegler once and was nicely impressed by him.

Pegler was a different person entirely from his writings. He was so sweet and kind that I couldn't imagine how that poison came out of his pen. You read his things and said, "That is not the man I met, who was so charming."

W.R. saw him only once. Pegler and his wife came up to San Simeon and we had dinner one evening and luncheon the next day. Then they motored down to Los Angeles. We didn't talk about anything in particular, just how nice the place was. Everybody always said that.

W.R. didn't write to Pegler about the Eleanor Roosevelt thing. He would wire the editor and say, "Would you kindly tell this gentleman not to write nasty things about a woman. I do not believe in hiding behind a woman's skirts."

They would think they had Pegler under control, and then, the next thing you'd know, there it was again.

W.R. wanted to fire Pegler, but he found out that he had a contract. He said to pay him off unless he behaved himself. Aside from Mrs. Roosevelt, Pegler was all right, but Mr. Hearst got awfully tired of his attacks. I got tired, and I got mad, too.

Pegler had referred to Mrs. Roosevelt as "La Boca Grande."

Later he suggested that his readers who visited London might want to drink a few pints and then desecrate the statue of F.D.R. in Grosvenor Square.

His statements about others would lead to court, and the many judgments against him form a unique case in the history of American journalism and jurisprudence. But he stayed with the Hearst newspapers until 1962, when he attacked W.R.'s memory and was fired.

I think it started at a party in Washington. Mrs. Pegler was invited, but then she was asked not to go because Mrs. Roosevelt was going to be there. A woman can influence a man, just like that.

If anything was wrong with a man, you could say: it must be his wife. Women have loads of influence, and they know it, too. But what good was it to the newspapers if one man, supposedly and apparently intelligent, was constantly roasting one faction of a family?

Marion disguised in *Operator 13*.

10

Over the hills to Burbank. Gary Cooper raises his voice. Rehearsals at
San Simeon. Purgatory in furs: the Warner Brothers lot. A fast one on
Jack and Harry. Marion retires. Some reflections on success.

*T*he whole darn Academy thing was started by W.R. He
wanted me to win an Academy Award. You bet your
life he did. When there was a party at the Hollywood
Roosevelt Hotel, he suggested it to Louis B. Mayer. But I missed out
—by a mile—or twenty miles. I never won one. I thought I would
cancel my membership. I used to say it was a plot.

If W.R. thought an Academy Award was for my benefit, it certainly was a lost cause. There were so many better actresses, and I
never did anything outstanding.

I guess he had hopes that I might. He thought I should have won
an Oscar for *Peg o' My Heart,* but I thought it was a corny story to
begin with, and a very inferior performance by the star.

I thought the Academy Awards were designed to create an incentive, but they were bound to create jealousy. You would go to the
show and think you were going to win and somebody else did. I've
forgotten who did win that year. I didn't. But I got a nickname,
Daisy.* Connie Talmadge was one of my best friends, and she thought
it up.

I stayed a member through the years, but I never went to any
more of the shows, after *Peg o' My Heart.*

W.R. thought that was my best film, and it did make a lot of
money, if that means success. *Little Old New York* and *Operator 13*

---

* Daisy Dell was the name of the character Marion played in *The Floradora Girl.* Speaking of flowers,
Morning Glory was the film that won Katharine Hepburn an Oscar that year (1933).

An MGM advertisement for *Peg o' My Heart.*

Below: Two of the stars of *Peg o' My Heart.*

Bottom: *W.R. thought I should have won an Oscar for PEG O' MY HEART, but I thought it was a corny story.*

METRO · GOLDWYN · MAYER

MARION DAVIE

an absolutely bewitch
creature in PEG O' MY HEA
When J. Hartley Manners wrote the st
play he asked for a lot...a child of the
and the sun whose natural charm was so g
that sophisticated London society would
down and worship her. In M-G-M-Cosmopolit
screen version Marion Davies is the very elfin c
ture that Manners must have dreamed about...'
O' My Heart" is a sensitive and beautiful production
Robert Z. Leonard, from an adaptation by Francis Ma

★ The reproduction above of an original painting of Marion Davies by William
is the third of a series of caricatures by famous artists of Metro·Goldwyn·Mayer

In *Peg o' My Heart*, Marion played the daughter of a poor fisherman. She would inherit a fortune if she would leave home to claim it.

made money, too, but they [MGM] used the booking system, and you could have all the detectives in the world and you'd never know where the money was going. There was no way to check up.*

Ilka Chase was in *The Floradora Girl*. She did a scathing book about Mr. Hearst, about the swimming pool and her mother.

The most amazing thing was that I got the part for her. I looked at twenty-two tests for that part. It was the second lead.

She came up to me outside the projection room one day and said she was Ilka Chase and that she was dying to get into pictures. She asked me if I'd seen her test. She said, "I'd give anything in the world, and I can do it . . ." I went back in and said I wanted Ilka Chase. How gullible I was.

We went to San Simeon to rehearse, and she asked if she could bring along her mother. I said, "Certainly." There were forty or fifty guests: actors, circus performers, stunt people, and political and society people from Newport, New York and Washington.

At a party I didn't seat her mother on the right of W.R., because her mother was merely an editor at *Vanity Fair*, and it would have been very poor form on my part. There were more important people at the party.

She then wrote a book about why I didn't put her mother next to Mr. Hearst. She didn't really say anything about me. She wrote about the swimming pool. She said Mr. Hearst goosed her in the swimming pool. But he was not that type. Besides, when there were loads of people swimming, W.R. hardly ever went in.

Well, I'd rather pretend I never knew

* Studio reports on twenty of Marion's films made between 1925 and 1934 showed costs of $14,401,-000 and a net loss of $823,000. See the table compiled on page 179.

her. I hate to be snobbish, but if I ever saw her, I'd look over her head.

Bing Crosby was a very fine man to work with. He was always in a very happy mood and he never paid any attention to anybody—he just paid attention to his work.

What amazed me was that when he started to sing before the orchestra, he could sing perfectly fine with a pipe or a cigarette in his mouth. With those enormous notes coming out. It didn't bother his throat a bit.

I said to him one day, "How can you do that when you're smoking?"

"It gives me that sort of husky quality."

He was very cute and very sweet, and he was crazy about his wife Dixie. And she was a darling.

Every time he'd be doing a scene, his eyes would be sort of . . . He had big blue eyes, and you knew his mind was way off. I knew where it was. He was wondering where Dixie was and what she was doing. He'd be very serious on the sets. He'd stay by himself and read a newspaper, and then he'd go to the phone and call up Dixie.

She used to tease him, and he'd tell me, "I love Dixie. She teases me so I can't think of anything in the love scenes."

So I said, "Well, in our love scenes, let's make it real. You pretend I'm Dixie."

"Oh, no. You're not nearly as pretty."

"I understand that—but just close your eyes."

We were making *Going Hollywood* and Bing had been making pictures at Paramount, and we had borrowed him. His first day, I stayed off the set, which is the polite thing to do, because when

RESULTS OF MARION DAVIES'S MGM PICTURES BASED ON STUDIO OPERATING REPORTS

Total MGM Releases For Year	Release Year	Title	Release Number	Production No.	Footage	Cost (M)*	Days in Production	Total Revenue (M)*	Profits/ Losses (M)*	Supervisor (Producer)	Director
40	1925–26	Beverly of Graustark	612	253	6627	$357	42	$ 756	$180	Thalberg	Franklin
	1925–26	Lights of Old B'way	615	239	6344	321	35	601	109	Thalberg	Bell
45	1926–27	The Red Mill	735	274	6337	488	51	663	<50>	Thalberg	Goodrich
	1926–27	The Fair Co-Ed	736	329	6330	316	36	666	131	Thalberg	Wood
	1926–27	Tillie the Toiler	737	297	6160	475	30	637	<64>	Thalberg	Henley
51	1927–28	Quality Street	827	313	6485	523	69	568	<188>	Thalberg	Franklin
	1927–28	The Patsy	828	345	7249	245	27	617	155	Thalberg	Vidor
	1927–28	Her Cardboard Lover	829	375	8460	343	36	663	84	Rapf	Leonard
53	1928–29	Marianne	920	427	10437	648	52	986	64	Hyman	Leonard
	1928–29	Not So Dumb	921	449	6972	331	24	501	<39>	Thalberg	Vidor
	1928–29	The Floradora Girl	922	478	7346	593	43	627	<216>	Lewin	Beaumont
	1928–29	Show People	935	360	7558	397	34	981	176	Thalberg	Vidor
49	1930–31	It's a Wise Child	109	C548	7509	408	17	491	<123>	Bern	Leonard
	1930–31	Five and Ten	110	C554	8358	594	41	550	<274>	Hyman	Leonard
	1930–31	Bachelor Father	111	C528	8335	502	22	706	<170>	Fineman	Leonard
43	1931–32	Polly of the Circus	209	601	6325	438	34	700	20	Bern	Santell
	1931–32	Blondie of the Follies	210	C626	8525	611	46	737	<141>	Thalberg	Goulding
40	1932–33	Peg o' My Heart	314	C664	8140	623	42	979	18	Considine	Leonard
	1932–33	Going Hollywood	315	C712	7298	914	47	962	<269>	Wanger	Walsh
38	1933–34	Operator 13	410	C738	7943	880	76	1010	<226>	Hubbard	Boleslavsky

* Stated in thousands.

Bing Crosby starred with Marion in *Going Hollywood*. He had big blue eyes. Every time he'd be doing a scene, his eyes would sort of . . . you knew his mind was way off.

Marion with Bing in the carriage scene from *Going Hollywood*. This was included in MGM's recent retrospective, *That's Entertainment!*

you're at a new studio, I know how nervous you can be, and he didn't know me.

But there was a certain star [Joan Crawford] who used to play Bing's records all the time on her set, and when she heard that he was working, she came over and sat under the camera.

Poor Bing couldn't do his scene, and they finally had to ask her to leave the set. Now how could you do a scene with somebody staring at you with big owl eyes?

I'll tell you why I liked Gary Cooper. I would say that in American history he could be a Bowie or a Jefferson. He was a wonderful man and very understanding, but in a way that you didn't know half the time.

You'd think that here's a very tall person who looks like Uncle Sam and you'd wonder: Is he? You'd find out he was.

When you were working with him, he was very considerate. He would always back you up. Gary would give the star the benefit of the scene. Only a real man does that, and Bing did that, too. Other actors don't.

When we used to do scenes, the director would say, "I cannot hear your voice—kindly talk louder." So either my voice would have to get low, or Gary's would have to get a little bit higher. And Gary refused to change, and he was right. How could he change his voice?

One day—I got mad—I said to the director, "Look, that's your job, to get us on a level. I can't talk to my toes, and certainly if Mr. Cooper talks higher, they'll say he's a pansy."

Gary looked so shocked at me. "What did you-all say?" he said.

I said, "Now don't disturb us while

Rocky and Gary Cooper.

Their Big Love Scenes

Marion Davies and Gary Cooper in a scene from *Operator 1.*

Marion co-starred with Gary Cooper in *Operator 13*.

we're working." And they heard his voice all right after that.

But every time Boley* would say to Gary, "Would you mind doing that over again in a different way?" he'd do it just the same way.

He was smart, because an actor knows more than the director. If the director knew more, he'd be an actor and get more money. And Gary had been engaged for his style, anyway, so why should he change it?

There are so many directors who want to change your whole system of doing work, your personality. They want you to change to something which is not yourself but might be somebody else. So Gary always stayed his same character. He'd say, "Yup," and he'd still go the same way.

I'd do anything. If they said my voice was too high, I'd go lower. I had no character. I should have said, "Look—this is me. If you don't like it, you know what you can do." And one time they did. We were on the back lot, making scenes, and they let two lions loose out there. That's what they thought of me.

I used to take my cook out there. We'd all be working, maybe a hundred of us, and we'd have luncheon in a big tent. Beans and potato salad and hot tamales and beer. I'd be watching Gary, and he would eat more than anybody in the whole cast. He'd have the beans, and God knows he loved hot peppers, and then after luncheon he'd just throw himself down on the grass and rest until he was called. Then he'd get right up and go, and he'd look skinnier than anybody else.

Now I would pack in the food, every bit of it, and I'd feel my costume getting tight. When they called me on the set, I'd say "Just a minute till I let my costume out."

---

* Richard Boleslavky was directing *Operator 13*, a Civil War story.

Hollywood Revue of 1929.

Polly of the Circus.

Going Hollywood.

Clark Gable was very fine to work with, and he didn't upstage. You get some leading men who want to steal the whole scene, but those four—Bing, Gary, Clark and Bob Montgomery—were fine to work with. I hope the rest of the hundred thousand leading men I had won't be jealous.

Everyone knew I was scared of horses, and in this one scene they had a lot of horses on the set. I was in the bungalow, and there was a long street, and I could see the stage about a block and a half off.

I was upstairs refreshing my makeup when I heard a noise, a clattering, and I looked out. I saw Raoul Walsh and Bing Crosby on two white horses. So I screamed down, "Lock the door!" It saved my life. They were feeling pretty high, and they were going to bring the horses right into my living room.

It would have been very funny, but I defeated them. I anticipated the punch line.

Marie Antoinette was the straw that broke the camel's back at MGM. W.R. wanted me to do it, and I was going to try my best. I wasn't sure I could make the grade, but I read all the histories about Marie Antoinette and went through the whole routine, and I could visualize myself as Marie Antoinette with a big white wig and an upturned nose. We were both disappointed.

He had wanted me to play Juliet, and I'd practiced that. Of course W.R. thought everything I did was wonderful. He said, "You're perfect for Juliet, because Juliet was a blonde, you know. She was not a brunette." But the studio said no. They said, "No. No. No. No

Juliet for Marion—she's a comedienne."*

The same happened with *The Barretts of Wimpole Street*. I couldn't be a sick, consumptive Elizabeth Browning, because, they said, "Marion's too lively. She's got to do comedy."

I was frustrated at each end. W.R. was much more mad than I was. He said, "I don't want you to ever have anything more to do with the MGM studio." We went down the road—but fast.

More literally, it was over the hills to Burbank. Marion's bungalow was also moved, in pieces, to the Warner Brothers studio.

I don't think Louis B. Mayer minded losing me so much. He did mind losing Mr. Hearst, if you know what I mean. Later he said to me, "We have lost our queen." What he meant was he had lost the power of the chess game—the visitors—and the press.

I went up to San Simeon and Jack Warner kept calling.** He was really very kind. I don't think I ever worked for anybody nicer, except Mr. Mayer. But I felt shy. I wouldn't go to the studio. When he called, I'd say no. "I'm sorry. I'll go when you present the script and we okay it." I said, "Let's do our rehearsing up here."

Jack said, "Oh, no. Now look, have a heart."

I said, "I'm terribly shy. Let's do it all here, and when it's ready, I'll come in the back door."

"You're homesick for MGM."

---

* Irving Thalberg produced, and his wife Norma Shearer, a brunette, played Juliet.

** He wanted to start production on *Page Miss Glory*, in 1935.

Marion with Sammy White in a dance sequence from *Cain and Mabel*. Clark Gable was Marion's leading man in this one.

Jack Warner was really very kind. I don't think I ever worked for anybody nicer, except Louis B. Mayer. This picture of Marion and Jack was taken at the Spanish Fiesta birthday party for W.R. in 1936.

Left: A Warner Brothers advertisement for *Ever Since Eve.*

I said, "It isn't that. It's just that I've got stage fright." And I really did.

We had the costumes all arranged up at San Simeon. Then I finally came down for my first test. I tried to crawl in the back way, but I couldn't. He had locked the back entrance, and I had to come in the front way.

Nobody molested me. I was perfectly all right. That was the trouble; they gave me the air. I had gone too far. I got the freeze-out. Nobody would talk to me. And I thought they'd like me for staying away, but they didn't like that at all. They thought I was a snob. When we started the production, it seemed awfully cold. I wasn't used to that. I was used to warmth.

I was only frightened because I thought I was really a lousy actress and that they were all good. I don't think they knew what stage fright was. I would sit in my dressing room by myself.

When you go to a new studio, you feel at a disadvantage. They're not wise to your little tricks, the little pranks you play. They think you're so nice, at least for a while. Then they find out that you're really an imp, that you try everything under the sun to wreck everything as far as it possibly can be wrecked.

I was only at Warners' studio for two years. I was supposed to stay longer, but I felt that I had worked long enough, and I wanted some time off for myself. Although I was only making two pictures a year, I couldn't enjoy myself. Even though I could travel for about three months a year, when I knew I had to get back to the studio by a certain date and that I couldn't eat too much or get sunburned or freckled, I couldn't really have a good time.

There was always a sign: NO FOOD ALLOWED ON THE SET—AND NO DRINKS. But I used to give the boys on the set beer and sandwiches. And Clark used to buy them ice cream cones all the time. They worked hard, and we didn't stop at five o'clock, exactly. "But," somebody would say, "we've got to go." And I'd say, "Well, anybody who wants to stay on gets beer and sandwiches." A little coaxing; that was all.

Over at Warner Brothers, in the summertime, it was 148 degrees up in the flies, where the electricians were, and it was 122 on the stage. Ice cream was quite efficacious, and Clark used to bring it every day.

The girls would faint on the set, even though they had those big airplane propellers with ice in front of them. They would faint like dead flies.

I had on a fur costume and had to do dances. They were taking bets on me. A lot of them lost, even the time I was up on the top with this Madame Pompadour number. They had to put ice on my wrists and chain me to the rail. I was just on a shelf, and I'd look down and think, Uh-oh. But I was used to the heat, because I had been in the *Follies* in the summertime with fur costumes. So it didn't bother me much, but I didn't dare look down. I kept looking up, and all I saw was the top of the stage. I was up there about an hour and a half; really, it was Purgatory.

Then the music started, and I felt the lights going on me, and I hiccupped. I was roasting. I kept wondering, How long is this going to last?

Finally, it took ladders to get me down. The costume alone weighed about fifty-six pounds. And the assistant director had told them to keep their shirts on because I was on the set, but I said, "Take everything off—including your pants." And they did. I was wild

I thought the least I could do for a man who had been so wonderful and great, one of the greatest men ever, was to be a companion to him.

because I knew how hot it was up there.

What made me finally decide to quit was something that happens to everybody. If you're a dramatic actress, you want to do comedy; and if you do comedy, you want to be a dramatic actress. I had big ideas for myself. I even wanted to do Shakespeare, even when I innately knew I couldn't do it. I thought I could do dramatics, but the other people didn't. And they were right.

Not that I was a comedienne, either. I just did stories with comedy in them. It was the story that counted, not the one doing the story. You're only as good as the story is written, and no better.

I also thought that if I ever wanted to go back to work again, I could always do so. But I never did want to go back.

I wanted to take life easy, and once you get used to the lazy way of living, you find out that you rather enjoy it. So I quit.

I did miss the studio for a while. When I had nothing else to do, I'd go back. It was postman's holiday; I'd go see how the other animals performed. We'd have a luncheon someplace, too. I got over that after a while.

Of course, W.R. had wanted me to quit a long time before I did, so there would be plenty of time for travel. He didn't know what to do with himself. And there's nothing more interesting in the way of pleasure or occupation than having something to do.

When you're working, you keep thinking of taking a long vacation and forgetting the whole thing. When you make the change, you have to make up your mind not to go back to the rut. I liked to have a good time, so I never went back.

I'd go to San Simeon, then to Wyntoon, then back to Los Angeles, and keep going back and forth. We didn't go to Europe again [after 1937]. But we had the beach house, and we went to Chicago once or twice, and I think we went to Florida one year. But I didn't care for it there. It had once been nice, but it wasn't anymore.

For a while I was trying to kid myself along that I didn't miss working. I could always go visit the studio and say, "I feel sorry for you . . ." They had to get up early, go through scenes hundreds of times, and get so tired they couldn't eat, just flop into bed. My happiest days had been on the stage. I had had more fun on the stage than in the movies. Not fun, exactly, but the exhilaration and excitement and the music and the glamour. Of all the things I did, that's what I liked the most.

That was when I was most insignificant. And that was why I liked it the best. I had no responsibility. I just held up the backdrops.

But the publicity pushed me along. I won't say that I was successful, because I don't know whether I was successful or not. I don't think anybody actually knows. That's up to the box office. But according to Mr. Mayer and Mr. Warner, there were no complaints on that score.

The old saying is, "It pays to advertise." I suppose that's all right, but I used to feel I had too much. If the producers gain by it, then you can't say you are overpublicized. If I was overpublicized, it hurt only me. It didn't hurt the picture.

When I did decide to get out—I made up my mind just like that—they said, "But you have a contract here."

I said, "I'm sorry. The contract's under the name of Cosmopolitan, and you signed the papers for Cosmopolitan to be released, and I go with it." Oh, was Jack Warner mad. And so was Harry Warner. They said I'd pulled a fast one.

But I just didn't want to work in pictures anymore. I'd been working awfully hard for quite a long time. At that time Mr. Hearst was about seventy-eight or so, and I felt he needed companionship. He was having some financial troubles at the time, too, and he was more upset than people realized.

I thought the least I could do for a man who had been so wonderful and great, one of the greatest men ever, was to be a companion to him.

W.R. cuts his seventy-fifth birthday cake.

11

The Great Depression. An empire endangered. Mr. Hearst's best friend. Hatrick produces a cool million. Marion makes a small loan, and takes two Boston tabloids for collateral. How Johnny put everything right. A tragic plane crash.

While most of the world suffered through the years of the great depression, W.R. continued to buy whatever captured his fancy. He filled warehouses in New York and California with pieces of art which even he could never find a place to show. He had architects working at San Simeon, Wyntoon, St. Donat's and Ocean House, attempting to cope with his expansive nature.

Income from his business ventures was diverted to pay for his reconstructions. His British magazine Good Housekeeping held the title to the castle in Wales.

As the depression and decade of the thirties continued, W.R. became more and more unpopular with the public. Labor and union problems began to afflict his publications.

Taxes also seemed an incredible burden for both W.R. and Marion. She petitioned for reduction of the corporation and income taxes that Roosevelt's administration had raised to new high levels. When the California taxes were raised, W.R. said, "Over 80% of my income will go in taxes—in fact, it may be nearer 90%."

In 1937, W.R. rebelled against the cost of living in California, and took a large party of friends and relatives on what was to be the last of the fabulous European trips.

We had visited Europe and we had gone to Venice. Anybody knows that in Italy you dare not eat vegetables or salad.

Arthur Brisbane knew better, but he ate them anyway, and the next day he developed a terrific fever.

We were at the Excelsior Hotel, on the Lido, and Alice Head, who used to be head of the Hearst magazines in London, was with us. That night the Duke of Valletta, who was supposed to be the next heir to the throne after the King of Naples, was giving a dinner party. Barbara Hutton was there, and many others. I got word that Arthur Brisbane had a raging fever, 106 degrees. But he wouldn't let us get a nurse, so Alice and I decided that I would take the night shift and she would take the day shift. His face was scarlet, but he didn't want any doctor. He was a very stubborn person.

He got up and left Venice one morning on Alec M'divani's* boat. He went from the Lido to Venice and caught a train to Paris. That was about a month before we left. I said, "He went alone?"

Alec said, "He acted very peculiar, because he said, 'I had to come all the way over here from America to get a fever.'"

We went to New York, then we went on to California. After we returned to New York, on Christmas morning [1936] the phone rang and Cissy Patterson said, "A.B. just died."

I said, "Good Lord, Cissy, aren't we in enough trouble? I better not say anything to W.R." But he had heard the phone ringing. He started to cry, because he really liked A.B.

A.B. was a big crook, incidentally, but W.R. liked him. He was the edi-

torial writer and had been the publisher of the [New York] *Mirror*.

Brisbane may have annoyed Marion because she knew he had amassed a twenty-five-million-dollar estate while he had worked for W.R. And he did not live to help W.R. and Marion when times got bad.

A.B. always wore the same suit when he came to see W.R. I used to wonder why, because I saw that he carried a suitcase. When he was staying at the beach house I asked the maid if she was pressing his things. She said, "No. He's got nothing in there but books." I went in his room and looked, and there was nothing but encyclopedias. I had no right nosing around, but I wanted to be sure he had a clean shirt. That doesn't mean he didn't have a great mind. He was brilliant.

He even died reading a book.

Cissy and I went over to his house, and Phoebe opened up the door and said, "Come in." She was smiling. She was half Indian, and they had five or six youngsters. Their daughter Sarah was married to Tex McCrary, who got to be publisher of the *Mirror* and then married Jinx Falkenburg.

There was a bottle of sherry, which was a relief. And they were all happy; they were on the loose. Brisbane had been too much of a disciplinarian. Phoebe said, "Would you like to see Arthur?" Cissy said yes, and we went in. He was lying there with an encyclopedia in front of him. She said, "Doesn't he look wonderful?"

Cissy and I then left. We went to "21" to talk it over and get plastered. That whole family had been tied in a knot for years, and now they were released.

The funeral was at St. Thomas's on Fifth Avenue, and it was revolting. The photographers were going up and

---

* Russian Prince Alexis M'divani had married the twenty-year-old Barbara Hutton, heiress to the Woolworth five-and-ten-cent-store fortune, in 1932. But they had divorced in 1935, before Brisbane died.

   If Ms. Hutton was at the party, as Marion remembers, she was then married to Danish Count Kurt Haugwitz-Reventlow. Later she would marry Cary Grant, then Prince Igor Troubetzkoy of Lithuania, then Porfirio Rubirosa of the Dominican Republic, then Baron Gottfried von Kramm of Germany.

down taking pictures while the service was on. W.R. and Vincent Astor were pallbearers, and there were hundreds of photographers in the church. I felt I was getting sick.

Afterwards we didn't go back to "21"; we went home, to the Ritz Tower. W.R. owned the Ritz Tower and had a huge apartment and offices there.

At the beginning of 1938, W.R. was in very serious financial trouble. His investments in New York City real estate and his boundless appreciation of art had caused a monumental drain on the finances of his empire.

John Francis Neylan, a trusted advisor to W.R., had been working diligently to try to stave off disaster, but he had resigned by this time, saying he was worn out. He had lost the strength to say no to W.R. Marion saw it differently. She thought Neylan was the villain.

In desperation, late in 1937, W.R. had relinquished financial control of the empire. He retained editorial control, but Clarence J. Shearn assumed responsibility for managing the business, with its debts of $126,000,000. Shearn immediately began cutting the losses. He shrank the size and number of publications and liquidated the real estate and collections of art. Still the financial problem persisted.

Canadian newsprint prices rose from $40 to $45 per ton. The increase meant $5,000,000 per year in additional costs to the Hearst Corporation.

W.R. was going to be sold down the river by the people he had placed his great faith in. He always misjudged people.

They were trying to get the control, but he didn't know it until it happened, and he was shocked. He was a broken man; he couldn't believe that the peo-

ple he had practically made would ever do a lousy trick like that to him.

When we had come back from Europe in 1937, they were piling up bank loans on him, trying to break him and take over. But thank God we came through all right.

The main one responsible was Jack Neylan, who had been in San Francisco and was put in charge of the financial end. Once he had made a statement to a very good friend of mine, saying, "If it's the last act of my life, I'm going to break Hearst in half."

W.R. had thought he had found his best friend in Jack Neylan. But he was the one who had arranged for the whole thing to collapse. I had heard W.R. say, "You, too?" And I thought, *Et tu, Brutus?* That was his best friend, the great, wonderful Holy Roman Catholic, John Francis Neylan, the biggest crook that God ever created.

Frances Marion knew him very well. She told me that one time he had come up to San Simeon and went over and hid in House B or C and didn't appear for four or five days. He used to go on awful benders.

She said she was there one night when he was loaded. He staggered into the living room and said, "Where is Hearst?'

Frances said, "I don't know where Mr. Hearst is. I always refer to him as Mr. Hearst, because I worked for him for a long time and I have great respect for him."

He said, "I call him Hearst."

She told him he was drunk and should go to bed. And he said, "I'll get that son-of-a-bitch if it kills me." Frances Marion asked why. He said, "Because I've always hated his guts."

She told me that a long time afterwards. I'd only just met him. He had a big bloated red Irish nose, and he was nearsighted and horrible.

He was the type of black Irishman

who was jealous of anybody he thought was a little more powerful than himself. W.R. had been very kind to him. He had made him what he was.

I found out about all that business complication mess because I was just going to the studio to finish one last scene, when Bill Hearst arrived at the house and said, "Where's the chief?" It was very early in the morning, but he said, "I think I'll go up and see Pop."

"Look, I don't think it's kind to wake him this early in the morning."

"This is a very serious matter. The empire's crashing."

"What?!"

"We need a million dollars, and the chief has to go east immediately."

It was an awful shock. I said to him, "Well, I'm going with him. But first, I have to go to the studio." But I thought I'd call the studio and say I'd be a little late. I called up my business manager, Edgar Hatrick, and said, "Get me a million dollars right away. I want to sell everything I've got—everything." And he did; he worked like mad, and he met me at the railroad station and gave me a certified check.

I hadn't talked to W.R. I thought: Why have him tortured, for a miserable million dollars, when he was worth three hundred million?

He was very worried, and after we had dinner in the dining car, he said, "I guess I'm through." They had said they were very sorry, but everything was going to crash. They owed over fifty million dollars to a bank in Toronto, and the bank was going to take everything over.

When I told him about the check I had, he said, "Don't give it to me. I'll tear it up. Anyway, what's a million dollars when there's fifty million dollars involved?"

I had a good answer for that. "Why are there only fifty million dollars in-

volved when there are three hundred million dollars involved?" I'm not good at arithmetic.

When W.R. wouldn't take my check, I went in and presented it to Tom White, the president of the Hearst Corporation. He was in the drawing room with Richard Berlin and Bill Hearst. Tom didn't want the money.

I said, "I heard you say that was all that was needed."

He said, "Well, it can't help." He meant well and, to be kind, he said, "It isn't a bad idea."

I said, "Now don't say anything to Mr. Hearst about this. He doesn't know about this."

But he knew better. "He does know, doesn't he? He wouldn't take it."

I said, "Take it. At least it will be a chance for you all to get your breath, to reason things out."

Tom said, "Well, God bless you—that's sweet."

At the Ritz Tower in New York, W.R. gathered everybody but me together for a conference in my drawing room. I heard the argument going on, and I hoped nobody would open that door. If they had, I'd have fallen in.

W.R. said, "We have to give Miss Davies some collateral for this. I don't want to take the money without collateral."

So they picked the two papers that were in the red—the two Boston tabloids. They were losing God knows how much money.

W.R. said no. "We'll give her the magazines." But they wouldn't let him.

Earlier, Joe Kennedy had offered W.R. fourteen million for those magazines, but since the magazines made fourteen million a year, I had said, "Don't accept it."

That was one thing I liked about W.R.—he had no idea of money at all. It didn't make any difference to him. But to be caught in a trap like that—

HEARST'S NEWSPAPERS IN 1936

Newspaper	Circulation		Time	Estb.	Editor	Publisher
	Daily	Sunday				
Albany Times	46,008	61,808	Morn	1853	G. O. Williams	Albany Evening Union Co.
* Atlanta (Georgia) American	84,459	191,600	Evg	1906	W. S. Kirkpatrick	American Newspapers, Inc.
* Baltimore News-Post	204,872	233,354	Evg	1872	Wm. Baskerville	American Newspapers, Inc.
Boston American	249,568		Evg	1904	A. L. Southwick	New England Newspaper Publishers
Boston Record	308,121		Morn	1813	J. P. Murphy	North Eastern Publishing Co.
Boston Sunday Advertiser		513,325	Sun	1904	J. A. Mallay	New England Newspaper Publishers
Chicago Evening American	437,842		Evg	1900	F. J. McCarthy	Evening American Publishing Co.
Chicago Herald-American	364,491	1,029,566	Morn	1881	G. A. DeWitt	Illinois Publishing & Printing Co.
* Detroit Times	306,784	397,214	Evg	1920	A. E. Dale	Times Publishing Co.
* Los Angeles Examiner	195,099	531,749	Morn	1903	R. T. Van Ettisch	L. A. Examiner Publishing Co.
* Los Angeles Herald-Express	284,245		Evg	1911	J. B. T. Campbell	Frank F. Barham
Milwaukee Sentinel	106,565	178,574	Morn	1837	Julius Liebman	Paul Block
* New York Evening Journal	683,739		Evg	1896	Wm. A. Curley	New York Evening Journal, Inc.
New York Mirror	554,939	1,183,349	Morn	1924	Emile Gauvieau	A. J. Kobler
* Oakland Post-Enquirer	54,571		Evg	1886	Howard H. Krueger	Post-Enquirer Publishing Co.
Omaha Bee News	48,703	121,982	Morn	1871	F. S. Hunter	Bee News Publishing Co.
	47,561		Evg			
* Pittsburgh Sun-Telegraph	164,531	390,778	Evg	1927	Royal Daniel, Jr.	Pitt Publishing Co.
Rochester American		77,483	Sun	1922	Ralph Young	Rochester News Corp.
Rochester Journal	48,300		Evg	1922		
* San Antonio Light	56,367	89,074	Evg	1881	N. D. Allison	Light Publishing Co., Inc.
* San Francisco Call-Bulletin	119,766		Evg	1856	J. A. Muzcahy	Call Publishing Co.
* San Francisco Examiner	168,700	431,959	Morn	1880	C. S. Stanton	Examiner Printing Co.
* Seattle Post-Intelligencer	98,189	208,687	Morn	1865	A. E. Dunning	Post-Intelligencer Co.
Syracuse American		110,874	Sun	1922	F. H. Hosmer	Syracuse Newspapers, Inc.
Syracuse Journal	63,479		Evg	1839		
Washington (D.C.) Herald	101,234	195,242	Morn	1906	Eleanor Patterson	American Newspapers, Inc.

* Controlled by Hearst Consolidated Publications, Inc.
Data accumulated from Ayer & Son's American Newspaper Annual and Directory For 1936 and Moody's Analysis of Investment for 1936.

he felt helpless. He didn't know what to do. He was absolutely a beaten man.

He didn't want to accept my money, but nobody else would step forth, even though the boys had trust funds, and the old woman had twenty times more than I had.

I went back to my room. W.R. walked in and told me about the Boston papers. I said, "I don't want any collateral."

He said, "Well, you've got to take them. I don't think it's any good, but they seem to think this is all right. I know it isn't, and I want to get you some decent collateral."

I said, "Listen, if that's what's worrying you, I'll take it. As long as I don't have to pay the expenses of what is in the red."

I got the Boston papers for collateral,* and those were the worst papers in the whole syndicate; they were stinkers. But the next day Walter Howey came to me and said, "Hey, boss, I'm going to Boston, and I'm going to take those papers out of the red."

Well, he did. It took him four months. They went way high in the black, and then they were begging me to give back the collateral. They wanted those two papers for the chain. They said they'd give me some of the money now and the rest later. I said, "You were quick enough to give them to me when they were in the red," but I added, "All right—take them."

It was a plot. They had it all planned. No doubt about it. It was ludicrous that we couldn't even borrow a million dollars. Later they said they needed more money. And I got him some more money. Rose and Ethel and I turned the money over from my grandmother's trust fund. When I see anybody in trouble, I'll fight like hell to get them out. Especially someone I love very much.

If they had really foreclosed on him and demanded all fifty million dollars, he'd have been sunk. They weren't smart. They didn't figure on me at all. They thought I was just a nonentity, a dullard, a stupid who sits in the corner with a dunce cap.

After that they hated me.

Meantime the Chase National Bank was moving in. I knew Babs Rockefeller very well, and Winnie and Nelson, too. I went to see Winthrop, but he wouldn't see me. I asked Babs, but she said, "I can't do anything with him."

W.R. then got a lawyer called Clarence Shearn, who got a loan from the Chase National Bank.

Shearn was an old friend of Mr. Hearst's. He said, "I will save your life . . ." One of those things. Lifesavers. You buy them in a package, but they don't do you any good.

Shearn was a little bit vicious. One day he called us at San Simeon and said he was in Santa Barbara and wanted to see W.R.

We went down for a conference at the Biltmore Hotel. I said, "Hello, Clarence . . . you know, it's an amazing thing, but you resemble Napoleon."

"Do I?"

I said yes. "In a way. Because you always scratch your chest. But as far as looks are concerned, you stink."

"You're just kidding."

"Not exactly," I said. "Look, Napoleon, would you have strength enough to go and get me a drink?"

"I'd be delighted to."

"Make it a pitcher—gin fizzes."

So he went off into the hotel, and W.R. said, "You shouldn't talk that way to him."

I said, "I'll crack his skull. I'll take

---

* The minutes of the meetings of the Board of Directors of Hearst's American Newspapers, Inc., show for the year 1938 a pledge of 8000 shares of the New England Publishing Company to Marion.

Standing, left to right: Hearst newspapermen Bill Curley, Edmond Coblentz, Frank Barham, Joe Willicombe, Richard Berlin, Tom White, and an unidentified man at Cissy Patterson's house in Washington, D.C., 1938. Seated with W.R. were Clarence Shearn, left, and another guest, thought to be visiting royalty.

him apart if I have strength enough in my hands."

Shearn came back with a pitcher and started talking about the great job he'd done, rescuing W.R.

I said, "Wait a minute, Napoleon. I'm here and I'm listening." He was telling W.R. what to do. I said, "You know, Clarence, you're beautiful. Anybody ever tell you you're beautiful?"

Well, W.R. finally got wise to him and fired him. He realized he was trying to take over the power. I think he was asking for a personal settlement of five or six hundred thousand dollars, and he finally got about three hundred thousand before he left. He was really abominable.

He used to call up the newspapers and tell them he didn't like the editorials or he didn't like the way the presses were running. He thought he was William Randolph Hearst.

When Clarence J. Shearn joined the effort to rescue the Hearst Corporation, he was an attorney and the counsel for the Chase Manhattan Bank, which held some of the notes. To restore the empire to profitability, he began to liquidate those newspapers which lost money. Some were merged, some closed. He sold the radio stations.

He cut salaries, including W.R.'s. That was reduced from $500,000 a year to $100,000. He ordered the sale of the

203

overinflated real estate holdings, and auctioned more of the art collection. St. Donat's Castle was put on the market.

For four years Shearn worked with the Conservation Committee to keep the organization together, but it was difficult for Marion to measure their accomplishments. She saw W.R. giving up his treasures and forgoing pleasures.

When some signs of new life were detected, W.R. thought he should again have complete control of his empire. But the Delaware chancery court rejected his suit on the grounds that the creditors must agree to a change in power. Shearn remained until 1944.

Marion says she suggested bringing in John W. Hanes. She had met him in New Haven, when she was a showgirl and he was, quite literally, a stage-door Johnny. He had become a banker and also an official of the U.S. Treasury Department—just what she thought they needed. Hanes joined the Committee and took on the task of restructuring the empire, sprawled among ninety-four separate entities. And he was able to resolve some of the tax problems.

Then Johnny Hanes came in and took over and things went fine from there on. But there was so much to that story, it was fantastic. We'll have to go over everything before it's printed.

I'd known Johnny since I was about three, and he had a great financial mind. Even though he had a southern drawl, he was still brilliant. And I suggested him.

W.R. had never heard of him, but I wanted him. He whipped things into order without being the master. He settled the financial problems beautifully when nobody else could have helped. Johnny pulled W.R. right out of the mess.

Once, while all this was going on, we were on the balcony at the Ritz Tower and W.R. said to Martin Huberth,* "What's that building over there?"

Martin said, "That's the Heckscher Building."

W.R. said, "Buy it."

"How can you when you haven't even got fifty cents in your pocket?"

"I have more than that . . ."

He had fifty cents in his pocket, so he wanted to buy the Heckscher Building, a great big edifice.

The twenty-five-story building on Fifth Avenue, occupying the block between 56th and 57th Streets in Manhattan, was for sale in 1938 for $4,250,000. But W.R. didn't buy it.

This was in the midst of that crisis, and he asked him that for a purpose. He wasn't being facetious. He just wanted to find out what the reaction would be. He was very smart and it was a very subtle way of testing somebody. Martin Huberth was very fine during the whole thing.

I'm not really sure where I did get that million dollars. Mr. Hatrick handled it. I thought I had borrowed it from Louis B. Mayer, but maybe it was from Jack Warner. It's too bad I didn't write a diary. But I don't believe in diaries.

Louis B. Mayer used to say, "I loaned you money." But I don't think he did. I thought I worked a year for nothing. Of course, when you worked for Louis B. Mayer it was nothing anyway, so what was a year?

That was a false idea that Louis B.

---

* A friend and confidant of W.R., Mr. Huberth was a real estate expert. He was appointed to the Conservation Committee and liquidated some of the Hearst real estate properties at the time of the financial crisis. His company, Huberth and Huberth, at 488 Madison Avenue, still manages the real estate affairs of the Hearst Corporation.

Mayer put in my head, and I hope his horse lost in the races. He told everybody that story and I was not at his studio at that time.

I didn't borrow from any studio. I had some stocks and some money from my grandfather and my mother. I just told Mr. Hatrick, "I don't care what you do—but get me a million dollars in a hurry." And he did. He didn't approve of what I was doing. But I was making a huge salary and it wasn't any too difficult.

Hatrick sold at a discount some of the many bonds in Marion's portfolio, and thus raised the money.

I was at Warner Brothers and I know I didn't get it there. Harry Warner wouldn't spend a nickel to see an earthquake.

Marion might have anticipated tremors when Robert Maynard Hutchins visited San Simeon. He had become president of the University of Chicago in 1929, at age thirty, and he remained in that office for seventeen years. Then he became chancellor of the University.

Renowned as the enfant terrible of education, he had, by the time he met Marion, degrees from Yale, Harvard, Tulane and West Virginia universities, and from Lafayette, Oberlin, Williams and Berea colleges.

Later he would have at least a dozen more honorary degrees. He had also passed the Chicago bar and had been elected to Phi Beta Kappa before becoming a director of the Ford Foundation and subsequently chief executive of the Fund for the Republic at the Center for the Study of Democratic Institutions in Santa Barbara, California.

Robert Hutchins came up to the ranch. He was the president of the University of Chicago at the time and a stranger to me. Cissy Patterson was there, and I think Mrs. Robert Hammond Hayes Smith from San Francisco, along with Mayor [James] Curley from Boston.

Hutchins, on my right, said to me, "Why aren't you eating any meat?"

I said, "I'm a theosophist."

He said, "Do you know what that means?"

"I suppose it means not to eat any meat."

I guess I was wrong. He said, "Very stupid." Then he said, "Can you play ping-pong?" I said yes.

After dinner we went outside and played. He gave an upper serve and hit me. I said, "Don't do that. That's not allowed."

He said, "How would you know? You're so stupid."

I said, "Well, I know that in ping-pong, the serve should be underhanded."

Then Cissy Patterson walked in. She said, "How dare you insult the hostess? You belong to the brain trust." And then they had a brilliant argument and she cut him down to size.

Marion and sisters Ethel and Rose in 1939.

205

He finally said, "There's only one intelligent person here."

I said, "Who is that?" He looked at my sister Rose, who was not too bright. Rose took his part against me.

I went into the powder room and started to cry because I thought I had done something wrong. But I hadn't. I couldn't cope with brains like that. His brains were too big for his head. Cissy said, "I'll fix him."

The next morning Dr. Hutchins said, "I'm leaving."

"So soon?" I said. "I thought you'd stay over the weekend."

He said, "No. I'm leaving." And he did. Cissy had told him to leave because he'd insulted me. He hadn't insulted me, just hurt my feelings, but I suppose his retort was, "How can you insult a person who has no intelligence?"

Right before the war, the president of the Philippines* was up. He found out, by the grapevine route, that we had two Filipino cooks, and they were the first people he wanted to see. I thought that was rather sweet.

The cooks were so flustered that they mixed everything up. I couldn't tell what kind of food we got, they were so excited. It tasted good, whatever it was.

W.R. loved to cook. He made scrambled eggs wonderfully. He could cook most anything. I would wash the dishes and he would dry them, or vice versa.

We worked by ourselves. We didn't need the staff of about fifty or sixty. We lived quite simply.

We'd do the jigsaw puzzles for hours

in the main living room. Twenty of us would be around and we'd pick out the pieces. It was childish, and I wouldn't do it now; it's awfully hard on the eyes. But we had a big table and everybody'd get in and there'd be arguments and little flirtations because the men would get in and pick out a piece for a girl and give her a wink. We had hundreds of puzzles.

It was fascinating. It was also a good way to waste time.

We used to look at my own films. Most of the other people were so bored they'd go to bed. And afterwards, after a late evening, Mr. Hearst would make Welsh rabbits and biscuits and coffee. He would get a big pan and put the cheese in it and then he'd bring it in and serve it.

One night I was so hungry for one and he put one next to me and I was talking to somebody. I thought, Will this woman ever stop talking? And when I reached for mine, it was gone.

Gandhi had eaten the whole Welsh rabbit. I saw him licking at the rest of the plate. I was so mad and I asked for another one, but W.R. said, "Sorry— they're all gone."

I said, "But Gandhi ate mine."

He said, "He'll be sick."

Gandhi wasn't sick. He was healthier than I was. I was sick because I didn't have one.

My father moved to California after my mother died. He came out for the funeral, then he went back east. He was still a magistrate then and had a job to do. But after about a year I asked him if he wouldn't like to come out and stay.

His first answer was no; but he finally did come out. However, he didn't like it; it wasn't the same life

---

* Manuel Quezon was the first president of the Philippines, elected in September 1935. A U.S. Governor General, Frank Murphy, from Detroit, had been the executive prior to that election.

206

that he had in New York with the court and all his cronies. But after going back east for a while, he came out again, saying, "New York is not the same."

I guess all his friends had died. He stayed at the Lexington Road house in Beverly Hills with my sisters and my niece and nephew.

It was an amazing thing: My mother had died when she was fifty-two, and my father was twenty-two years older than she was. He died when he was eighty-two, I think, but he said he was seventy-eight. Rosie said he told her he was eighty-seven, and my niece said he told her he was ninety-eight. I never figured out exactly how old he was. He died* when I was making my first movie at Warner Brothers, *Page Miss Glory*.

The trouble with people who fib, like my father, is that you tell everybody a different story and you expect them to believe it. I guess I took after him, that way.

He didn't do work when he came out to California. He met the magistrates and went around with them. He'd get dressed and go out wearing spats. I'd say, "What have you got spats on for?"

He'd say, "Because I belong to the gay nineties."

He'd take his cane, but he didn't walk with it; he'd twirl it around. He even wore a monocle. He was very suave.

He got along fine with W.R., because W.R. would just be perfectly quiet and let my father talk. W.R. knew that nobody could argue with him. It was just like when he was on the bench; his mind was always full of politics, the Constitution and the Civil War.

He came to the studio now and then

to watch the movies being made. He didn't like Hollywood at all. I hate to use a four-letter word, but he didn't think much of the movies. He thought that it was all very *dull*.

My father didn't particularly like San Simeon. He was a kind of wry, independent character who was not impressed by anybody.

He would gather all the younger girls around him and tell the darnedest fibs about when he was in the Civil War. He wanted an audience. He told a story about how he pulled General Burnside's whiskers off by mistake as he was riding along with a message. They all believed it, but if he had been in the Civil War he'd have had to be a hundred and seventy years old.*

I didn't know he was bribing them all the time. On Christmas Day, the year before he died, I went downstairs to have some breakfast, and they all said, "Your father gave us each a hundred dollars."

"Oh, how wonderful," I said.

There were a lot of those young flibbity-gibbities, girls around eighteen or nineteen. I thought that was all right, and I wondered what he was going to give me.

When I went to my room, my father's valet, John, knocked on the door and gave me a note. There was a five-dollar bill in it. I was furious. I went over to House B and said, "What is this for?"

He said, "It's your Christmas gift."

I said, "What nerve you have, Dad. You give all these girls a hundred dollars each, and you give me five."

He said, "What's wrong with that? They need it and you don't."

I had no answer to that. I thought of saying, "Maybe you need it more than

---

* On April 26, 1935, when Marion's father died, he was just past his eighty-second birthday.

* Not exactly. Papa Ben was born in 1853 and would have been eleven years old when the Civil War ended. Many a drummer boy became a veteran at that age.

I do," but I didn't dare, because he was so right. He was a Solomon, all right. He could judge things.

My father was very active until about two weeks before he died. It was cirrhosis of the liver, or something. I'm not quite certain. He was buried in the Hollywood Cemetery, where we had a mausoleum. We had more than half the family wiped out within two years. First my mother, then my niece, then my father, then Reine and then Ethel. The dates I don't actually know. I just thought it was only a few years when the whole family was wiped out.

Irene (Reine) was born in 1886 and died in 1938.

Ethel was born in 1889 and died in July 1940.

Charlie was born in 1891 and died in 1906.

Rose Marie was born in 1895 and died September 20, 1963.

Marion was born January 3, 1897, and died September 22, 1961.

Bernard J. Douras was born April 14, 1853, and died April 26, 1935.

Rose Reilly was born in 1862 and died January 25, 1928.

Dorothy Plunket called me from Los Angeles. We were at the ranch and it was winter.* She was a guest of Sylvia and Doug Fairbanks, and she said she wanted to see me.

"I'm only going to be here one or two days—do you mind if we fly up?" she said. She was with her husband Terry [Lord Conyngham] and she said, "We have another guest [bobsled champion James Lawrence] with us. Is it all right if we bring him along?"

"Certainly," I said.

"Would you send the airplane down for us? We have no way of getting there."

I said yes, "But, look, Dorothy, don't leave Los Angeles later than two, because the fog starts rolling in. It's treacherous on the cliffs."

She said she wouldn't. I was with Dorothy Mackaill, who was beating me at gin rummy, and no one else was at the ranch except Mr. Hearst, and he was resting that afternoon. When I thought the Plunkets should have arrived—it only took an hour to fly up—I went down to the phone in the office. I looked out the window and the sky was very bad.

I rang the man at the teletype, Jack Adams, because he could radio the airplane. He said, "Well, I don't know. They should be in by now." I told him to try to get a message to the pilot to explain that the ceiling was low. He said he'd try.

Then I heard the sound of a motor over the ranch and I said, "My God, that's the plane. It must be." It was way up over the castle. I called back to Jack. He said, "For God's sake, hang up—he's in trouble. Hang up! I'm trying to call him. He can't come in!"

I hung up, but he couldn't make contact. Something was wrong. I rushed down to the plaza, but I couldn't hear the motor anymore. I said, "I wonder what happened? Maybe he's gone back to Santa Maria or San Luis." The next thing I heard was this terrific sound. He had tried to land, but thinking they would hit a mountain, he had given the damn thing the gun and it had gone shooting up and then straight on down, in a nosedive. Then I saw the flames.

The whole thing was in flames. The fire department started going like mad, but it was too late. They were gone, burned to death. Only Lawrence was saved.

The reason he got out was that the plane hit the ground at the tail end, breaking in half, and he was tossed

208

Marion in *Five and Ten*. She was wealthy enough to lend a million dollars to W.R. when he needed it in the crisis of 1938.

out. One of the rental cars was going by, and Steve, the rental man, saw all of the smoke and Lawrence lying there in flames. He hopped out and beat the flames off and saved him. Lawrence was in the hospital for a year. There was nothing left of the rest of them but their heads, so they told me.

Then I called up Doug Fairbanks and I said, "Get up here quickly. Something terrible has happened. Will you call Fanny Ward?"*

Doug said, "What happened?"

"Dorothy and Terry were killed. They were late."

"Yes, she was late. They didn't get to the airport until almost three."

"I wish to God you'd phoned me— or somebody'd phoned me—I'd have told her not to go at that time."

Well, Doug got up there as fast as he could. Then he said, "You have to call Fanny."

"I can't do it," I said. "I'm a nervous wreck." I had fainted when the plane crashed—the only time in my life I'd ever fainted. I just fell right down on my back, and Dorothy Mackaill was running around, yelling for somebody.

I was just a wreck. To look at a crash, to know that your friends are in it, is a terrible experience. Well, I called Fanny in Palm Beach. I didn't ask to talk to her; I spoke to her husband, Jack Dean. I didn't know her very well, just slightly, and I hadn't seen her for a long time. I told him what had happened and he said, "Oh my God— well, you've got to tell Fanny . . . I can't." So again it was up to me.

I was so darn nervous I could hardly open my mouth. "I have some bad news for you," I stuttered. Then I told her. She started to scream.

It was about two days later that we had to go to the funeral. There was an awful flood. The Los Angeles River

was up to the bridge. We weren't allowed over the bridge. We had been to the funeral for the Plunkets and were supposed to go to Glendale for the pilot's funeral, and they were waiting.

We couldn't get to the pilot's funeral. Nobody was allowed in Glendale.

In Long Beach a bridge had been washed away and a man was electrocuted, and in Santa Monica there were floods in the canyon, and some houses were washed away. It was very bad.

I didn't get over that shock for quite a long time. It was a terrible thing to see and know two of my best friends were there. It was just another reason why I hated flying—but I hated flying even before then.

Subsequently an instrument-landing system was installed at San Simeon, the first such private installation in the world.

Well, that was at San Simeon.

How often it seemed that in the midst of gaiety and frivolity, the phone would ring. Then there would be tragedy.

A German baron came from Europe on his yacht. Apparently he was an adopted son who was supposed to have murdered his father and taken all the money, but I didn't know that at the time. When he arrived he sent up a letter of introduction from a friend I knew in France. There were about eight in his party, and they had luncheon. Then he asked if we'd go down and have the courtesy of having dinner on his yacht.

Mr. Hearst wouldn't say no, so we went down on the yacht, a fairly big one. A little French girl dressed like a sailor came dashing up. She couldn't speak a bit of English. I don't think she could have been more than fourteen years of age. Well, the baron screamed at her to get out, and I thought it was kind of peculiar.

When we went back to the castle we discovered that we didn't have enough room for his guests and our guests, too, so two people had to go down and stay on the yacht that night.

One was Lloyd Pantages. He told me that in the middle of the night he heard terrible screaming and banging noises. He went to see what was the matter and broke the door down. He found that little girl. She was stark naked and all the sailors were taking a whack at her.

He told me this the next day. I told Harry d'Arrast to get rid of them.

Harry did. They left, and we heard there was a fight on the ship. It was a real mystery ship. The girl had gone completely insane.

Then the baron went to Paris and left her behind. He said he could not take her along.

I talked to W.R. about it and he said, "We'll have to take care of her." I told Harry to tell the doctor to take care of her and that Mr. Hearst would pay her expenses until she was well enough to go home, and then he'd get her home, if she had any family.

But that wasn't all. I got word from the district attorney that the doctor had attacked the girl himself. She was only a kid in a little sailor suit.

The doctor charged W.R. six thousand dollars, but I said, "Don't pay him." I didn't tell him what Harry had told me. It shows how you can get in trouble by just meeting up with strangers. It was the most fantastic thing that ever happened to me, and I was shocked.

If I had known at the time, I'd have had them all arrested. After that Barbara Hutton met the baron, and there were reports that she was going to marry him, but somehow she got out of that all right.

Plenty of romances started there. The watchmen were around, so nobody could do anything off the beam. That was a strict rule. They had to be in their rooms at a certain hour, and nobody could be in anybody else's room.

W.R. was right, in a way. There were young girls, and they could have gotten involved. The moonlight is very efficacious there. He had a place called the Cloister. It was way upstairs, and that was for the girls, next to the library.

The bachelors stayed in the duplexes. There was no connection. Let's not call it Presbyterian, but let's say he was very careful. And there was one good thing about it—nobody stayed too long.

There was a story that someone walked into the swimming pool nude, but it was just a legend. It could never have happened. There were always lights around the pool, and all the watchmen.

W.R. didn't want to have anything happen. He was very, very austere, and he always demanded that the girls wear wraps over their bathing suits. He thought they might catch cold.

It was for his own protection, too. Somebody might get raped or murdered and he'd have been accused. Nobody got away with anything.

Marion.

12

We hadn't been to Wyntoon for a long time, until the war started. We were told to get out of San Simeon, so we went.

San Simeon looked like a birthday cake, and it was a target. I didn't want to go and W.R. didn't want to go, but somebody, the federal government or the state, told us to get out. W.R. said, "If they blow it up, I want to stay with it."

"But I don't," I said. "I don't want to be blown up just for a castle."

W.R. said, "We can go down in the cellar and hide."

"No thanks. Close it all up and let's get to Wyntoon."

W.R. said, "Well, I'm not evading the war."

I said, "I don't want to be shot for no reason." It would have been perfectly okay if I'd had a gun and could fight somebody— which I couldn't, because I'd wiggle. But I didn't see why we should stay right in the line of fire. They could see us from miles away, and W.R. had been the one who first started to write about the yellow peril.

I said, "If they're after anybody, they're after you. They're going to look for San Simeon, and we'll all go up in a blow of smoke." Then we went to Wyntoon.

W.R. ran the papers from there with a wireless and the ticker. We knew when the Japanese got loose one night. They had an internment camp about thirty miles away.

The camp was not for prisoners of war. In a hysterical, now regrettable moment of fear, the government suspended the civil rights of the Nisei communities. Though some efforts were made to repair the damages, many lives were ruined, businesses destroyed and homes seized in the wake of the forced evacuations. There were several camps in California; one of them was near Wyntoon.

One was electrocuted in the electric wire. The rest were headed our way. We had extra guards out; the Japanese hated W.R. at that time. They couldn't have gotten in, but if they had, you know what would have happened to us.

I didn't know what they were complaining about, because they had lovely menus in their camps; I had a copy of the menu. They had the most wonderful breakfasts, and chicken for luncheon, and anything they wanted at night. But still they were dissatisfied. They created a furor all the time, and it was a constant strain all during the war.

The castle at Wyntoon was a wonderful place. W.R. loved it because it had belonged to his mother, but up to that time we had been there only one or two weeks a year. There were watchmen on duty, but one night in 1935 one of them had fallen asleep, and the main house, the Gables, had burned down. We weren't there at the time.

W.R. had rebuilt the whole thing. He should have been an architect. It was simply magnificent. It was like a whole city—half city and half country.

There was the Cinderella House, the Bear House, the Sleeping Beauty House, the River House, the Cottage House, the Honeymoon Cottage, the Chalet, and the Bend. There were nine houses in all, plus the manager's and staff housing.

It was more or less German architecture, but not all Bavarian. And the Bend House was very early American. From there a bridge went over to the main house, the one that had burned down.

Wyntoon was much more beautiful than San Simeon, as far as natural scenery goes. There was a wonderful falls where the McCloud River came right down from the mountains and flowed past each house. Mr. Hearst wrote a poem about it, the "Song of the River"; I think it was the most beautiful thing ever written.

If you wanted to go fishing, you just took a rod and put it out your window and went to sleep. The river was right underneath every window. But there was no boating, because the river was too swift. I loved the sound of the rushing water and the wind in the tall pine trees.

The nights were wonderful for sleeping, with the fireplace blazing. There was a calmness about it that really appealed to me.

The deer were beautiful; they'd dance all around the place. But they would eat the flowers, and of course the gardeners didn't like that.

Our happiest times, I think, were at Wyntoon. It was less formal than San Simeon, and there was more life to it. There were two swimming pools and two tennis courts; a motion picture theatre, and ping-pong and croquet. And the hills were marvelous for riding.

Winter I liked best. The snow came down in white flakes, just like little quarters. But I tried skiing one day and almost broke my leg, so I said, "Nothing doing!"

One night, I was sleeping in my room. I had a Dutch fireplace which was run by electricity. Suddenly I

At Wyntoon there was the Cinderella House, the Bear House, the Sleeping Beauty House, the River House, the Cottage House, the Honeymoon Cottage, the Chalet and the Bend House. At one of W.R.'s birthdays, the cake reproduced this entire village.

heard a bang—smash—bang—smash. The room filled with smoke, and flames were coming out of the stove. I thought I couldn't get out. If I jumped out the window, I'd be in the river and get taken down to Weehawken or someplace at ninety miles an hour.

The flames were getting worse, and I ran into the closet, but I thought I'd better not open the window, because that would create a draft.

I thought I'd get on the balcony if I could, but then I still couldn't jump into the river. Everything was made of wood. I just stayed and trusted fate, and finally the door broke open. It was W.R. He said, "Get out—quickly!"

He had a blanket, and he put it over me and dragged me out. The moment he got me out, there was an explosion. I didn't have any clothes, but I didn't care. I was awfully glad I was out. I'd have stayed there, because I didn't

Overleaf: Wyntoon. *It was more or less German architecture.*

215

know what to do. W.R. saved my life.

It was a short circuit from that stove. The wardrobe caught fire, and it went through to the attic.

The fire at the Bear House turned out to be inconsequential. The big fire was at the main house, the Gables, and that was about two or three months later. It began at about five-thirty one afternoon. I was in the Bear House, reading, per usual. Reading doesn't do me any good, because it does not improve my mentality—whatsoever. When I get into a book I just want to go on turning the pages. I just don't want to get out of it.

I was wondering if W.R. was awake, so I sent for his valet. I wanted something to eat. I had not had any luncheon yet, though I had had breakfast early in the morning.

We had to go way over to the Gables, about a mile away. W.R. was awake, but he didn't want to eat. He thought it wouldn't be a bad idea to wait until dinner. Dinner was at nine, so I said no. "I'd prefer to get something. I'll go in the kitchen and get it myself."

I rang up Joe Willicombe and said, "Look, I'm hungry."

"You can't go near the Gables—it's on fire."

"You're kidding!"

"Don't go near the place—it's crumbling."

"Didn't you notify Mr. Hearst?" I asked.

He said, "Why should I bother him?"

I said, "Oh, Lord . . ."

He really said, "Why should I bother him about a little fire?" And W.R. had all those antiques in the place! I went

The McCloud River, from the River House. *There was a sort of discussion about how fast the river ran and how cold it was. I think it was Joe, Jr., or Jack [Kennedy] who said, "I'll swim across it."*

into W.R.'s room, where he was writing.

We couldn't hear the fire engines, because it was a mile away. I said, "There's a fire at the Gables."

He tried to get Willicombe, but there was no answer. I thought we would take a car and go, but there was no car outside. I had to take it on the run, and it's quite a long run.

Half a mile away you could see the place going up. When I got to the bridge, there was a terrible explosion, and the whole front blew out. Two of the firemen were very badly hurt.

The most fantastic thing was that Walter Howey was asleep at the time, and the smell of smoke woke him. His door was closed, and he got up, opened the door and got the smoke in his face. He sat on the windowsill and went backwards, and landed in the top of a tree and had to be pulled down.

W.R. gave him his own clothes but they hung on him. W.R. was very tall, about six feet two, I think. So with every fire, there's always a laugh.

Carmen Pantages must have lost a hundred thousand dollars' worth of jewelry, but she just thought about a sweater for her daughter. She was only out for two seconds before the whole thing exploded.

One of the guests was the man who owned the New York *Inquirer*. He was in the shower when it happened. He couldn't smell the smoke in the shower, and when he got out and opened the door, it was blazing. He had to run out practically stark naked.

The fire started from an electrical shortage. Right underneath Walter Howey's room, right over the living room. From there, it went up.

That night we had dinner in the kitchenette. W.R. cooked. When somebody wanted something else, they cooked. All we wanted was something to drink, and we got that from the town. Just a little wine, but it helped a bit.

Everyone was sort of depressed.

W.R. was awfully sorry about the guests losing all their belongings, and he got them outfitted immediately. He sent to San Francisco for tailors and dressmakers to come up. And Magnin's sent dresses and suits to replace everything that the guests had lost.

The guests were telling stories, anything to get our minds off the fire. W.R. didn't appear to take it too badly, but I knew he felt bad about it. The only thing left was the big iron chandelier that had belonged to his mother and had been saved from the first fire, in the Castle. All the antiques, all his pottery and silver were gone.

They had tried to get the piano out the window when the fire first started. Instead of thinking about the beautiful paintings and the chinaware and silverware, they had worried about the lousy piano, which didn't amount to anything at all.

W.R. said, "I'll build a better house."

"Next time, make it fireproof," I said, "and don't put in any antiques, and no piano."

The Bear House was the smallest house. It had paintings by Willy Pogany, a great artist. He had painted all those gorgeous paintings of Cinderella on the concrete outside the house.

The Sleeping Beauty House was not yet completed, and the other house was the River House, with all the lovely antiques of the Colonial period.

The guests had the Cottage House on the river, between the river and the road.

The Swiss Chalet was on the right; the staff lived there. That was a beautiful building.

About a mile away from the village was the main house, where we used to have our food. A mile from there was where we watched the motion pictures. That was a very fine old home made of stone and built in 1876.

During the war we used to take the first aid courses, and we'd go to the theatre and bandage someone up. Once we used all our bandages practicing on a very fat man.

We did that for two hours a day, and then we'd do respiration. The women were the nurses, and the men were the specimens we'd practice on.

I think there were more rooms at Wyntoon than there were at San Simeon. We could have a hundred people there; there was plenty of room. The dining hall was not as big, though. It was very simple.

Of course we had a lot of guests all the time. When there weren't too many, we used to sit and play that game the Navy invented, acey-deucey. W.R. always used to win, and I'd get so mad I'd throw the whole thing on the floor and say, "I won't play with you. You cheat."

He would say, "If to win is to cheat, you'd better learn how to cheat." I used to get furious.

The Lindberghs were at Wyntoon during the war. They were charming, but we were pestered by the villagers. They kept calling up, asking if they could have autographs. Knowing how reticent the Colonel was about giving autographs, I thought I'd approach him through Anne.

I said, "There are so many people who adore Colonel Lindbergh—they want his autograph. And yours, too. They're mostly children."

She said, "Children? Well, I'd be delighted."

I told the phone operator to tell the mothers to bring the children out—but for the mothers and fathers not to ask for autographs. I thought there'd be only a few, but there were hundreds.

Anne and the Colonel sat the whole

afternoon—both of them—autographing. They had wanted to talk to W.R. about some important thing, but they spent almost the whole afternoon with the children. It was the sweetest thing I ever saw.

I didn't know what he was talking to Mr. Hearst about. Anytime anybody wanted to have any conversation with him, I'd go out. I think it was something about Russian planes; he wanted to go into active service, but he was disqualified.

He thought that perhaps Mr. Hearst could help him out that way. Roosevelt had turned him down. W.R. did work on it, I think, but there was a peculiar feeling there.

He wanted just to go and fly, like any G.I. boy does. Eventually I think he did, and that was what he wanted.

Anne Lindbergh and Jean MacArthur [the General's wife] looked so much alike, and they had that same sweetness. I would say, if anybody asked me, that they are the two greatest women in the world. No doubt about it.

For all the suffering and tragedy that they had gone through, they were still so pleasant. The theory is that a man is only as good as his wife, or the woman who inspires him.

I believe it to be true.

We had two tennis courts.

We used to have Elizabeth Ryan and Alice Marble and the Englishman that Lorraine Walsh married, Fred Perry, and Frank Shields come in.* We'd have contests.

One champion would take a lousy player, like me, and it was vice versa

on the other side. The only thing you could do when you were on the side of a great tennis player was yell for a chair. You just sat and watched the action going on.

W.R. played in those tournaments. He didn't ask for a chair. He didn't have to. He had the most wonderful forehand drive.

He usually played with Alice Marble, or he played singles. That was awfully hard, and I wouldn't say they were entirely kind to the host, but he did all right.

Of course there were the bridge games and the arguments that went with them. Back and forth. You know how everybody argues over bridge. I figured out that a husband and wife should never play together as partners, because they can have signals. God help the wife or the husband who missed the signal. There were so many fights I decided that we should split partners.

We played a lot of bridge in the afternoon, after the tennis and swimming, when there was nothing else to do.

We never played for money. Sometimes I wish we had, because it would have taught people a lesson. You should not get up against very good players unless you know the game. But gambling was not allowed. You could gamble under the table if nobody caught you. W.R. was against gambling. He said it was bad for the morale and also for the pocketbook.

Maureen O'Hara was up. She made a big decision while she was there. We said to her, "You know, you're a very, very beautiful girl, and you have a great career. But which do you like better? Marriage or a career?"

---

* All were world-famous tournament tennis players in the 1940s.

We were at the big table one afternoon and everybody was needling everybody else. Maureen said, "Nothing in the world will stop me from love. Marriage comes first. I'm not a bit concerned about a career. When you're in love, you don't think about a career."

Well, she got both; she was lucky. And Bill Price hadn't asked her then, but she had decided to marry him.

Barbara Hutton was up there with Cary Grant just before they got married. She was very much in love with him, and I'm positive that he was in love with her. He was very sweet with her. He would say, "How about a walk?"

Barbara doesn't like any exercise at any time. I'm the same way. My exercise is going from chair to chair. She said, "I don't feel like a walk."

Cary said, "Well, let's just go a little way." They'd go off, and the next thing I'd see, he was carrying her in his arms.*

Wyntoon was a romantic place; that was where the romances ripened. You could always see the moon at night.

Cary was always gracious and charming to women. He put women on a pedestal, and some women don't belong on pedestals. I never worked with him, though I wish I had. I knew him a long time. He was a very fine person, with a warmth that was not put on; it came straight from his heart. When he said, "I'm glad to see you," you'd know that he meant it.

He told wonderful stories, mostly Cockney. He had a great sense of humor, and I knew him for quite a long while, and he was always the same.

Barbara always had been the quiet

type. I don't think she was feeling well. She went on a long diet and lost her vitality. I don't think she weighed more than ninety pounds. Very little, she was, and very thin, but very nice. He was crazy about her, and very cute, and they got married right after they left us.

I was sorry when that marriage broke up. But you can't tell whose fault it was.

Joe Kennedy was up to Wyntoon one night. He had just come back from Europe, where he'd been an Ambassador.* He was in a corner with John Boettiger, who was married to Anna Roosevelt.

John Boettiger said to Joe Kennedy, "What right have you to go against the principles of my father-in-law?"

Joe Kennedy said, "Now, wait a minute. I have not in any way said I'm not in accord with what your father-in-law says. Let's not argue now."

Now Anna was getting very uncomfortable. Joe said, "I'm not going to stoop to argue with you."

I said, "Let's have a drink."

Joe Kennedy said, "No, thanks."

He was squaring off with this guy, and it got so hot that Anna said, "Do you mind if we go to the powder room?" We let them fight it out.

In other words, John Boettiger was trying to prove to Anna that he was sticking up for her father, when he was really against him. He was double-twisted, and I could sense it, and I think Anna could, too.

I wasn't quite crazy about John. He was too belligerent. He'd lord it over Anna all the time, acting like a Prussian. She went through hell with him,

---

* It led to the long-standing Hollywood gag about Grant and the dimestore millionairess: Cash and Cary.

* To England's Court of St. James.

One champion would take a lousy player, like me, and it was vice versa on the other side.
The only thing you could do when you were on the side of a great tennis player was yell for a chair.

and he gave her an awful life. He always wanted his martini and a whole Roquefort cheese and all the beer and whiskey, in his room, just for himself.

Joe Kennedy was a very good friend of W.R.'s, and I always liked him. He was a good Irishman.

Two of his sons were with him one time. There was a sort of discussion about how fast the river ran and how cold it was. Nobody could swim in it, but I think it was Joe, Jr., or Jack who said, "I'll swim across it."

We said, "It's impossible—it can't be done," but he did it. He did it even though it was freezing and the current was going like mad.

We were all watching him. I don't think W.R. was there, because he was writing or he was busy, but all the guests went to watch. He went like mad, and he made it just like a little Trojan. It was ice cold there, and very wide, but he did it.

Hamilton Lewis was a visitor at Wyntoon. He said he was suffering very badly with asthma. I think he was a senator.

I don't know where he was a senator from, but he had a toupee and a little red beard mixed with gray.*

I said, "I'll have this infra-red light put in your room, and you just stay under it five minutes, and do the same tomorrow."

He fell asleep, and the light was on for twenty-five minutes. He was almost burned to a crisp. They rang me up at the Gables and said the Senator was very sick and asked for a car. He wanted to leave immediately. I went over and said, "What's wrong?"

He said, "I've got to get out of here. I'm all burned." I think he thought I had a plot against him, but he was just burned a little. I never saw him again.

Ina Claire arrived. She had married what's-his-name—the one eligible bachelor in San Francisco. She had copped him off. They came to Wyntoon, where we were having luncheon. I said, "Let's go see the falls."*

The falls is a place to get lost in. You have to drive over to the River House, and from there on, you walk. You go up a narrow path to a gorgeous falls. I thought I knew the way, because I'd been there so many times.

There were about eight of us. I led the way. They should have known better than to follow me, because I'm no leader. I don't know how to lead myself, much less anyone else.

We were lost for four hours. If I'd known as much then as they told me afterwards, we'd have been all right. They said follow the river and see which way the river goes—then you can get back to where you started. I should have known that theory, but I didn't.

We went over branches and logs. Hope Hearst's legs were scratched. All of our legs were. I broke a toe. Ina Claire said, "I came from San Francisco to have a good time. And look —my shoes and my only suit are ruined."

By then it was getting dark and we couldn't go any further. We might have landed in Oregon for all I knew. Ina said, "You don't know anything, you stupe."

I said, "That's right."

That's right.

---

* James Hamilton Lewis, a resident of Chicago, was U.S. Senator from Illinois, 1931-1937.

* Ina Claire had been a Ziegfeld girl, also a film and stage actress. She was divorced from actor John Gilbert before her marriage in March 1939 to Harvard-educated San Francisco lawyer William R. Wallace.

We sat down and waited for help. Hope said, "Supposing a bear comes around?"

I said, "All you have to do is hug the bear—don't let the bear hug you first." We sat there and Ina worried about her suit.

Everybody was looking for us with flashlights. Eventually we got back all right. I was so tired I went to my room, and after a bath to get the sand out, I went to sleep.

Ina was so furious she left that night. And W.R. didn't get her a new suit and new shoes. He said that we were out on our own that time. He said, "Don't ever do that again unless you know exactly which way the river's running."

I had to give Gandhi a bath and wash his eyes out. I was more concerned about Gandhi than anyone else.

I promised I wouldn't ever do it again. Until the next time.

Two babies were born at Wyntoon. Not that it's of any interest. One was Al Berger's, who was a driver for us; and Lillian, one of the maids, had a child which I'm the godmother of. She called the baby Marion. She had married the butler.

A doctor was up there all the time, a Dr. Dickerman, a surgeon from the Mayo Clinic. One night Harry Ruby's wife, Eileen Percy, got violently ill and was in awful pain. The doctor came and operated. If he hadn't, she'd be dead. Her intestines were all twisted up.

There was a hospital in the town, only fifteen minutes away. They needed it for the mill people.

Bill Lundigan came up, and in the middle of the night I got the call—he was sick. He was screaming in pain,

and I called for Dr. Dickerman. He operated on him for acute appendicitis.

We had three very sad burials there.

The first one was Gandhi, and I never forgot that night. Gandhi was about fifteen, and he'd promised me he'd live to be fifty. He didn't feel well, so I had a nurse take care of him. Gandhi was over at her quarters and he was lonesome for me. And I was lonesome for him, too. He used to stay in bed and warm my feet. That night I felt I'd lost my hot-water bag.

The next day I phoned and asked Marsha, the nurse, to bring Gandhi back. She said, "He's sick."

I went over and found him standing in a little bit of a wicker basket with his head nodding. She said, "All last night he kept walking around and looking and smelling."

"He was looking for me. Why didn't you bring him over?"

"I just had the vet here, and the vet said he's dying."

"Dying?" I said. "Oh, no—not Gandhi." I looked at Gandhi and said, "Come here, fellow." He looked at me, as much as to say, "You left me flat, you bitch."

I said, "How would you like to come back to my house? Providing that you don't do naughties on the floor?" Which he always did. I had to wipe them up, but it was good exercise for me.

The nurse said, "You better wait until the vet comes again."

The vet came and said that Gandhi was pretty sick. He thought he might have eaten something, but Marsha said he hadn't eaten a thing all day. I said, "Take him over to my room—immediately." He wouldn't walk. They wrapped him in a blanket and brought him over, and I put him in bed with me.

W.R. said, "Aren't you going for dinner?"

I said no. "I'm going to stay here with Gandhi. Gandhi's not feeling well."

"Of all the absurd things I've heard!"

"Look, he's my baby. He's not feeling good, so I'm going to stay."

I fell asleep, and when I woke up and moved my feet, there was crap. Gandhi was at the bottom of the bed, and he had crapped in it.

I took Gandhi, put him on the floor and took the sheet and cleaned it off and washed my feet and got the bed all fixed and got in again.

Gandhi was insulted because he was on the floor, and he kept looking at me. The vet came in, with the nurse and W.R.

In the meantime, Gandhi had crapped again, and they saw it. I wish they hadn't. Everybody gets diarrhea, and it doesn't mean you're going to die. If it did I'd have been dead ten years ago.

They had a conference, and then W.R. took me in the bathroom and said, "Now, this is one time I want you to be brave."

"What's the matter?"

"They have to put him out."

"Over my dead body," I said. I saw Gandhi looking up with those two appealing eyes.

The nurse gave him a shot and he went.

I tore the place apart. I broke everything I could lay my hands on. I almost killed everybody, I was so furious.

If they'd left him to me, I could have taken care of him. You always feel that way about your own dogs. You don't want anybody else to make the decision.

It wasn't W.R.'s fault. It was the nurse's. She said he was dying. How did she know?

Gandhi used to stay in bed
and warm my feet.

Well, Gandhi was buried at Wyntoon, across the long court, up on the hill.

There are three gravestones. One is for Gandhi, one for Helen, the dog that he whelped, and the third was for Heinie, the prize dog that we bought in England that went to his death by running right in front of an automobile.

They were all dachshunds.

Gandhi I named after Mahatma. I used to call him Mahatma Coatma Collar Gandhi. Helen was named for Helen of Troy, and Heinie was named for Heinz Variety 57. I used to call him 57.

When Gandhi died we had the Irish priest from McCloud conduct the services. The whole staff was up there. It sounds silly, but it's so heartbreaking when they go. You feel that not only have you lost your best friend, but a part of your life has gone.

I was very upset about Gandhi. I didn't think I'd ever get over it. When we buried him, everyone expected I would have hysterics. But I didn't. I just held it inside.

Helen had gotten ill, and the vet said that she'd been eating too many bones. They were not chicken bones but beef bones, and that should be a lesson to anybody who owns a dog. Too many bones are not good.

When Helen died, Mr. Hearst just had her in his arms. He cried and cried. He wrote a beautiful article about Helen in his column "In the News."

We'd go up the hill every once in a while just to say a silent prayer at their graves. And we put flowers up there all the time.

One time there was a porcupine fight. We had at that time two dachshunds named Fritz and Hans. You couldn't keep them in a room. They were wandering all around the place, and one night we got a message from the manager that he had found the dogs and had to take them to the hospital.

It was terrible. Quills through their ears, their nostrils, right through the stomach and everything. Every place but the eyes. We couldn't get the doctor at that time of the night, so the foreman said he'd take the quills out.

I had to hold them and he just had to wrench them out. They were bleeding like mad, but they survived. And the next night they tried to find that porcupine to start the fight all over again. We had to chain them up.

I didn't think dachshunds were fighting dogs; I thought they were only gopher hunters. But they were wild with rage and furious to realize that they didn't win the battle.

We had to lock them up for about two weeks to calm them down.

One night a bear broke into the pantry. Mrs. Engstrom, who was the cook, used to go outside and hand the bears sandwiches. So they always used to hang around the kitchen.

I said, "Don't encourage them. Don't go near them. One time and you're all through." She said she would stop. We had the yard fenced in, but one morning I went over to the pantry, and the ice box was wrecked.

A bear had gotten in from one of the little windows and had sat on top of the ice box and tried to open it. He broke it open, took everything out and threw the plates around. Then he went out the window and left. I guess he was hungry and felt that he wasn't going to get anything from the outside.

I saw him running when I got there. I just missed him, thank goodness. He looked about seven feet tall, and don't let anybody tell you that he was harmless. I don't think any animal is, if you come right down to it.

W.R. didn't mind the bears, but he said, "I wouldn't advise any of the guests to go too near to them. They are not to be trusted." But he wouldn't allow anyone to shoot anything there.

One night, almost at the end of the war, we were unusually late for dinner because W.R. had some work to do, and we had just sat down at about quarter to ten.

We were outside, over by the swimming pool and near the lights. At eleven o'clock I heard something, like a plane in trouble. Then, in just two split seconds, there was the most awful explosion, and the windows blew right out of the main living room.

A plane just missed the house and the office and went right on through and hit the mountain and exploded. I could see the flames, but you couldn't get there because of the river. It was a long way, and we started trekking.

Carmen Pantages got the first aids and blankets and all the necessary things. There was Walter Howey and Carmen and myself and a chauffeur, and we walked and walked. We ran, but we still couldn't see what was going on, because the plane landed on the other side of the mountain.

We had been going for three hours when we heard horses. It was the Boy Scouts and the Army. They said, "Don't bother going any farther—you can't make it. You can't get across the river."

They had gotten through because they had horses. We gave them our first aid things and started home. We didn't get back until nine in the morning, and we were exhausted.

Marion as she looked in the film *Five and Ten*, the story of a poor little rich girl who some viewers thought resembled Barbara Hutton.

The black velvet dress I had on that night was torn to shreds. W.R. was waiting for us, and he said, "Now, relax. You look a mess."

"I'd just like to have a cup of coffee. Do you know what happened? We tried to get there, but we couldn't."

"I tried to tell you that you couldn't possibly cross that river."

"You ought to have a plane here for an emergency."

"There is a plane, but it couldn't get in there."

Just then I saw a little character limping across the bridge. I said, "Is that one of the workmen?"

He said no. We saw that it was a boy. We took him to the River House. W.R. said, "That was the pilot. He jumped."

He had been lying in the river all night and was suffering from shock. His only explanation was that he had given word to the other boys to jump. All he could remember was that there was a stowaway on the plane. He landed in a tree with a parachute and then fell out of the tree and lay in the river all night. He was only seventeen years old, and I said we'd just have to keep him quiet and let him rest.

One of the men walked up and said, "Mr. Hearst, I'm sorry to tell you, but we have to take this boy to the hospital. He has to be questioned."

They insisted on taking him to the hospital. We found out that the plane had exploded, and it was a good thing I didn't get to the scene. It took two days for the fire to burn out. All that was left were fingers in the trees and toes all over the place and halves of legs.

I kept thinking about it, the bodies all split and burning, and I thought it was horrible. I think it was an Army transport, and this seventeen-year-old kid was the pilot. Eight boys and the stowaway were killed.

The next day I got up courage enough to go see him. He was shaking like a leaf. I had a box of candy for him. I thought that might make him feel better.

I heard the Army men say, "Did you give any word?" He said yes.

They said, "You had no right to jump, without giving them orders."

"I did. I did."

"You jumped first. Who was going to control the plane when you had jumped?"

He said, "I—I told them to jump."

One of them said, "You jumped and left the plane to crash, and it killed all eight boys. Possibly a ninth.

"All right. You're either up for a court martial, or you're going to fly right back to Washington. I give you two days to get on your feet and fly back to Washington. Explain it there."

I thought it was pretty cruel. They didn't see me and they left. I went in and said, "Don't cry."

"I'm not crying. I just don't want to go up again."

"It wasn't your fault—those things happen so quickly. Here's some candy for you."

"I didn't mean to do anything."

"Shhh—don't tell me," I said. "Keep it a secret. Take a piece of candy. You'll get strength enough to go to Washington."

"Do I have to go?"

"Look—I'm not the President of the United States. I can't tell you not to go. If the Army tells you to go, you have to. You'll have to prove to them that you have the courage to get in a plane. It's tough. I wouldn't do it myself. What are you going to do—hide in a corner?"

"I did."

I said, "Don't try it the second time —it's no good." And, honest to God, I never saw such a suffering little boy in my life. He was shaking like a leaf.

I made him eat the candy. I said, "You know, it's kind of nice here. Don't think you have to go if you don't want to. You can rest. All you have to do is just hide. That's the true American spirit, isn't it?"

"No," he said. "I'll go."

"I'm not telling you to go. I'm just suggesting something." I said, "Are you married?"

He said yes.

I said, "How long have you been married?"

"About two months."

"Then you have something to look forward to. Where's your wife?"

"She's in Chicago."

"So you can fly east and see your wife. Isn't that a happy thought? You want to see her, don't you?"

"She won't want to see me when she knows I'm a coward."

"Who said you were a coward? Shame on you. She'll be so happy to see you; just think of the love in her eyes when she sees you." He ate some more candy and got over the shakes after I talked to him awhile. That night I brought him some food.

He couldn't sleep. His eyes were wild, and I thought he was going crazy. I said, "It's a very funny thing—I just love the smell of a hamburger. Nothing in life like food to make you feel good and give you strength and make you think that nothing matters. You know, I do many bad things in my life that I really hate, but when I eat food

I think, It's not so bad, after all." I said, "Now look—all you have to do is just to say, 'I'm as good as anybody else—I can do it. I'm not afraid.' "

"But I'm supposed to go alone."

"That's right. You're on your own. If anything happens, you have only yourself to blame."

"I wish you hadn't said that."

"Forget about this. It was a bad dream, and you're going on to a new life, and you're going to be happy. Your wife is waiting for you. That's your incentive to be brave."

He went. He was guilty, but they gave him a break because he was a kid and because Mr. Hearst intervened. They dismissed the charges. He flew east by himself and he made it; that was his test.

I got a letter from him about six months afterwards and it said how happy he was. His wife was going to have a baby. He was all fine and fit and ready to go into the service again.

After all, self-preservation is the main thing in life.

He had lost his bearings and couldn't find the airport. When he looked down at the swimming pool, he thought it was a landing field because there was a whole square of lights in the trees.

When he saw it wasn't the field, he tried to get up. He went through the village and over the mountain, and he hit. I said to W.R., "Keep those lights out of that pool. Don't ever put them on again."

I was a major during World War II.

13

Life with Little Willie. The Japanese raid on Santa Monica. Toy drums
and wild Indians. The very fine host Mr. Hearst, not socially minded.
He knew the whole beginning of life, and wrote to
no one else but me.

During World War II, I was a major in the California
Guards, and I used to go to the hospital and we'd have
review. I was at the beach house when we had the raid.
We thought it was the Japanese, and the guns were going like mad.
I was having a dinner party. All the lights in the house went out, and
I jumped under the table. I crawled on all fours and tried to turn on
the lights, and my own watchman rushed in and said, "Turn out
those lights!" He brutalized me. "There's a raid going on—the Japanese are attacking us."

W.R. was up on the upper top balcony of the beach house
watching the raid. Bullets were going over his head, shells were flashing like mad, and you never heard so many guns in your life. It
lasted for half an hour. People were fainting.

There was firing all up and down the whole coast. I heard that
two Japanese planes were shot down.

Well, it was terrible.

*The guns of Santa Monica were fired one night early in 1942 at
an unidentified plane. But the plane was not shot down. Californians
had been anticipating an enemy attack for quite some time after Pearl
Harbor, and air raid wardens patrolled the streets—ordering lights
out and citizens in.*

W.R. would send long letters to his editors and publishers. He

233

liked to write more than he liked to dictate, so many times he sent them letters in his own handwriting.

His eyes were perfect. He didn't use glasses. I wished I had his control of the English language, not flowery but positive, and the strength of the words he used, and the expressions and the anecdotes he put in parentheses, like: (This reminds me of when I was a little boy and I picked up a book and I saw something that I thought was funny and I found it wasn't.) Like that, he would give them a little dig.

W.R. didn't care for radio and television. Every once in a while, when he would read the *New Yorker* and see some cartoon, he'd laugh and say, "Isn't that funny?"

He would read the magazines and the papers. I used to say that having all the papers and magazines around the house created cockroaches—that was an old thing my mother had believed. But W.R. was absorbed in them. He knew radio and TV were the coming thing, but he was a newspaperman, and for him, naturally, the printed word was most important.

W.R. found a cartoonist in *Esquire* that he wanted. He thought the man was brilliant, and he got him for the editorial page. His cartoons ran in the *Examiner,* usually at the top of the page, after Mr. Hearst got him a contract.

He was a little bit of a fat fellow, and his wife was very skinny and blonde and dumb-looking. Like most blondes are.

I was no exception to the rule.

W.R. was a very fine host, but he was not socially minded. He would greet the people, then he would disappear. He would go to the architect's office, or maybe he would work on his editorials.

He would pay no attention to the guests, except at mealtimes, when he would be very polite, and then he would disappear again. That was probably the best way for a host to be. It made the guests feel at home. They could wander around and do what they wanted.

The place cards were always down before W.R. came to the table. We would all go in and sit down, and he'd listen to the discussions, but he wouldn't say much. Looking at him, you would say he was not even listening, but he was. Still, it was like water off a duck's back; it meant nothing. He generally was thinking of something else.

He gave toasts only on special occasions. He never wanted to make a speech on his birthday, but they'd all scream for him to say something. He would say only one or two words, and sit down.

He'd always drink a toast to me, which I thought was kind of cute. He wasn't one to make speeches, and when he had to do two or three radio broadcasts, I never saw a man so nervous in my life.

One time he had to do one on politics. They set up the things in the office, and we were all in a jovial mood. We had had a little champagne. When W.R. was nervous, he had a little quiver in his voice. His face would get kind of pale and he'd be nervous for about a minute. Then he'd get himself under control.

His throat used to bother him, and he had an operation in Cleveland, about 1940. His diverticulum had to be operated on. First they string it out and then they chop it off. It was a very serious operation, and after we got back home, it bothered him again. They thought they'd operate again, but it went away. It did affect his speech a

W.R. wasn't one to make speeches, and when he had to do two or three radio broadcasts I never saw a man so nervous in my life.

234

bit; afterwards he spoke much better. Then he got his voice down to a very even level, and the broadcasts sounded fine.

He used to like to read historical books, like Thackeray and Dickens. He liked Dickens very much. W.R. had an immense amount of feeling inside. He was very emotional, but not outwardly. Very few people understood this.

He'd stay up all night long writing his article, the column, "In the News." He'd sleep in the morning, after he had breakfast. We'd have luncheon and dinner together.

I was sewing for the Army and the Navy, making hospital shirts and masks. It was loads of fun. I wonder why we didn't get any complaints from the hospital saying, "This seam is wrong."

Everyone wanted to go up to Wyntoon because they thought it was a place for protection. Little did they know that there was a Japanese camp less than fifty miles away. And it was right in a line from Seattle to Los Angeles, so if the Russians had wanted to come, it was on their way. They'd get to Wyntoon before they got to Beverly Hills.

But there was an influx of people all the time. Coming in for a day or two and staying quite a while. You know the kind. So we had a little family, maybe five hundred people there, possibly more.

W.R. didn't feel that he was being taken advantage of. He used to get a little bored occasionally, but he liked to have a lot of people around him, up until the last five or six years. Then

W.R. wrote little notes to me every day. He would shove them under the door and wait until I woke up. He wouldn't allow anyone in the house to wake me up. I was spoiled.

they made him nervous. I said, "Well, it's just like eating too much cake. You get fed up with a lot of people all the time, and then you want to quiet down. If you don't, your system's ruined."

After that we led a nice quiet life.

He was concerned about the families at Wyntoon that were working in the lumber mill there. He used to try to inspect the places, and every Sunday he had all the youngsters over for a barbecue.

I'd have to sit back and wait until they got fed and went swimming. There was an orchestra for them on the tennis court. I'd just have to step into the background and watch.

My tongue was hanging out for food, and all those little brats would come first and eat it. I was a great humanitarian. I wanted to grab a hamburger out of somebody's hand.

They had hot dogs and Spanish beans and tortillas and frijoles and enchiladas and chicken wings. I used to be hungry because sometimes my luncheon would be my breakfast, too.

It was the same routine every Sunday. They'd stay the whole afternoon. They would have to leave about six o'clock; and I could hardly wait. The place would be a mess, and it would take a day or so to get it cleaned up.

W.R. took great pleasure in seeing other people having a good time. I think he felt he ought to get some people in who might appreciate things. He saw to it that the children always got some sort of toy before they left.

The toy drums almost drove me crazy. He didn't care about the money. If there were five thousand, it didn't make any difference. He just had that feeling that children have to have a break in life.

And they broke everything. They broke the springboard one day. They'd get like little wild Indians and destroy everything. But W.R. couldn't see that side. He never complained.

Of course it was only during the good weather. In the winter nobody could get through. The snow was piled high and we couldn't even get out.

You might think W.R. did not have a good childhood—but he had a wonderful childhood.

Oh, maybe he didn't have that kind of fun when he was young. Maybe he was taken to too many antique galleries and did too much studying. But his mother and father were crazy about him.

W.R. told me a story about when he was young and his mother decided to take him to Paris to live in a pension. She wanted him to learn French.

He had gotten hold of a gun somewhere, and he shot at the ceiling. The chandelier came crashing down. The "mama" of the pension said to Mrs. Hearst, "I think you better take your son away from here, because he has just shot the ceiling out." So then they called him Little Willie, the bad boy. But all little boys are full of mischief.

W.R. wrote about Little Willie *in his papers on several occasions. One example that graced a page read:*

When Willie was a little boy,
Not more than five or six,
Right constantly he did annoy
His mother with his tricks.
Yet not a picayune cared I
For what he did or said,
Unless, as happened frequently,
The rascal wet the bed.

He used to tell me these stories about himself. He enjoyed retelling them.

There was the time when he burned his arm on becoming a member of the

Even after Marion had retired, the publicity continued. This piece appeared in the Sunday supplements in September 1946.

with Louella O. Parsons

By LOUELLA O. PARSONS
Motion Picture Editor
International News Service

C AN A glamorous, successful star who retires at the height of her exciting career be happy living away from the plaudits of an admiring public? After spending three weeks with Marion Davies, who left the screen when she was admittedly the most popular comedienne, I want to say it's entirely possible to find happiness and contentment in retirement if you have the caliber of mentality and a helpful interest in other people's problems.

Very few actresses have left the satisfying limelight at their zenith.

Marion Davies and Mary Anderson, who left the stage years and years ago when she was the toast of the New York stage, are the two outstanding examples of famous women who gave up their careers when they were at the top of their profession.

So many, many letters have come to my desk asking me for some news about Marion Davies. Is she going to make another picture? Why doesn't she give us some of her delightful comedies? So I asked Marion's permission to tell you something about her.

At first she said, "I am not in public life now. Wouldn't your readers rather hear about the actresses who are making pictures?"

I convinced her that these loyal fans want to know about her, how she looks, what she does and something of her many interests.

I'll try to give you a word picture of Marion Davies and you can see for yourself from this lovely photograph taken a few weeks ago exactly how she looks, how slim and lovely. Her weight, 115 pounds, is the same as it was when she was in pictures. I don't know any woman who leads a busier, pleasanter life than Marion. Sitting out in the sunshine I thought as I looked at her how wonderfully the years have treated her.

She looks younger than any of the stars who were on the screen at the time she was a top comedienne. But more important, in her maturity she has become a lovely, gracious woman with character, intelligence and the sparkling wit for which she was always famous.

I didn't have to ask her if she is happy away from the screen. Her face shows it and she is busy from morning until night sewing, knitting and superintending her many charities, principally the Clinic which gives free medical attention to children. She is absorbed, too, with her new interest in Beverly Hills real estate. She shows uncanny judgment, according to those who know how to evaluate the estates she herself discovered and purchased.

The weeks I spent with her while I was recuperating were such happy ones. Marion is the most completely selfless person I know and her beauty of character has grown with the years. As I watched her one afternoon making a dress for the child of one of the help, I was reminded of the verse of my school days. Paraphrasing it I could only think she has indeed grown in stature since I first met her, a shy blonde little girl of sixteen.

One reason for this is because she is constantly improving her mind. You cannot mention a book she hasn't read. The facility with which she separates the wheat from the literary chaff continues constantly to amaze me. She not only has an appreciation of present-day literature, she is up on the literature, mythology and history of yesterday, both medieval and ancient.

She sees a motion picture every night and she knows all the up-and-coming youngsters.

Frequently as we watched a picture she would point out a new face, saying:

"Look, Louella, at that girl— she has ability; or that young man shows promise and should be watched."

I found myself listening to her and mentally deciding to talk to some of the young people when I got back on the job. She was especially interested in Beverly Simmons, a child we saw in a Universal picture.

"She has that same something that makes Margaret O'Brien such a special little girl," Marion said.

"Tell me, Marion," I asked, "don't you ever long for the excitement of making pictures?"

"No," she said, "I don't expect to ever make another picture unless something special comes up. I love motion pictures but I wouldn't want to play in some of the stories now being made. I like gay, happy, romantic comedy dramas with perhaps a tear or two. "Besides," she laughed, "I have too much to do to spend the time required in a studio."

I thought of the many Davies fans who have begged her to come back. I think Marion feels she never wants to disappoint those who saw her in "The Patsy," "Little Old New York," "Peg of My Heart," "The Fair Co-ed" and other delightful comedies which might today help clear up the muggy atmosphere of the too many gangster movies.

P S I forgot to say Marion is champion ice cream eater of the world. I asked her if she attributed the fact that she looks 22 years old to eating at least two quarts of ice cream a day. She laughed and said:

"I do act as if I were working for an ice cream company the way I eat it, but I just happen to love it better than any food in the world."

Marion Davies

Harvard *Lampoon* staff. He had five little cigar marks for his initiation.

But he didn't talk very much about Harvard. There were many stories about the fact that he didn't graduate from Harvard, but they were not true.*

For example, the one about the pink satin slipper that was planted in front of his room. But the reason he left Harvard was that, from his work on the *Lampoon,* he got excited about the newspaper business. He didn't want to go to school any longer; he wanted to become a newspaperman. He asked his father if he could have the San Francisco *Examiner.* That was the only newspaper his father owned that was no good. His father must have thought he was crazy, but he gave it to him and told him, "Go to work on it." Well, it got to be the best one of all the papers.

One time W.R. was up for Mayor of New York and they threw the ballots in the Hudson River. He was very young, and he said that it must have looked like he was going to win, because they took wagons and trucks and threw all the ballots in the river.

But that was long before my time. And he didn't go into any politics while I knew him.**

I asked him once about the pro-German thing, and he said that his wife gave a party for the German Ambassador [Count von Bernstorff]. From that, he got the reputation of being pro-German. He was always pro-American, but his wife might not have realized that she might be entertaining the wrong people.

In the last part of the war, I started staying up most of the nights and sleeping most of the days. W.R. was working on his column, and practically the whole night long he'd be up in his rooms, writing.

It would be broad daylight when he finished working, and we'd go look at the river. It was a beautiful place.*

We didn't talk about his column. I never knew what he was writing from one minute to another. I don't think he knew either until he got himself closeted up.

Once in a while we'd talk about the circulation of a paper. He'd ask me which cartoon I liked best, or what did I think about the editorials, or if there was enough news.

At Wyntoon we got the San Francisco papers, the *Call-Bulletin* and the *Chronicle.* The *Chronicle* was never as good as the San Francisco *Examiner,* which was the best paper of all.

He knew the names and subject of anything I'd bring up. He'd say, "Let me get you a good book on that." I often wondered where he got that knowledge, because I'd never seen him read a book.

You could ask him any question about ancient history, about the Greeks or the Gauls, or the neolithic or paleolithic period, and he'd rattle it off, just like that.

He knew the history of every great emperor; he knew the whole beginning of life, from the oceans and the fish. He must have read before he knew me; I never saw him read. He was always writing.

---

* W.R. attended Harvard University from 1882 to 1885. He was dismissed from studies and had no academic degree until he was sixty-four years old. Then Oglethorpe University in Atlanta conferred upon him an honorary Doctorate of Laws. He, in turn, conferred upon Oglethorpe $100,000 and some four hundred acres of land.

** W.R. was elected to the U.S. Congress twice, in 1903 and 1907. He ran for Mayor of New York City in 1905, but he lost in a close election that was contested for irregularities. He was a candidate for Governor of New York in 1906 on the ticket of the Independent League and the Democratic Party, but he lost in another close count. He had hoped to run for president in 1908 but didn't. His last effort for political office was his second try for Mayor of New York City, in 1909, on the Independent League's ticket.

---

* Marion was known at times to refer to Wyntoon as Spittoon.

He could interpret any Greek or Latin word, and he knew French and Italian and Spanish, and he could speak the languages as well as read them. I used to wonder where he got all that knowledge.

He worked the crossword puzzles because he loved them, and he played solitaire because he said it gave him time for relaxation.

W.R. used to dictate correspondence. It would be typed up and he'd sign it. He wrote little notes to me every day. He would shove them under the door and wait until I woke up. He wouldn't allow anyone in the house to wake me up. I was spoiled.

He wrote to no one else. Not his lawyers or editors or his sons. They got either a telegram or a typewritten letter. He hadn't written or talked to his wife for at least twenty-five years. She never wrote to him, either. There was no feeling, nothing. They were separated and never saw each other. Hers was café society and his was different.

I used to answer him back. He used to keep all my little notes in a drawer right next to his bed. But they were stolen from the house.

I still have his.

A fragment of one such note read:

*Oh the night is blue and the
  stars are bright
Like the eyes of the girl of
  whom I write.
And the day is a glimmer of
  golden light
Like the locks of the girl of
  whom I write.
And the skies are soft and the
  clouds are white
Like the limbs of the girl
  of whom I write,
But no beauty of earth is so
  fair a sight
As the girl who lies by my
  side at night.*

I didn't pay any attention to politicians.

14

I had eaten lobster or something and I went into a coma. I was poisoned and I had an awful attack and thought I was going to die.

I was at San Simeon when that happened. Right after luncheon I doubled up and I hardly could get over to House A. I was on the floor, screaming at the top of my lungs. I didn't know what had happened to me.

W.R. sent for a doctor, by airplane from San Luis, and he said it was appendicitis. But W.R. wouldn't let him operate. He called San Francisco and they wanted me up there. So I had a pill of codeine, but it didn't do any good. I was really cramped up. I couldn't move. Everything inside me was going like mad, and it was horrible. So I had another codeine, and then I remember I was in an ambulance and then in a plane and then I'm on a stretcher in San Francisco.

They gave me the Murphy Drip. That was the last stage. It's a pipe they put up you—to get the water out of your system. You just lie there and go drip, drip, drip, all night long.

Of course, I got the wrong room. Next to the kitchen. I was trying to sleep and they had gotten the pipe in wrong. I called the nurse and said to send for the doctor. "Take this thing out of me. I'm going crazy."

She said to me, "Ahhh, signs of life."

I said, "This is no time to be funny. Tell them to stop rattling the dishes in the kitchen and get me out of here."

She said, "You can't."

Well, it was four in the morning and she said the doctor had gone to bed. I'd been there for five days, but I didn't know where I was.

I said, "The pipe is in wrong. I'll tear it out."

She said, "Don't you dare touch it."

Well, I was going to have a fight with her. I said, "You let me alone or I'll kill you." So she sent an intern to me. But he couldn't do anything without the doctor. I could see the fear on his face.

I said okay. He said, "You must be feeling better."

I said, "Look, I couldn't feel worse." And I was there three weeks and I was going to kill everyone in that hospital.

That was the week that Roosevelt died, and then they had the United Nations conference and there were Arabians at the Fairmont.*

They took my suite, the whole floor, and asked for all the beds to be taken out so they could sleep on the floor. I had to go to the Huntington House, which was opposite.

I could see Molotov but I didn't meet him. I could look out the window and see him. He made a very nice impression, as far as looks were concerned.

W.R. met Molotov, and though there was a difference of opinion, W.R. thought that he cared, that he had a sort of amenability toward being sensible. Molotov looked like he might have had a little brains in his coco. He was old; he looked a bit calmer than the others.

They looked like wild, violent, tearing reds who wanted to kill everybody. They had that big fat fellow, a horrible person, Malenkov, and the other, the chief of police.*

About Malenkov, Mr. Hearst said— and I never forgot it—"A person who's fat, with a fat face and a fat figure, has a meanness in him." And they were chubby guys. And they were tough.

I thought there would be a revolution in Russia. But most of the Russians know of nothing beyond their iron curtain.

Now W.R. was very, very, very rigid about the Communists. He was almost rabid, and he predicted another world war unless America could keep her money and defenses. And if we could get South America and Mexico in with us, then the western hemisphere would be perfectly fine. But he thought we were spending too much money and we shouldn't be bothered by foreign wars.

Like the fighting in Korea. He put it this way: How many Englishmen and Scots are there? Six with bagpipes and violins. They're playing music and the Americans are being killed. And are they going to protect us if we get into a war?

The English will have a happy holiday and so will Scotland. The English used to pay the Indians to scalp the Americans. So W.R. used to say, "Keep out of foreign entanglements."

---

* Vyacheslav Mikhailovich Molotov was Foreign Minister, representing the Soviet Union at the Founding Conference of the United Nations. Subsequently he represented the Soviet Union at the United Nations in New York. Later Nikita Khrushchev would post Molotov to Outer Mongolia, as Ambassador.

Georgi Maksimilianovich Malenkov was the deputy Prime Minister of the Soviet Union at that time and succeeded Joseph Stalin as Prime Minister in 1953. Later he and Molotov were accused of conspiring against the Communist Party, and he was assigned to work in a hydroelectric plant.

Lavrenti Pavlovich Beria was the chief of the secret police and a Marshal of the Soviet Union. He served with Molotov and Malenkov in a ruling triumvirate after Stalin died. Convicted of treason, he died two days before Christmas, 1953, before a firing squad.

---

* The U.S. President died on April 12, 1945, and the Charter conference of the United Nations began officially on April 25. It would last until June 26, when it was signed by representatives of fifty nations.

W.R. thought that a president was not supposed to leave the United States, and Wilson broke that rule. Then Harding went to South America. Then Roosevelt went over to Malta when they should have come to see him.

Now they have all of our money and we still have to go and see them. Well, W.R. thought we were an independent country and we didn't belong to England or Ireland or Italy or France or any goddamn country. He thought we had to fight for our own rights and that we were really floating on ice, then.

General MacArthur was the grandest man in the world. W.R. thought MacArthur was one of the greatest men since George Washington. He had met him on several occasions and was very much impressed.

He knew his policies, and he didn't have to know the person very well to judge them. W.R. had the most profound respect for him, for his mentality. Mr. Hearst followed every move MacArthur made.

He said, "He can't make a mistake. He's too good, too honest." But, he said, "There will come a day when people won't appreciate him." We found that out when we had the haberdasher.*

We had buttons made and started campaigning for MacArthur for president in 1948. But you can't campaign on two blondes. I understand that. It winds up that you work against him, not for him.**

I had met the General at MGM, when I was doing Bachelor Father [in 1931]. He came on the set with W.R. I think then he was a governor or an ex-governor of the Philippines. We all had luncheon over in the bungalow.

I was busy, and I have a one-track mind. I didn't pay any attention to the politicians, politics, or society. I would just sort of be orientated, but I'd keep thinking about something else.

I think George Bernard Shaw said that anybody who doesn't have a one-track mind will never be a success in life. In a way, that theory is true. If you jump from thing to thing, then you're nothing. You become a parasite, and then you become a borrower, and then you're a beggar.

W.R. was happy with most of the newspapers, but not all of them. He was constantly working on them, trying to get them to see what he wanted done.

He said to me once, which is so true, "It is so much more difficult to get people to do what you want them to do than to do it yourself."

The papers came first. The magazines came next. He didn't really bother about the gold or silver mines or the paper mills. After all, he paid the experts to run them.

He owned a million-acre ranch called Babicora in Mexico, in Chihuahua. The government took over half of it away for the agrarians. There were a lot of cattle there, and two or three silver mines and two gold mines, but W.R. didn't pay any attention to them. The main focus of his mind was on the newspapers, just the newspapers.

He had a theory: The people should know the truth. He said, "A free press; but if the press breaks the faith . . ." He meant that freedom was for the public but not for the columnists. He had to watch that faith all the time. So many times, interviews would be falsely written.

He would read not only his own pa-

---

* A reference to President Harry Truman's business venture.

** Patricia Van Cleve Lake, Marion's niece and companion, was involved in many of Marion's activities, including the 1948 campaign. Like Marion, she was a striking blonde.

pers but the other papers, to find out what they were doing. He watched his own like a hawk, to see if they were stepping out of bounds.

He used to say, "I don't read criticism of myself, because I know what they're saying. I know they don't approve of me. If I read all that, I might lose faith in myself."

I didn't believe in that theory. I got great delight in reading nasty articles about myself. I thought it was best to be mentioned rather than ignored. But still I would get a little bit mad, for a minute. But then, you could learn something from a little criticism.

I guess I didn't. I never was a very good actress, but I tried my best. Maybe W.R. had the right theory. He said that the critics would get you so down, you would be in a furious mood and wouldn't believe in anything. Since all I had to believe in was my own ability, and I didn't have any of that, I couldn't believe in anything.

I did hear the criticism in the early stages, but it went in one ear and out the other. I was the captain of my soul, and I wanted to do what I wanted to do, regardless of what people thought. I happened to have a little mind, and I would not have other people interfering in my life. And I think everybody should say that.

No one ever criticized me to my face. You can be criticized anywhere for anything, but never once did it happen.

There were two factions. Some would say, "Ummm, better not talk to her." That was Louella Parsons and Hedda Hopper. If you talked to one, you were no friend to the other. This wasn't so in Europe, and in New York I didn't go around much with the café society set. I was theatrical.

It might have made a little difference in that I was working for a living then. There might have been one or two little burrs, but they didn't mean anything to me.

The only open attack on living in sin, being a mistress and all that, was from Al Smith when he was campaigning for something or other. President, maybe.

He made a stump speech, and then W.R. wrote an article and said he had no respect for a man who would do that. Then Mr. Smith made another speech. He started in on "the man who attacks me." There was a little bit of a legal thing, I guess. He didn't mention *my* name, but everybody knew who he meant.

Of course Mr. Hearst was opposed to Mr. Smith. He didn't like his politics, didn't think he was conservative enough.

Maybe he didn't like his brown derby; I don't know. W.R. wrote a few articles in the paper, and then Mr. Smith figured out that he couldn't get even with a newspaperman, so he tried to attack me, by the grapevine route.

When anybody ever said anything to W.R. about me, he would be ready to kill them. He didn't care about himself, but he wouldn't take anything about me. He really stuck up for me.

I think he liked me.

We used to play singles at tennis and go swimming and yachting. When I caught a big fish, he helped me reel it in. He told everyone not to say that he helped me.

Everything seemed to jive just right. We sort of liked the same things.

We sort of liked the same people, up to a point.

We used to play backgammon a lot, or gin rummy.

W.R. didn't like bridge. He thought it was a stupid game, because the partners always argued. We used to play Monopoly. I always used to win that, and he said I knew more about real estate than he did.

In Time *magazine, August 1, 1955,
an article under Real Estate, headed
"Tycoon Davies," read: "A onetime
Hollywood queen and a longtime
friend and helpmate of newspaper tycoon William Randolph Hearst last
week talked about her 'current con-
suming interest': real estate. Said Marion Davies, now fiftyish, 'Land is the
most important thing in the world because it's God-given, and should be
developed.'*

"*Her most recent action proving her
words is the purchase of Palm Springs'
$2,000,000 Desert Inn . . .

"*Her reasons for buying were not
always dictated by potential profits.
'I went on a house-buying spree one
day, bought about eight houses in one
day. I don't know why I did it; I didn't
like most of them.' But she likes the
comparatively small 27-room house in
Beverly Hills that she now lives in . . .

". . . she tore down some old brown-
stones at 57th Street and Park Avenue
in Manhattan that were bringing her
$8,000 a year, got the Tishman Realty
and Construction Company to put up
and lease the 22-story, aluminum-
sheathed Davies Building. It pays her
about $120,000 a year. Down came a
block of flats on her property at 55th
Street and Madison Avenue, and now
abuilding is the 17-story Douras Building, named for her father, onetime
Manhattan Judge Barney Douras,
which will bring her about $50,000 a
year. By improving property she owns
on 57th Street between Fifth and Sixth
Avenues, she added still more to her
revenues, bought control of Fifth Avenue's Squibb Building. Still to come
are improvement of two pieces of
property in Los Angeles near the 'Miracle Mile' and development of residential acreage in Bel Air, Beverly Hills and
Santa Monica.

"*Marion appreciates the talents of
her lawyers, whose guidance has*
helped her earn an estimated annual
net income of $400,000 a year from
real estate.

"*Lawyer Arnold Grant estimated last
week that 'she could liquidate for spot
cash right now for $12 million or $13
million, I suppose. If these holdings
were mine, I wouldn't sell for $20
million.' "*

Now, every organization needs a
leader, and I was wondering why
things at the papers were going so
haywire. When they would come up
against the smallest kind of a snag,
they immediately would flock to W.R.,
and he would have to solve their
problems.

Right to the bitter end, they bothered him day and night. They were being paid excessive salaries and he
wanted them to make the decisions,
but they were not equal to it. Some of
them might have been afraid their decisions would be wrong, but if they
knew they were right, they should not
have run to W.R. and bothered him. I
thought, They are being paid—to use
his brains?

These were editors and publishers
themselves, and they would run to him
all the time. Bill Curley ran the most
successful paper in the whole institu-
tion, the *Journal,* but now that he's not
working on it, it's brainless. He never
bothered W.R.

Mr. Campbell ran the *Herald* beautifully, and Mr. Hearst only met him
once. There was the difference between a good editor and a bad one.
Mr. Carrington used to say, "This happens to be the pet paper of Mr. Hearst,
and therefore I have to be very careful." I thought he should have used
his own mind occasionally, but he
didn't have one.*

---

* John B. T. Campbell was the managing editor of
the Los Angeles *Herald-Express.* Carrington
worked in Baltimore.

Some of his editors went haywire. They tried sensational stuff, and people don't like that all the time, especially when the papers go into the home and the youngsters see them. Like the Tallulah Bankhead diary. That was nice stuff for the kids.

W.R. wouldn't allow that.

Then John Hanes came in, but he never took over. Of course nobody could tell W.R. what to do. If they tried to, that was the time for him to go forward. Mr. Berlin would say, "Now don't buy so many antiques."

And W.R. would say, "What's that got to do with the price of eggs?"—he got that phrase from me—and that would stop them.

And things would go on just the way they were.

But they were not running things properly, and they wanted to blame it on him. It was up to them to run the organization as they were supposed to, not to bother W.R. They promised me they would never give him any bad news. But then I should never have gone to sleep, because they got to him, even when I asked them not to.

Their running to him accomplished nothing, because he'd say, "I'm paying you to work. Why do you bring your problems to me?"

Especially the financial problems. Mr. Hearst was not financially minded at all. He didn't care anything about money, and he wasn't interested in the finances. He'd say something like, "If you can't do it, I'll have to get somebody else." Not those words, exactly, because W.R. was very kind, but that was what he meant. Then they would get panicky.

Of all the opposition papers, the one he admired most was the Los Angeles *Times*. That was the prime one. He thought the Los Angeles *Mirror* would go way ahead, like the *Daily News* in New York, because there isn't a town in the United States that doesn't like at least one tabloid. He wanted a tabloid himself, but they kept talking against it.

Now I can't really talk about it, but just between us, W.R. owned the Los Angeles *Daily News*. They used to call it the Los Angeles *Option* in their conversations, but W.R. owned fifty-one per cent. There was something about one newspaper owner not being allowed to have more than two newspapers in one town. Three is bad luck.

The idea of the tabloid was to protect the Los Angeles *Herald-Express*. But I don't think it worked. In the first place, the *Daily News* wasn't really a tabloid. It was in-between. They call it a three-quarters or a bastard paper.

W.R. never touched it; he just owned it. That was a military secret, but Manchester Boddy knew it, and so did Mr. Robert Smith, the editor, who was later the publisher.

Money went into a new press and other things. They wanted it to hang on as protection for the *Herald,* but I failed to see the point. If anybody had bought the *News,* I suppose it would have hurt both the *Mirror* and the *Herald.* Any more competition might have affected the evening papers, but not so much the morning papers. He said he had control of it as a shield to protect the evening papers.

In a way, it was a kindly gesture toward Mr. Chandler.

Some years earlier, Mr. Harry Chandler had made a kindly gesture to Mr. Hearst. When W.R. had financial problems and mortgaged San Simeon, it was through a bank controlled by the Chandler family that the money was obtained.

Bill Curley ran the most successful paper in the whole organization, the Journal. *But now that he's not working on it, it's brainless. He never bothered W.R.*

249

Cornelius Vanderbilt, Jr., was the original publisher of the Los Angeles Illustrated Daily News, *which first appeared on green paper on September 3, 1923. After W.R.'s effort to keep the paper alive, a San Diego publisher, Clinton D. McKinnon, made a fresh effort in 1949, but on December 17, 1954, the* Daily News *tabloid,* Sunset Edition, *carried its own obituary.*

Within ten years of W.R.'s death, Los Angeles was a two-newspaper town. The Times *had closed its afternoon* Mirror, *and the* Herald-Express *was merged with the* Examiner *to become the* Herald-Examiner. *The simultaneity of these changes would arouse some judicial interest for antitrust proceedings, but no charges were brought. The Chandler organization's Los Angeles* Times *now dominates the morning paper field, and Hearst's strike-ravaged* Herald-Examiner *has little opposition in the barren afternoon.*

Not that he was afraid of anybody, but he didn't want an outside influence to come in and pick up that paper, the Los Angeles *Daily News,* which was a lame duck. And there was a threat from Marshall Field. I knew him, and he didn't use very nice tactics.

W.R. thought the Chicago *Tribune* and the New York *Daily News* were maybe the two best papers in the country. He owned the New York daily *Mirror,* and that one was doing all right. In Chicago he owned the *Herald-American,* and they couldn't get it straightened out.

Well, the Hearst Corporation would have a meeting every three months, and they would discuss things like the printing and new presses and color and those sorts of things. They always wanted to improve things. Like the Sunday supplements.

But it would cost ten million dollars for new color presses, and they had just paid ten million dollars for a new black-and-white press. They just didn't have the foresight to think of color and rotogravures.

I was always very nice to Mr. Hearst's boys, and we got along fine until the night that Mr. Hearst died.

I imagine they thought he had changed his will, and that was why it started. George and John weren't there, and Randolph was somewhere, but not in the house.

David and Bill were right in the office that night. It was pretty awful. They didn't know what they were talking about.

David said to me, "You trying to run the papers?"

I said, "No."

He said, "Who ordered that?" He showed me the third page of the Los Angeles *Examiner,* where there was a story about a children's party at the Mocambo [a nightclub on Sunset Boulevard].

I said, "Your father ordered it."

"I don't believe it. You're trying to run the papers."

"Look—I don't want to run the papers, for God's sake. All I am is a messenger boy. W.R. orders a thing, and I have to telephone it. If you have any objections, go in and talk to your father."

This was just before Mr. Hearst died. There had been a party for poor kids who didn't have homes or any place to go. I had contributed some money for it, and Hopalong Cassidy* was there, and I thought it was all right. Mr. Hearst had ordered page three, the whole page, for the story, and David was blaming it on me. He said that I was trying to monopolize the paper for my own publicity. Well, maybe he was trying to put on an act. I never heard of anything sillier.

---

* Western actor William Boyd.

I think it was just kind of a stirring up of a feud that was beginning. They knew that something was happening upstairs; otherwise they wouldn't have dared to talk to me the way they did. They were taking the chance that I wouldn't talk to W.R. In fact, they knew I wouldn't. I never had. But this was brutal.

I left the room. Maybe they thought I was going upstairs, but I went in the living room and cried my eyes out. When I came back, Bill said, "I think you've gone a little bit too far."

I thought it was an act. I said, "All right . . . if I've done anything wrong, I'm sorry. I'm just a messenger boy for your father, and I don't know anything about the newspaper business."

David said, "He's got secretaries."

I said yes, "But lots of times the secretaries are asleep, in the middle of the night," which was true. At three or four in the morning he'd say, "Would you call up the *Examiner* and say that I don't like the crossword puzzle . . ." He'd pick out everything, and I'd call and say I was talking for Mr. Hearst.

It was absolutely preposterous. I was no newspaperwoman. I wasn't even an actress, though I had intended to be one.

Yet, I liked to think that W.R. was at his happiest when he was with me. That's a very conceited thing to say, but we always did have a good time. I'd be sewing, he'd be working. I'd be reading, he'd be working. We'd have an occasional conversation. With a great long friendship, and love, you don't have to talk. You are perfectly contented to know that somebody's just there. That means a lot, that complete tranquility.

He would say, "I know you are young, and wild, and want to have a good time. But I'm tired of so many people. Why don't you try to quiet

W.R. would say, "I know you are young and wild and want to have a good time. But I'm tired of so many people. Why don't you try to quiet down?"

down? Read a book or sew or do something."

I said that was all right, but it was awfully difficult for me at first, especially at the beach house. But once it was conquered, I couldn't lose it. I had stopped making motion pictures. I tried to follow his idea, but I was like a pony or a horse that has not been quite trained. There were still newspapermen and guests around, and relatives. It wasn't easy to relax, but gradually I got the hang of it. There really was never a moment's peace with all the comings and goings, in and out, all the time.

The night before he died, there were blazing lights in the hall, and everybody was talking at the top of their lungs. He had no chance to rest. I was furious; I went out and asked them to go downstairs.

Right to the last moment, W.R. was tortured with people. He wanted to lead a quiet, peaceful life, but we only had it for a little while. A very little while.

There were seven nurses, and they got officious and said, "You must do this." The newspapermen came, and there was no way to avoid them. I had no way to help him.

We were at San Simeon and he had had a slight attack. Not a heart attack, but indigestion. He had eaten too much. The altitude was too high at San Simeon. It was only 2700 feet, but it was bad for his heart. Now, you don't feel any heart trouble until you're over 5000 feet, but we went for that corny idea and moved to Beverly Hills. Then it was quiet, for a while, for three months.

Then one night we had strange nurses in the house, and from then on everything was chaos. The nurse who slept in his room snored, and he couldn't sleep.

When we were back at San Simeon, I had my room in House A, and he had his room over on the other side. Through the door lattice, I could see that his lights were always on, all night long. I'd walk in and say, "Are you going to bed or are you not?"

He'd say yes.

I'd say, "Turn the lights off."

Well, half an hour later he would still be writing or playing solitaire or thinking. There were millions of things for him to do, and he had a fantastic mind. Yet he was so human.

His feeling for people was so strong. And he was kind. He was depicted as a strong, masterful character who made hard bargains, yet he never made any negotiations at all. He never cared about money. He was no bargainer.

The studio made all the film deals. If the question would come up where L. B. Mayer might say, "I think this is too much," W.R. would say, "I'll pay more out of my own pocket." That was a good quality. I loved that quality. But it could be dangerous sometimes.

I like generous people. I was acquainted with one for thirty-two years, so I can appreciate them. Generosity is a very rare, rare gift. You can never tell who is a generous person. We're always on the outside; we never really know.

W.R. didn't believe in canned charity. He believed in personal action. He gave millions to the Red Cross and the Community Chest and the Knights of Columbus, but he felt the personal way was better. You could be sure of it, without the percentage taken off.

One of W.R.'s pet projects was the University of California, up in San Francisco. His mother had had something to do with it, and he gave them huge sums of money, as his mother had.

A LOVE AFFAIR IN TELEGRAMS.
OVER THE YEARS MARION RECEIVED HUNDREDS OF WIRES FROM W.R.
HERE ARE EXCERPTS FROM SOME OF THEM:

May 8, 1918, from Mount Clemens, Michigan:

"I will come to New York and spoil your parties . . ."

May 15, 1918:

"Develop your talents . . . you can do it if you want."

August 2, 1923, from San Simeon, after reviewers praised one of her films:

"I knew your genius would be recognized."

May 18, 1928, from La Junta, California:

"We never know how many more years we have . . ."

April 23, 1929, en route to New York from Albuquerque, New Mexico:

"Dusty California is the Eden of the world. . . . Adam had to leave Eve behind."

May 29, 1929, from Albany, New York, after trying to reach Marion by phone:

". . . but operator could not find you. Where were you? Explanations are in order."

November 22, 1930. W.R. and Marion had returned from Europe. W.R. remained in New York, while Marion hurried back to California to work on a movie. She didn't stay long because W.R. telexed to her:

"Patient is on the blink . . . [bring] your nurse's uniform."

W.R. became interested in the Lawrenceville school. He had met a Dr. Jacobs from there, a nice old gentleman who came to visit at San Simeon.

There were really a lot of schools around the country that he gave money to. I never checked, but it must have been millions, and I know there were a lot of them.

From San Simeon we'd go to the church in Cambria. We didn't go all the time, but we did for funerals, and there were lots of those. At first there was a tiny church where we went on Sundays, and W.R. would look around.

The next time, it wasn't the same. It was enlarged, had heating in it, and a new organ. I said, "Things must be picking up in Cambria."

It had been maybe three months since the last time. Afterwards we stopped to talk to the priest. He was

Marion in costumes from some of her later pictures.

Irish, and with his brogue I couldn't understand a word. But I suspected something when I heard him say, "You're a fine man, Mr. Hearst . . ." And, of course, I found out that W.R. had had the whole little church fixed over. He hadn't said a word to anybody.

W.R. should have been an architect, but he would have been terribly expensive for anybody. He was always changing things. But he just lived for plans, and anytime you wanted to find him, he would be in the architect's office. It was that way at San Simeon.

When there was the atom bomb scare, W.R. wasn't worried about himself. He had a bomb shelter built downstairs because he was worried about me. This was at Lexington Road, but he wasn't satisfied with only that one; he had another put into the garage.

Later, I had that bomb shelter knocked out of the garage. It was the only garage I had, and it only held one car. The bomb shelter in the basement became a storeroom. That was all right.

W.R. was going to build another bomb shelter on the side of the hill. The first thing you were supposed to do was throw yourself under the bed and not get near a window. Then the next thing was to run downstairs and turn the pilot lights off. How could you do all those things and still run to your bomb shelter? Besides, I said, "Where are we going to put the cars?" So on that question he had garages built for six cars.

W.R. thought we were going to be bombed, but I said, "What's the use of worrying about it?" He wanted to be prepared. But I thought the best thing to do was to jump under the bed. He didn't. He went to all the expense of building bomb shelters, with bathrooms—but no windows or anything pretty—and they have never been used.

Marion and W.R.

Looking back. Thoughts on living. Ingrid Bergman and the old Presbyterians. Thoughts on Mr. Hearst. Companionship and devoted love:
that was our pact. He was very kind. I was a faker. He thought he was
building up a star.

I was always on W.R.'s side, so there was nothing to argue about. And W.R. was always on my side. That's why I liked him so much. If anybody was in trouble, regardless of what it was, he would help. I think that is a great trait.

I liked a lot of people, but there were plenty of villains. That'll be the next chapter. There were two types of villains. One who says something to you that you don't like and one who takes an attitude so you feel they don't like you.

W.R. would help his enemies. He would help the people who didn't like him. He never held a "knocker" toward anybody.

That's a word Bing Crosby used about me, that I never held a "knocker." Maybe I changed a bit, but W.R. was that way. He would never listen to anybody who would say anything against anybody else. He didn't believe in tearing people down. He believed in building them up.

I didn't know Ingrid Bergman at all, but when I discovered the difficulty that she was in, I called up the Los Angeles *Examiner* to put in an article saying that I agreed with her.

The word came out that a women's club was going to ban her because she was in love with another man [Roberto Rossellini] and would marry him except that her husband [Dr. Peter Lindstrom] was standing in the way.

She was persecuted; I would say that they nailed her to the cross. If a woman of her great character can go ahead with her love, why should she be criticized? I told W.R. that I thought Ingrid Bergman should be commended and that she was a great person, with a beautiful face.

That women's club was a bunch of old Presbyterians. W.R. agreed with me. I sent her a cable and she answered it. She was very kind.

However, the legal man at the paper took it upon himself to cut the article out of the second edition.

By that time, the story in the first edition had been picked up by the wire services—and was soon printed by other newspapers.

He went to see W.R. and said, "What Miss Davies has done is horrible." He said that I wouldn't be acceptable to the women's clubs—as if I cared. Then W.R. sent for me and said, "I think you've made a mistake. My lawyer said the women's clubs won't like this."

I said, "Don't make me laugh." I showed him the Los Angeles *Times* and their story that "Marion Davies says, 'I think Ingrid Bergman is a great woman, beautiful and with great integrity.'"

W.R. said, "Did the *Times* get it first?"

I told him that his lawyer had cut it out of the *Examiner*. He said he was going to fire him. I said, "You tell him."

He called him and said, "How dare you do that to Miss Davies? When she gives an order to the *Examiner*, it has to go through. And don't you dare countermand it.

"If you ever do that again, I'm going to bounce you out. As far as the women's clubs go—well, Marion is not working in pictures any longer, and if they haven't got the humanity in their souls to be kindly toward a great woman, if they haven't got an open mind, then they are no good. And you can cut the women's clubs out of the papers . . ." He was really furious, and that was the end of that.

Ingrid wrote me a very nice letter and thanked me.

She was really in a desperate situation. She had given every cent to her husband to put him through school. He was afraid that he was going to lose his money bag. How could a man be so mean? He tried to tear down her character, which nobody in the world could do. She is the most beautiful, kindly lady in the world.

The story was in the Los Angeles *Examiner* the next day. They printed my telegram, and W.R. said I was right.

I just had to stand up for the principle. After all, I did have feelings. And I knew how she felt.

She had been brutalized by a horrible creature, and I knew about this, because I had a maid, Maria, who had worked at her house. She told me that one night he tried to get into her room. That didn't come out in court.

Miss Bergman recently said, "I was very pleased to find that there were two sides to a coin." She remembered when she was hospitalized, having her child, and stories and headlines all over the world were against her. A nurse brought in the first bouquet of flowers. The message of congratulations was signed Marion Davies.

I had plenty of opportunities to get married, myself. But how can you marry someone when you're in love with somebody else?

I couldn't think of anybody else when I was in love. Whether I could get married or not, I didn't particularly care. How could I break myself away from love just to say that I wanted to be a married woman? That meant nothing. I thought love and companionship were much more important.

That's exactly what it was. Companionship and devoted love. That was our pact.

No. 3 Nell Gwyn
(Posed by Marion Davies) **Pin-Up Girls of History** by Henry Clive
See John Erskine's Story on Page 2

Marion posed as Nell Gwyn, and W.R. ran this in the Sunday supplement *The American Weekly*, carried by several of his papers.

Metropolitan Critics Hail "Little Old New York" as a Film

REMARKABLE PORTRAYAL OF A CENTURY AGO

MARION DAVIES ACCLAIMED AS GREAT ARTIST

"Theatre, Star, Picture, Direction, All Call for Superlatives," Says S. Jay Kaufman in Evening Telegram.

"STAGE VERSION ECLIPSED"

"Heroine's Role Couldn't Be in Better Hands," Says Sun and Globe; "Lives the Part," Evening Mail.

Supplementing the Metropolitan morning newspapers in their unstinted praise of the great Cosmopolitan film spectacle, "Little Old New York," and of the rare excellence of the work of the star, Miss Marion Davies, the reviewers of the evening newspapers combined in pronouncing the new offering a great triumph.

The premiere of the film masterpiece, which occurred at the new Cosmopolitan Theatre, Columbus Circle, gorgeously decorated by that peerless scenic craftsman Joseph Urban, was attended by a representative first night audience.

Never has there been expressed by the critics such unanimity of approval of a film as that accorded "Little Old New York."

Following are extracts from the comments of the evening newspaper reviewers:

C. J. KAUFMAN in the Evening Telegram —Theatre, star, picture and direction—they all call for your superlatives. Perhaps we should put Miss Marion Davies first. She was acting, and doing several of her scenes were starting. And the doesn't animate and "act up" for the camera. She seems to know what the character would do, and does it. A very pleasing success is hers.

STAGE SETTING LOVELY.

The theatre is Urbanesque, which is another way of saying that it is beautiful. The stage setting is particularly lovely. And he has reduced its hollowness without reducing the number of seats.

The picture, "Little Old New York," is from a Johnson Young play, to which several scenes have been added. And interests all the way.

And the direction by Sidney Olcott, who by his work puts himself in the Griffith class. The reproduction of old New York, the whipping post scene, the first steamboat, the baking service, and storms of others—are given every value there is in them.

BOWLING GREEN in 1807 has been faithfully reproduced in the newest Cosmopolitan production, "Little Old New York," starring Marion Davies, that last Wednesday night opened the new Cosmopolitan Theatre on Columbus Circle. Many of the most interesting episodes of this great historical film are laid on the streets of lower Manhattan in the early days of the nineteenth century, and to reproduce Bowling Green in its entirety the largest armory in New York City was used as a motion picture studio. More than four hundred persons took part in the famous whipping-post scene, when Patricia O'Day, masquerading as a boy, breaks up a prize fight by calling out the fire department on a false alarm and is taken to the village whipping-post for punishment. Marion Davies in "Little Old New York" has settled down for a long run at the newest of Broadway cinema palaces. Victor Herbert and his orchestra play at both performances daily.

Miss Davies Called 'One of Best Actresses' and 'One of Greatest Artists on Screen'

WHAT the critics of the leading New York morning newspapers think of Miss Marion Davies's triumph in "Little Old New York," the magnificent film play of the early days of the metropolis, is indicated by the following brief extracts from their reviews:

QUINN MARTIN, NEW YORK WORLD—If we

ture and a fine achievement for its director, Sidney Olcott. The Park emerges as perhaps the loveliest theatre in this highly theatrical borough.

HARRIETTE UNDERHILL, NEW YORK TRIBUNE— It is doubtful if Miss Davies ever dreamed that she would become what she has become—one of the best

what New York was at the beginning of the nineteenth century gains some measure of satisfaction from the picture. It attempts to depict the spirit of the life of the day when Forty-second street was at Bowling Green was considered another part of the world.

MISS DAVIES IMPRESSED.

In this setting is brought Patricia O'Day, an Irish miss who impersonates her brother as a boy. Miss Davies impressed

---

The rumor about my having children has come up many times, and many people say that W.R.'s twins are my sons, but I don't see how they ever could be. Randy and David and I were almost the same age. They say that Randolph looks very much like me, but I don't see any resemblance. What about birth certificates and all the papers and the proof that they were mine? I would have been glad to have both David and Randy with me, if anybody could prove it. Then, I just might say I wish it were true.

The twins are a bit younger than I, but not that much.* You have to figure that I didn't even know W.R. until after the twins were born. So where my boys could be, I was damned if I knew. Of course I was working all the time, then, on stage and in the pictures.

When W.R. met me he was fifty-eight, going on fifty-nine. When we came to California, he was well into his sixties, but the rumors went on and on, like about the Thomas Ince mur-

---

* Eighteen years younger.

der. It was absolutely ridiculous, but people lose their sense of time.

If I had a daughter, I would say, "Get started young. Take the dancing lessons; take posture and poise, and dramatics and diction. Prepare yourself for a good theatrical career." Girls always have a sense of the theatrical. Girls like powder and having their hair fixed. They love lace dresses and party dresses. I was always in front of the mirror when I was young. I was like a statue, showing off, posing; that's how you know you belong to the theatrical life.

If you don't make the grade, then you can be a secretary or a salesgirl.

I didn't make the grade myself; I was pushed. If I hadn't been pushed, I would have gotten a job selling gloves at a counter. I wouldn't have been happy doing that.

I can't say I was ever unhappy, not at all. I asked for what I got, asked when I was very little. My sisters were actresses, and I was surrounded by show business. I loved it. It was just like a fairy tale, and I was fascinated.

Still I say the best years of my life were in the background, holding up the backdrop on the stage. We were just a big, happy family. It was a big, gay party, every bit of it.

When I was young I just lived for the stage. I even hated my own home, because it wasn't as glamorous. I thought, like every poor idiot does, that I had a career. Marriage never entered my mind. I was going to be another Pavlova. If only I had stopped to realize how stupid I was. I had no talent for the theatre. I had no talent, period. I had the ambition that my life was made for a career and I was never going to leave the stage. But I had no talent

even for the pictures, just a little tap dancing. So something, fortune or luck, pushed me along. Otherwise I'd have been Bertha, the sewing machine girl.

When I was about seventeen, I got the second lead in a play that only lasted a week. I think it was called *Words and Music.*

It was discovered in the rehearsals that I couldn't speak a line, so I did things in pantomime, but I couldn't do that very well. Finally I wound up just being dressed in an American flag, and singing one song, "Little Butterfly from Japan."

I found out later that W.R. had backed the play, and then I thought he had done it on purpose, to show me up, to prove that I couldn't act. He didn't care about his money, but I think he was upset when I realized the truth about myself. He maintained that I could do anything I wanted to do. He said that I could dance and sing, and that an inferiority complex was a screen that people hide behind. He said that when I said I couldn't sing or dance, it was really no excuse.

He was very kind about those things. But I was a faker.

When I first went into motion pictures, I thought it was very drab and dull. It was nothing like the stage, so I wasn't very happy doing pictures. I just kept thinking of the stage, the stage.

All my life I wanted to have talent. Finally I had to admit there was nothing there. I was no Sarah Bernhardt. I might have been a character, but any kind of character. I had none of my own.

W.R. argued with millions of people. He thought I could do anything—Shakespeare's plays, any sort of a part. He thought I'd be the best. There were quite a lot of people who didn't have the same theory.

"AMONG THOSE PRESENT" *as seen by* RALPH BARTON *at the premiere of* MARION DAVIES'S *new super production* | "*Little Old New York*" *at the New Cosmopolitan Theatre on Columbus Circle. This design will be drawn on a special curtain.*

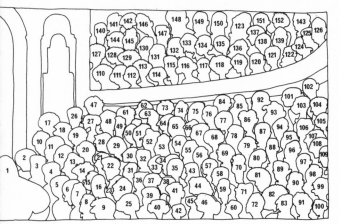

1 Victor Herbert	53 Rex Beach	107 Penrhyn Stanlaws
2 Rida Johnson Young	54 Elsie Janis	108 Mrs. Jerome N.
3 Luther Reed	55 S. Jay Kaufman	Bonaparte
4 Martin Beck	56 Allan Dwan	109 Arthur Horslow
5 A. L. Erlanger	57 Ray Long	110 Mrs. Harry P. Whitney
6 Arthur Somers Roche	58 Dr. Frank Crane	111 Mrs. Reginald C.
7 Harrison Fisher	59 O. O. McIntyre	Vanderbilt
8 Norman Hapgood	60 Gloria Swanson	112 Mrs. Samuel J.
9 John Drew	61 Florence Nash	Wagstaff
10 Anne Morgan	62 Glenn Hunter	113 Mrs. Carroll L.
11 Elisabeth Marbury	63 George S. Kaufman	Wainwright
12 Elsie de Wolfe	64 Marc Connelly	114 Anna Fitzla
13 Charles Dana Gibson	65 Pirie MacDonald	115 Howard Chandler
14 Dean Cornwell	66 Roland Young	Christy
15 Bayard Veillier	67 Percy Hammond	116 Mrs. Biddle Duke
16 William Le Baron	68 Gilda Gray	117 Nicholas Longworth
17 Harriette Underhill	69 James R. Quirk	118 Mrs. Nicholas
18 Raymond Hitchcock	70 Robert E. Sherwood	Longworth
19 Rupert Hughes	71 Alan Dale	119 Grace George
20 Louella Parsons	72 Bebe Daniels	120 William A. Brady
21 Rachel Crothers	73 Alexander Woollcott	121 Blanche Bates
22 James Montgomery	74 Quinn Martin	122 George Creel
Flagg	75 Karl Kitchen	123 Christopher Morley
23 Grover Whalen	76 Lyn Harding	124 Mrs. O. H. Belmont
24 Hon. John F. Hylan	77 Anita Stewart	125 Arthur Brisbane
25 Marion Davies	78 Morris Gest	126 William Randolph
26 Frank R. Adams	79 Samuel Goldwyn	Hearst
27 Daniel Frohman	80 Sam H. Harris	127 Elsie Ferguson
28 Messmore Kendall	81 Jacob Ben-Ami	128 Lillian Albertson
29 David Belasco	82 Billie Burke	129 Irene Castle
30 Deems Taylor	83 Florenz Ziegfeld	130 W. T. Benda
31 George D'Utassy	84 A. D. Lasker	131 Maury Paul ("Cholly
32 Frank Crowninshield	85 George Jean Nathan	Knickerbocker")
33 Lillian Gish	86 Scott Fitzgerald	132 Lynn Fontanne
34 David Wark Griffith	87 Louis Joseph Vance	133 Alfred Lunt
35 Dorothy Gish	88 Vincent Astor	134 Kenneth MacGowan
36 Hartley Manners	89 Al Jolson	135 William Collier
37 Laurette Taylor	90 Montague Glass	136 Sam Bernard
38 Irene Bordoni	91 Henry Blackman Sells	137 Mrs. Turnbull Oelrichs
39 William Frederick	92 Charles Hanson Towne	138 Ruth Chatterton
Peters	93 Irvin S. Cobb	139 Henry Miller
40 Will Hays	94 Ring Lardner	140 Stephen Rathbun
41 John Emerson	95 J. J. Shubert	141 Carl Van Vechten
42 Anita Loos	96 Lee Shubert	142 Fania Marinoff
43 Joseph Urban	97 Adolph Zukor	143 Dudley Field Malone
44 Ethel Barrymore	98 A. H. Woods	144 Ludwig Lewisohn
45 Marcus Loew	99 Avery Hopwood	145 Reginald Vanderbilt
46 Fannie Hurst	100 Irving Berlin	146 Nicholas Muray
47 Kelcey Allen	101 Neysa McMein	147 Meredith Nicholson
48 Nita Naldi	102 Robert C. Benchley	148 Robert W. Chanler
49 George Palmer Putnam	103 Franklin P. Adams	149 Charles Dillingham
50 George M. Cohan	104 Heywood Broun	150 John Murray Anderson
51 Alma Rubens	105 Ruth Hale	151 M. le Duc de Richelieu
52 Don Marquis	106 "Zit"	152 La Princesse Bourbon

Marcus Loew did big business with this picture

and so can You! For "CECILIA of the PINK ROSES" is a nationally advertised production starring beautiful MARION DAVIES

It will win for you as it did for Loew!

Directed by JULIUS STEGER

SELECT SP PICTURES

I did I don't know how many pictures. In those days they made them in a hurry. She would remember this one if only because Cecilia was her middle name. It was released in September 1918.

I did get a few crank letters every once in a while and I heard the gossip, but it never came inside the house. I was very well protected from every angle. I did get a bomb once, for Christmas, but it looked funny. The spelling looked like Spanish. It looked like it said Maria Davies. It was investigated for months, but we never found out who sent it.

That was a little worse than the pranks I played. It could have destroyed me, and my neighbors, too. I just played little tricks at the studios.

I never saw the picture *Citizen Kane* but my sister Rose did, and she said, "I'll kill him,* it's terrible. You can't even see the picture, because it's all dark."

I said, "Why are you saying it's terrible?"

"It's against you. They have you playing and hiding behind curtains."

I said to her, "Rose, there's one tradition that I have that was taught to me by W.R. Never read criticism about yourself." Once I made a mistake and read some criticism of myself, and it did get me riled up. After that I didn't read any critics and I paid no attention.

A man working on the *Telegram* in New York wrote a scathing article about the picture *Cain and Mabel;* he said I should be washing dishes. Little did he know that I loved to wash dishes, and I liked to dry them, too. But he went on and on and on. I sent him a telegram saying, "I'm mad at you." That was all I said, and I never got an answer. It was silly of me, and stupid, and he was probably right.

---

* Orson Welles.

Marion going to tea at St. Donat's Castle in Wales, 1935. *All my life I wanted to have talent. Finally I had to admit there was nothing there. I was no Sarah Bernhardt. I might have been a character, but any kind of character. I had none of my own.*

W.R. never went to see *Citizen Kane* either. The Hearst newspapers put a ban on it, as far as publicity went, but W.R. wasn't little that way. His theory was that no matter what anybody said, no matter what they wrote, you didn't read it and you didn't listen.

W.R. said, "Yesterday's newspaper is old news." But plenty of people talked about *Citizen Kane*. They would say that it was terrible and I had to go see it. But we never did.

I had no anger toward Orson Welles. After all, everybody is created to do their very best, and he probably thought that was his way to make money. Who was I to say I didn't like the way he did his picture? I was not built that way. I liked to keep the waters calm.

And I heard about Aldous Huxley. I don't think I ever met him, nor did I read his book, but I wanted to.*

When W.R. was really interested in something, he would go in heart and soul. Not just a little bit, but all. He did the same with my pictures as he did with his newspapers. He never made the remark, "I feel the pulse of the public." He seemed to know what the public would like, and he opposed anything that mothers wouldn't bring their children to see. He wanted nice, clean, honest pictures.

He wanted me to keep my career. He had signs all over New York City and pictures in the papers, and I was always meeting people. I thought it got to be a little bit too much, but W.R. didn't.

I said, "Maybe somebody else could do it, somebody who has talent." But the way he advertised me, I don't think anybody could. I said, "This is irritating to the general public. They read it, and then they go see the picture, and they think it isn't what they thought they were going to see." But I couldn't stop him.

In New York City there were big signs, blocks and blocks of signs, and people got so tired of the name Marion Davies that they would actually insult me. W.R. thought he was building up a star. He saw me, in all his good faith, as an actress, or that I had the ability to be one.

I hope, before he died, he found out I wasn't. Still, I think he thought I was.

Beverly Hills, California, 1951.

---

* *After Many a Summer Dies the Swan* was considered a parody on life at San Simeon.

Marion in *Page Miss Glory*.

ABOUT THE AUTHOR

Ten weeks after W.R. died, Marion was married to Horace Brown, who had been a captain in the merchant marine. Theirs was a simple elopement to Las Vegas, to the El Rancho Vegas Hotel. If the newspaper reporters didn't get her age right, they were quick to point out that it was her first marriage.

It was seen to be a union made in her desperation over the loss of W.R., and to give her support in the coming battles. She was an officer of the Hearst Corporation and held W.R.'s voting rights, and though she thought of herself as a member of the family, all these relationships were soon ended.

The captain stayed on, though Marion would several times think of divorce and have the papers filed. They said the captain looked like a young W.R., but that was almost all that friends would say about him.

Marion had been operated on for malignant osteomyelitis early in the summer of 1961. Then there were complications.

In southern California, summertime often lingers on. Nature shows little interest in the calendar. But for Marion, the turn of the seasons, when it came, was symbolic. Her last milestone was that autumnal equinox.

Acknowledgments

For permission to use excerpts from copyrighted material, grateful acknowledgment is made to the following:

TIME, The Weekly Newsmagazine, for excerpts from "Tycoon Davies," reprinted by permission, copyright © 1955 by Time Inc.;

Bernard Geis Associates, Inc., publishers of *HARPO SPEAKS!* by Harpo Marx and Rowland Barber, copyright © 1961 by Harpo Marx and Rowland Barber;

T. B. Harms Company, publishers of "Why Was I Born?" by Jeorme Kern and Oscar Hammerstein II, copyright © 1929 by T. B. Harms Company; copyright renewed.

The publishers wish to thank the following for photographs which appear in this book:

Mrs. Valentine Davies, Los Angeles

Miami-Metro Department of Publicity and Tourism, Miami

Mr. Bob Board, Hollywood

The State of California, Sacramento

UCLA Medical Center, Los Angeles

The William Randolph Hearst Collection at Los Angeles County Museum of Art, Los Angeles

Morris Rosenfeld & Sons, New York

All uncredited photographs were taken from the personal collection of Marion Davies.

Index

Numbers in boldface indicate pages on which illustrations appear.